Praise for *The Real Lincoln*

"This is a scholarly, lucidly written work that is bound to generate robust, even heated, controversy. It may very well end up revolutionizing our understanding of one of the great American icons."

—RALPH RAICO, professor of history,
Buffalo State College

"To the legions of Americans who regard Abraham Lincoln as a racial saint and a national demigod, Thomas DiLorenzo's *The Real Lincoln* will come as a rude awakening. Unlike his mythic representations as Honest Abe and the Great Emancipator, the real Lincoln dedicated his political career to the establishment of a corrupt system of high tariffs and corporate subsidies, and he was willing to plunge the nation into a bloody cataclysm in order to achieve his lifelong political aspirations."

—ROBERT HIGGS, PH.D., author of
*Competition and Coercion: Blacks in
the American Economy, 1865–1914*

"*The Real Lincoln* is not for weaklings. But for those who prefer historical truth over ignoble fiction and republican self-government over oppressive empire, read this book. Professor DiLorenzo superbly unmasks tyranny in the personage of Lincoln and the apparatus of centralization he set in motion."

—MARSHALL DEROSA, professor and
chair of social sciences, Florida Atlantic University

THE REAL LINCOLN

*A New Look at
Abraham Lincoln,
His Agenda, and
an Unnecessary War*

THOMAS J. DILORENZO

FORUM
An Imprint of Prima Publishing

Published by Prima Publishing, Roseville, California. Member of the Crown Publishing Group, a division of Random House, Inc.

FORUM and colophon are trademarks of Random House, Inc. PRIMA PUBLISHING and colophon are trademarks of Random House, Inc., registered with the United States Patent and Trademark Office.

Library of Congress Cataloging-in-Publication Data
DiLorenzo, Thomas J.
The real Lincoln : a new look at Abraham Lincoln, his agenda, and an unnecessary war / Thomas DiLorenzo
p.   cm.
Includes index.
ISBN 0-7615-3641-8
1. Lincoln, Abraham, 1809–1865. 2. United States—Politics and government—1861–1865. I. Title.

E456.D55 2002
973.7'092—dc21
[B]   2002016960

02 03 04 05 QQ 10 9 8 7 6 5 4 3
Printed in the United States of America

First Edition

Visit us online at www.primapublishing.com

CONTENTS

ACKNOWLEDGMENTS

THIS WORK GREW from a speech I gave on "Lincoln as Progenitor" of the twentieth-century American state at the Mises Institute's fifteenth-anniversary conference in Atlanta in November 1997. I would like to thank Lew Rockwell, Jeff Tucker, and the staff of the Institute for providing me with a forum for discussing these ideas and for publishing some of my earlier work.

I would also like to thank Robert Higgs, editor of *The Independent Review,* published by the Independent Institute of Oakland, California, for publishing my essay, "The Great Centralizer: Abraham Lincoln and the War between the States," in the July 1988 issue of the *Review.* The advice of two anonymous peer reviewers was also very helpful. This essay formed the backbone of the present book.

Former Prima Publishing acquisitions editor Steven Martin approached me about writing the book, and I thank him for doing so. I also gratefully acknowledge the financial support for my research provided by the Earhart Foundation and the Sellinger School of Business and Management at Loyola College.

My wife, Stacey, provided tremendous support and encouragement, as always, but I still won't list her as a co-author.

FOREWORD

IN 1831, long before the War between the States, South Carolina Senator John C. Calhoun said, "Stripped of all its covering, the naked question is, whether ours is a federal or consolidated government; a constitutional or absolute one; a government resting solidly on the basis of the sovereignty of the States, or on the unrestrained will of a majority; a form of government, as in all other unlimited ones, in which injustice, violence, and force must ultimately prevail." The War between the States answered that question and produced the foundation for the kind of government we have today: consolidated and absolute, based on the unrestrained will of the majority, with force, threats, and intimidation being the order of the day.

Today's federal government is considerably at odds with that envisioned by the framers of the Constitution. Thomas J. DiLorenzo gives an account of how this came about in *The Real Lincoln: A New Look at Abraham Lincoln, His Agenda, and an Unnecessary War.*

As DiLorenzo documents—contrary to conventional wisdom, books about Lincoln, and the lessons taught in schools and colleges—the War between the States was not fought to end slavery. Even if it were, a natural question arises: Why was a costly war fought to end it? African slavery existed in many parts of the Western world, but it did not take warfare to end it. Dozens of countries, including the territorial possessions of the British, French, Portuguese, and Spanish, ended slavery peacefully during the late eighteenth and nineteenth centuries. Countries such as Venezuela and Colombia experienced conflict because slave emancipation was simply a ruse for revolutionaries who were seeking state power and were not motivated by emancipation per se.

Abraham Lincoln's direct statements indicated his support for slavery. He defended slave owners' right to own their property, saying that "when they remind us of their constitutional rights [to own slaves], I acknowledge them, not grudgingly but fully and fairly; and I would give them any legislation for the claiming of their fugitives" (in indicating support for the Fugitive Slave Act of 1850).

Abraham Lincoln's Emancipation Proclamation was little more than a political gimmick, and he admitted so in a letter to Treasury Secretary Salmon P. Chase: "The original proclamation has no . . . legal justification, except as a military measure." Secretary of State William Seward said, "We show our sympathy with slavery by emancipating slaves where we cannot reach them and holding them in bondage where we can set them free." Seward was acknowledging the fact that the Emancipation Proclamation applied only to slaves in states in rebellion against the United States and not to slaves in states not in rebellion.

The true costs of the War between the States were not the 620,000 battlefield-related deaths, out of a national population of 30 million (were we to control for population growth, that would be equivalent to roughly 5 million battlefield deaths today). The true costs were a change in the character of our government into one feared by the likes of Jefferson, Madison, Monroe, Jackson, and Calhoun—one where states lost most of their sovereignty to the central government. Thomas Jefferson saw as the most important safeguard of the liberties of the people "the support of the state governments in all their rights, as the most competent administrations for our domestic concerns and the surest bulwarks against anti-republican tendencies."

If the federal government makes encroachments on the constitutional rights of the people and the states, what are their options? In a word, their right to secede. Most of today's Americans believe, as did Abraham Lincoln, that states do not have a right to secession, but that is false. DiLorenzo marshals numerous proofs that from the very founding of our nation the right of secession was seen as a natural right of the people and a last check on abuse by the central government. For example, at Virginia's ratification convention, the delegates affirmed "that the powers granted under the Constitution being derived from the People of the United States may be resumed by them whensoever the same shall be perverted to injury or oppression." In Thomas Jefferson's First Inaugural Address (1801), he declared, "If there be any among us who would wish to dissolve this Union or to change its republican form, let them stand undisturbed as monuments of the safety with which error of opinion may be tolerated where reason is left free to combat it." Jefferson was defending the rights of free speech and of secession. Alexis de Tocqueville observed in *Democracy in America,* "The Union was formed by the voluntary agreement of the States; in uniting together they have not forfeited their nationality, nor have they been reduced to the condition of one and the same people. If one of the states chooses to withdraw from the compact, it would be difficult to disapprove its right of doing so, and the Federal Government would have no means of maintaining its claims directly either by force or right." The right to secession was popularly held as well. DiLorenzo lists newspaper after newspaper editorial arguing the right of secession. Most significantly, these were Northern newspapers. In fact, the first secession movement started in the North, long before shots were fired at Fort Sumter. The New England states debated the idea of secession during the Hartford Convention of 1814–1815.

Lincoln's intentions, as well as those of many Northern politicians, were summarized by Stephen Douglas during the senatorial debates. Douglas accused Lincoln of wanting to "impose on the nation a uniformity of local laws and institutions and a moral homogeneity dictated by the central government" that would "place at defiance the intentions of the republic's founders." Douglas was right, and Lincoln's vision for our nation has now been accomplished beyond anything he could have possibly dreamed.

The War between the States settled by force whether states could secede. Once it was established that states cannot secede, the federal government, abetted by a Supreme Court unwilling to hold it to its constitutional restraints, was able to run amok over states' rights, so much so that the protections of the Ninth and Tenth Amendments mean little or nothing today. Not only did the war lay the foundation for eventual nullification or weakening of basic constitutional protections against central government abuses, but it also laid to rest the great principle enunciated in the Declaration of Independence that "Governments are instituted among Men, deriving their just powers from the consent of the governed."

The Real Lincoln contains irrefutable evidence that a more appropriate title for Abraham Lincoln is not the Great Emancipator, but the Great Centralizer.

—*Walter E. Williams*
John M. Olin Distinguished Professor of Economics,
George Mason University, and nationally syndicated columnist

THE REAL
LINCOLN

CHAPTER 1

INTRODUCTION

Anyone who embarks on a study of Abraham Lincoln . . . must first come to terms with the Lincoln myth. The effort to penetrate the crust of legend that surrounds Lincoln . . . is both a formidable and intimidating task. Lincoln, it seems, requires special considerations that are denied to other figures. . . .
—ROBERT W. JOHANNSEN,
LINCOLN, THE SOUTH, AND SLAVERY

MORE WORDS have probably been written about Abraham Lincoln than about any other American political figure. According to one source, more than 16,000 books have been written on virtually every aspect of Lincoln's private and public life. But much of what has been written about Lincoln is myth, as Pulitzer Prize–winning Lincoln biographer David Donald noted in his 1961 book, *Lincoln Reconsidered*. Donald attempted to set at least part of the record straight; but, if anything, the literature on Lincoln has become even more dubious in the succeeding decades.[1] Anyone who delves into this literature with an open mind and an interest in the truth cannot help but be struck by the fantastic lengths to which an entire industry of "Lincoln scholars" has gone to perpetuate countless myths and questionable interpretations of events. Many of these myths will be examined in this book.

In the eyes of many Americans, Lincoln remains the most important American political figure in history because the War between the States so fundamentally transformed the nature of American government. Before the war, government in America was the highly decentralized, limited government established by the founding fathers. The war created the highly centralized state that Americans labor under today. The purpose of American government was transformed from the defense of individual liberty to the quest for empire. As historian Richard Bensel has observed, any study of the origins of the American state should begin no earlier than 1865.[2]

This aspect of the War between the States has always been downplayed or even ignored because of the emphasis that has been given to the important issue of slavery. Lincoln will forever be known as the Great Emancipator. But to understand the real Lincoln one must realize that during his twenty-eight years in politics before becoming president, he was almost single-mindedly devoted to an economic agenda that Henry Clay labeled "the American System." From the very first day in 1832 when he announced that he was running for the state legislature in Illinois, Lincoln expressed his devotion to the cause of protectionist tariffs, taxpayer subsidies for railroads and other corporations ("internal improvements"), and the nationalization of the money supply to help pay for the subsidies.

Lincoln labored mightily in the political trenches of the Whig and Republican parties for nearly three decades on behalf of this economic agenda, but with only minor success. The Constitution stood in the way of the Whig economic agenda as one American president after another vetoed internal improvement and national bank bills. Beginning with Jefferson, Madison, and Monroe, Southern statesmen were always in the forefront of the opposition to this economic agenda. According to Lincoln scholar Mark Neely, Jr., Lincoln seethed in frustration for many years over how the Constitution stood in the way of his political ambitions.

Lincoln thought of himself as the heir to the Hamiltonian political tradition, which sought a much more centralized governmental system, one that would plan economic development with corporate subsidies financed by protectionist tariffs and the printing of money by the central government. This agenda achieved little political success during the first seventy years of the nation's existence, but was fully implemented during the first two years of the Lincoln administration. It was Lincoln's real agenda.

Roy Basler, the editor of Lincoln's *Collected Works,* has written that Lincoln barely ever mentioned the issue of slavery before 1854, and, even then, he did not seem sincere.[3] Chapter 2 explores the doubts that many others have also expressed about Lincoln's supposed commitment to racial equality. The average American—who has not spent much time reading Lincoln's speeches but who has learned about him through the filter of the "Lincoln scholars"— will be surprised or even shocked by some of his words and actions. He stated over and over again that he was opposed to political or social equality of the races; he was not an abolitionist but denigrated them and distanced himself from them; and his primary means of dealing with racial problems was to attempt to colonize all American blacks in Africa, Haiti, Central America—anywhere but in the United States.

Chapter 2 also shows the extent to which Lincoln's views on race were consistent with those of the overwhelming majority of white Northerners, who discriminated against free blacks so severely that several states, including Lincoln's home state of Illinois, amended their constitutions to prohibit the emigration of black people into those states. Such facts raise serious questions about the extent to which racial injustice in the South motivated Lincoln and the Republican Party to wage a long, bloody war.

Chapter 3 poses a key question that almost no one has addressed in much detail: Why didn't Lincoln do what much of the rest of the world did in the nineteenth century and end slavery peacefully through compensated emancipation? Between 1800 and 1860, dozens of countries, including the entire British Empire, ended slavery peacefully; only in the United States was a war involved. It is very likely that most Americans, if they had been given the opportunity, would have gladly supported compensated emancipation as a means of ending slavery, as opposed to the almost unimaginable costs of the war: 620,000 deaths, thousands more maimed for life, and the near total destruction of approximately 40 percent of the nation's economy. Standardizing for today's population of some 280 million (compared to 30 million in 1865), this would be roughly the equivalent of 5 million deaths—about a hundred times the number of Americans who died in Vietnam.

Chapter 4 outlines Lincoln's real agenda: Henry Clay's "American System." For his entire political life Lincoln was devoted to Clay and Clay's economic agenda. The debate over this economic agenda was arguably the most important political debate during the first seventy years of the nation's existence. It involved the nation's most prominent statesmen and pitted the states' rights Jeffersonians against the centralizing Hamiltonians (who became Whigs and, later, Republicans). The violence of war finally ended the debate in 1861.

Chapter 5 discusses the long history of the right of secession in America, beginning with the Declaration of Independence, which is properly viewed as a "Declaration of Secession" from England. The New England Federalists attempted for more than a decade to secede from the Union after Thomas Jefferson was elected president in 1800. Until 1861 most commentators, North and South, took it for granted that states had a right to secede. This doctrine was even taught to the cadets at West Point, including almost all of the top military commanders on both sides of the conflict during the War between the States.

Lincoln's insistence that no such right existed has no basis whatsoever in history or fact. He essentially invented a new theory—that the federal government created the states, which were therefore not sovereign—and waged the bloodiest war in world history up to that point to "prove" himself right.

Chapter 6 deals with the odd nature of the claim by so many Lincoln scholars that Lincoln "saved" the Constitution by suspending constitutional liberty *in the North* for the entire duration of his administration. He supposedly had to destroy constitutional liberty in order to save it.

Quite a few Lincoln scholars have labeled Lincoln a "dictator" for launching a military invasion without the consent of Congress; suspending habeas corpus; imprisoning thousands of Northern citizens without trial for merely opposing his policies; censoring all telegraph communication and imprisoning dozens of opposition newspaper publishers; nationalizing the railroads; using Federal troops to interfere with elections; confiscating firearms; and deporting an opposition member of Congress, Clement L. Vallandigham, after he opposed Lincoln's income tax proposal during a Democratic Party rally in Ohio.

Even though many have labeled these acts as "dictatorial," they usually add that Lincoln was a "good" or "benevolent" dictator. In reality, these precedents did irreparable harm to constitutional liberty in America. Some writers, such as historian Garry Wills and Columbia University law professor George P. Fletcher, have voiced their approval of Lincoln's assault on constitutional liberty because they believe that the Constitution stands in the way of their cherished goal of "egalitarianism." They openly celebrate the fact that Lincoln led the way in subverting constitutional government in America.

In addition to abandoning the Constitution, the Lincoln administration established another ominous precedent by deciding to abandon international law and the accepted moral code of civilized societies and wage war on civilians. General William Tecumseh Sherman announced that to secessionists—all of them, women and children included— "death is mercy." Chapter 7 details how Lincoln abandoned the generally accepted rules of war, which had just been codified by the Geneva Convention of 1863. Lincoln famously micromanaged the war effort, and the burning of entire Southern towns was an essential feature of his war strategy.

Lincoln's political legacy is explored in chapter 8 in the context of how, during Reconstruction (1865–1877), the Republican Party essentially plundered the South for twelve more years by instituting puppet governments that constantly raised taxes but provided very few public benefits. Much of the money was simply stolen by Republican Party activists and their business supporters. The adult male ex-slaves were immediately given the right to vote in the South (even though blacks could not vote in several Northern states), while most white male Southerners were disenfranchised. Former Union General and newspaper editor Donn Piatt, a close Lincoln confidant, expressed the opinion that using the ex-slaves as political pawns in such a corrupt way poisoned race relations in the South beyond repair at a time when racial reconciliation should have been the primary objective.

Lincoln's policy of crushing dissenters with overwhelming military might was continued after the war with the federal government's eradication of the Plains Indians by many of the same generals who had guided the North's war effort (particularly Grant, Sherman, and Sheridan). The stated purpose of this campaign against the Plains Indians was to make way for the government-subsidized transcontinental railroads. The quest for empire had become the primary goal of government in America.

Chapter 9 describes Lincoln's economic legacy: the realization of Henry Clay's American System. Many (primarily) Southern statesmen had opposed this system for decades because they viewed it as nothing more than the corrupt "mercantilist" system that prevailed in England during the eighteenth and early nineteenth centuries, and they wanted no part of it. Indeed, many of the original colonists fled to America to escape from that very system. So powerful was Southern opposition to the American System that the Confederate Constitution outlawed both protectionist tariffs and internal improvement subsidies altogether. Lincoln's war created the "military-industrial complex" some ninety years before President Eisenhower coined the phrase.

The notorious corruption of the Grant administrations was an inevitable consequence of Lincoln's success in imposing the "American System" on the nation during the war. The "Era of Good Stealings," as one historian described it, proved that the concerns of Southern statesmen, from Thomas Jefferson to Jefferson Davis, were well founded.

Chapter 10 explains how the death of federalism—the decentralized system of government that was established by the founding fathers—was perhaps the biggest cost of Lincoln's war. Although Lincoln is generally credited with having "saved the Union," in reality he *destroyed* the idea of the Union as a *voluntary* association of states by forcing the Southern states to remain in the Union at gunpoint. Lincoln can be said to have saved the Union only in a geographical sense.

It was not to end slavery that Lincoln initiated an invasion of the South. He stated over and over again that his main purpose was to "save the Union," which is another way of saying that he wanted to abolish states' rights once and for all. He could have ended slavery just as dozens of other countries in the world did during the first sixty years of the nineteenth century, through compensated emancipation, but he never seriously attempted to do so. A war was not necessary to free the slaves, but it was necessary to destroy the most significant check on the powers of the central government: the right of secession.

CHAPTER 2

LINCOLN'S OPPOSITION TO RACIAL EQUALITY

———————◆◆◆———————

The whole nation is interested that the best use
shall be made of these [new] territories. We want
them for the homes of free white people.
—ABRAHAM LINCOLN, OCTOBER 16, 1854

ABRAHAM LINCOLN was a master politician and, as such, was a master of rhetoric as well. It is doubtful that any American politician has ever matched his skills in this regard. But his actions frequently belied his beautiful prose; and, like most successful politicians, he was not above saying one thing to one audience and the opposite to another. Lincoln's speeches and writings offer support for both sides of many issues.

Lincoln is usually thought of as a great statesman rather than a great politician, but that distinction can be misleading. Lincoln was, first and foremost, a consummate politician. Lincoln biographer David Donald described Lincoln as "the master wirepuller who operated the [Illinois] state political organization first of the Whig Party and, after its decay, that of the Republicans."[1] Lincoln's law partner, William Herndon, once recalled that Lincoln was "the smartest parliamentarian and cunningest logroller" in the Illinois legislature.[2] Lincoln himself once said that his political ambition was to become the "De Witt Clinton of Illinois," so impressed was he with the former governor of New York, who introduced the spoils system to America.[3] Economist Murray Rothbard was even more forthright in his assessment: "Lincoln was a master politician, which means that he was a consummate conniver, manipulator, and liar."[4]

Lincoln has gone down in history as a champion of equality; indeed, some political scientists, such as Harry V. Jaffa, have even argued that Lincoln literally redefined the purpose of American government as the pursuit of equality rather than individual liberty.[5] This is a problematic inter-pretation, however, for Lincoln stated over and over that he was opposed to racial equality. Perhaps his clearest statement of opposition to racial equality was his response to Senator Stephen Douglas in an 1858 debate in Ottawa, Illinois:

> I have no purpose to introduce political and social equality between the white and black races. There is a physical differ-ence between the two, which, in my judgment, will probably forever forbid their living together upon the footing of per-fect equality; and inasmuch as it becomes a necessity that there must be a difference, I, as well as Judge Douglas, am in favor of the race to which I belong having the superior posi-tion. I have never said anything to the contrary.[6]

Lincoln also said that he was not and never had been "in favor of making voters or jurors of Negroes, nor of qualifying them to hold office, nor to intermarry with white people."[7] He was indignant over Senator Douglas's insinuation that he might favor racial equality and dismissed the idea by saying, "anything that argues me into his [Douglas's] idea of perfect social and political equality with the Negro is but a specious and fantastic arrangement of words, by which a man can prove a horse chestnut to be a chestnut horse."[8]

Lincoln is often hailed as a champion of the dictum in the Declaration of Independence that "all men are created equal." However, not all Lincoln scholars agree; some have even mocked the idea that Lincoln was upholding the equality principle of the Declaration. *Ebony* magazine editor Lerone Bennett, Jr., disagrees with the standard interpretation. "On at least fourteen occasions between 1854 and 1860," Bennett writes, "Lincoln said unambiguously that he believed the Negro race was inferior to the White race. In Galesburg, he referred to 'the inferior races.' Who were 'the inferior races'? African Americans, he said, Mexicans, who he called 'mongrells,' and probably all colored people."[9] These words contradict the Declaration.

On the topic of emancipation, Lincoln said, "Free them, and make them politically and socially our equals? My own feelings will not admit of this. . . . We cannot, then, make them equals."[10]

He also strongly defended the right of slaveowners to own their "property," saying that "when they remind us of their constitutional rights [to own slaves], I acknowledge them, not grudgingly but fully and fairly; and I would give them any legislation for the reclaiming of their fugitives."[11] That is, he promised to support the Fugitive Slave Act of 1850, which obligated the federal government to use its resources to return runaway slaves to their owners. (Under this act, fugitive slaves had no legal safeguards, such as a trial or a hearing. A federal slave "commissioner" was paid $10 if he ordered a slave's return but only $5 if he granted a slave's freedom. Citizens were called upon by the federal government to capture runaway slaves, and there were fines and prison sentences for anyone who concealed a runaway slave. At the time, the act had been upheld by the U.S. Supreme Court and by the supreme courts of every Northern state. Lincoln was clearly in the mainstream of Northern public opinion here.)

While adamantly opposing "social and political equality" of the races, Lincoln took the contradictory position of also defending—at least rhetorically—the natural rights of all races to life, liberty, and the pursuit of happiness, as enumerated in the Declaration of Independence, and referred to slavery as a "monstrous injustice."[12] But blacks could never in fact achieve equality if they were denied all the other rights that Lincoln would deny them—to vote, to become jurors, and so on. It was a textbook example of a masterful, rhetorically gifted, fence-straddling politician wanting to have it both ways—in favor of and opposed to racial equality at the same time—in an attempt to maximize his political support.

If Lincoln had an idol and a role model, it was the Kentucky slaveowner Henry Clay, whom he described as "my *beau ideal* of a statesman, the man for whom I fought all my humble life."[13] Clay was "the great parent of Whig principles," said Lincoln, and the source of his own political views. "During my whole political life I have loved and revered [Henry Clay] as a teacher and leader."[14] (More will be said of Lincoln's devotion to Clay's "Whig principles" in chapter 4.)

In his eulogy to Henry Clay, delivered in Springfield, Illinois, on July 6, 1852, Lincoln mustered his best rhetorical talents to praise Clay as a "majestic form" who supposedly "beat back the storms of anarchy" with his "mighty mind" and "gallant heart," the "mighty sweep of that graceful arm," and the "magic of that eloquent tongue."[15]

When Lincoln began explaining Clay's policy positions in the eulogy, writes Lincoln biographer Robert W. Johannsen, he was in fact "describing his own."[16] On the issue of slavery, Lincoln's position was virtually identical to Clay's. "I can express all my views on the slavery question," Lincoln announced, "by quotations from Henry Clay."[17] This position was, as Johannsen described it, "opposition to slavery in principle, toleration of it in practice, and a vigorous hostility toward the abolition movement."[18]

In the eulogy Lincoln claimed that Clay, like himself, had a "deep devotion to the cause of human liberty," even though Clay was a slaveowner. Clay was opposed to slavery "on principle"; however, he not only owned slaves but also was opposed to eliminating slavery. In Lincoln's words, "[Clay] did not perceive, as I think no wise man has perceived, how [slavery] could be at once eradicated, without producing a greater evil, even to the cause of human liberty itself."[19]

It's hard to imagine a clearer example of circular reasoning: Slavery is an affront to human liberty, but ending slavery would supposedly be even worse.

Lincoln denounced the abolitionists as zealots who "would shiver into fragments the Union of these States; tear to tatters its now venerated constitution, and even burn the last copy of the Bible, rather than slavery should continue a single hour."[20] Moreover, the "name, and opinions, and influence of Mr. Clay" (and presumably of Mr. Lincoln as well) "are fully, and, as I trust, effectually and enduringly, arrayed against [the abolitionists]" who were at the time receiving their "just execration" by the public.[21]

Lincoln was a highly skilled lawyer who, from 1837 to 1860, tried literally thousands of cases and was frequently employed by other lawyers as a consultant. He was one of the top attorneys in the Midwest, and his clients included the Illinois Central Railroad, then the largest railroad in the world. By the 1850s his income averaged about $5,000 per year, three times what the governor of Illinois was paid.[22]

Lincoln tried all kinds of cases, from those dealing with disputed wills, taxes, foreclosures, and debt to slander, assault, murder, divorce, and horse theft. He argued before the Illinois Supreme Court dozens of times and once appeared before the U.S. Supreme Court. In twenty-three years of litigation he never defended a runaway slave, but he did defend a slaveowner.

His client was a wealthy Illinois farmer named Robert Matson who brought slaves into Illinois from Kentucky during part of the year to work his farm. Matson's mistress became angry with him and threatened to sell the slaves in another state. Anthony Bryant, a freed black who was

Matson's overseer, smuggled the slaves away to an inn-keeper's house, and Matson brought suit to have his slaves returned.

Lincoln defended Matson before William Wilson, the chief justice of the Illinois Supreme Court. The slaves' at-torney argued that since Illinois was not a slave state, the slaves had to be set free. Lincoln countered that the Illinois Constitution did not apply because the slaves were only seasonal workers and did not reside in Illinois the entire year; they returned annually to Kentucky, which was a slave state. On October 17, 1847, the Illinois Supreme Court ruled against Lincoln and emancipated Matson's slaves.[23]

Lincoln was widely regarded as "a lawyer's lawyer"; and so, one could argue, it was no more unusual for him to represent a slaveowner than it would have been for him to represent a murderer. The Constitution guarantees every citizen the right of legal defense in criminal cases. But isn't it odd that Lincoln, who professed to be so bothered by the existence of slavery, attempted to condemn several dozen men and women into permanent, lifetime servitude for a modest legal fee?

LINCOLN AND COLONIZATION

ACCORDING TO ROY BASLER, the editor of Lincoln's *Collected Works,* as of 1857 Lincoln had no solution to the problem of slavery "except the colonization idea which he inherited from Henry Clay."[24] When, during the war, he was asked what should be done with the slaves were they ever to be freed, he said, "Send them to Liberia, to their own native land."[25] As president, Lincoln held a White House meeting with freed black leaders and implored them to lead a colonization movement back to Africa. He developed plans to send every last black person to Africa, Haiti, Central America—anywhere but the United States.[26]

In his eulogy to Clay, Lincoln made much of Clay's colonization idea. Clay was one of the founding members of the American Colonization Society and was its president when he died in 1852. The movement to send all blacks back to Africa was one of Clay's "most cherished objects" under "his direct care and consideration," said Lincoln, and "the association of his name with it has probably been its very greatest collateral support."[27] Lincoln approvingly quoted Clay as saying that "there is a moral fitness in the idea of returning to Africa her children" since "they will carry back to their native soil the rich fruits of religion, civilization, law and liberty."[28] How they would do this after having been deprived of an education and of the fruits of religion, civilization, law, and liberty in the United States was not explained. Nevertheless, sending all blacks back to Africa would supposedly be a "signal blessing to that most unfortunate portion of the globe."[29]

To this Lincoln added that Clay's colonization idea, first proposed in 1827, could mean the "ultimate redemption of the African race." Moreover, every year since then had "added strength to the hope of its realization," he said. "May it indeed be realized!"[30] Some ten years later, December 1, 1862, in a message to Congress, Lincoln reiterated his earlier assertions: "I cannot make it better known than it already is, that I strongly favor colonization."[31]

Eliminating every last black person from American soil, Lincoln proclaimed, would be "a glorious consummation."[32] This was apparently always Lincoln's position. In his famous Cooper Union speech on February 27, 1860, he advocated the peaceful "deportation" of blacks so that "their places be . . . filled up by free white laborers."[33] As a member of the Illinois legislature in 1857, he urged his colleagues to appropriate money to remove all of the free blacks from the state of Illinois.[34]

When Congress ended slavery in the District of Columbia in 1862, it simultaneously appropriated $600,000 as an initial authorization to send the freed slaves back to Africa. Lincoln appointed as his Commissioner of Emigration James Mitchell, a former leader of the American Colonization Society, who planned to send the freedmen not to Africa but to the Danish West Indies, Dutch Guiana, British Guiana, British Honduras, Guadeloupe, and Ecuador—anywhere but Washington, D.C., in particular and the United States in general.[35]

Lincoln gave colonization such a high priority that he also instructed his Secretary of the Interior, Caleb Smith, to work out plans for colonization and asked Senator Samuel Pomeroy to supervise resettlement efforts. Pomeroy proposed a Central American colony called "Linconia."[36]

The Lincoln administration also signed a contract with businessman Bernard Kock to establish a colony in Haiti. Kock turned out to be a crook and an embezzler, which must have been a deep disappointment to Lincoln, who "continued to believe that removal [of blacks] was the true solution to the race question."[37] Historian P. J. Staudenraus, who wrote the definitive book on the American Colonization Society, explained that

> The American Colonization Society's leaders watched in amazement as Lincoln's administration, spurning Liberia, toyed with first one plan and then another. In vain they urged the harried war leader to send emigrants to the African republic. Lincoln privately agreed with President Roberts of Liberia that Africa was the logical place for American Negroes, but he continued to endorse Central American ventures.[38]

America's preeminent abolitionist, William Lloyd Garrison, bitterly denounced Lincoln because of his infatuation with attempts to preserve the United States for whites through colonization. "President Lincoln may colonize himself if he choose," Garrison fumed, "but it is an impertinent act, on his part, to propose the getting rid of those who are as good as himself." Lincoln, in Garrison's eyes, "had not a drop of anti-slavery blood in his veins."[39] Garrison was furious that Lincoln held a meeting in the White House with freed black leaders and asked them to lead an exodus of blacks out of the country. Garrison began calling Lincoln "The President of African Colonization" and referred to the meeting as a "humiliating" and "impertinent" spectacle.[40]

Lincoln has become such an American icon that when one delves into the historical literature, one discovers that much of the Lincoln historiography is not so much an attempt to explain history as to devise rationalizations or excuses for Lincoln's behavior. An example of this phenomenon is an essay by historian Gabor Boritt on Lincoln and colonization. As just described, Lincoln was very clear—for literally decades—about his views on colonization and about their origins with Henry Clay and the American Colonization Society.

But to Boritt, Lincoln only "evoked in a vague way colonization."[41] Although Lincoln was bitterly denounced for his colonization proposals by America's greatest champion of abolition, William Lloyd Garrison, to Boritt his "fundamental rationale for colonization remained noble, as far as nobility was possible on behalf of such a proposal."[42]

Boritt admits that Lincoln was "the leading proponent of black emigration" out of the United States, but then offers a series of questionable rationalizations: Lincoln only "started" a colonization movement and did not succeed in shipping all blacks out of the country; he was "uncharacteristically sloppy in his thought" on this topic (but, presumably, on no others); he would have changed his mind with "more intensity of thought"; Americans would supposedly favor emancipation (which few did) if they thought all the freed slaves would be shipped out of the country; and, in a particularly Orwellian twist, he was an honest liar ("This is how honest people lie," says Boritt).[43] Historians like Boritt have created a literary and historical fog bank that makes it extremely difficult to understand the real Abraham Lincoln.

LINCOLN'S OPPOSITION TO THE EXTENSION OF SLAVERY

LINCOLN HAD NO INTENTION of doing anything about *Southern* slavery in 1860. In his First Inaugural Address he announced that "I have no purpose, directly or indirectly, to interfere with the institution of slavery *in the States where it exists*. I believe I have no lawful right to do so, and I have no inclination to do so" (emphasis added).[44] He also promised, in the same address, to strengthen the Fugitive Slave Law even though lax enforcement of it or none at all would have quickened slavery's demise.

None of the four political parties that fielded presidential candidates in the 1860 election advocated the abolition of Southern slavery. Doing so would have meant political suicide because—except for the small abolitionist movement—public opinion was not in favor of abolition at the time. When the issue of slavery was raised by politicians, it was discussed in terms of the *extension* of slavery into the new territories, not abolition of the institution in the South. But even then, opposition to the extension of slavery was not always based on moral grounds. Although there were undoubtedly some sincere abolitionists who believed that disallowing slavery in the new territories would contribute to its eventual demise everywhere, a more prominent concern was that slaves would compete with white labor in the territories, which the Republican Party wanted to keep as the exclusive preserve of whites. Lincoln explained the rationale for this very clearly when he spoke in Peoria, Illinois, on October 16, 1854:

> Whether slavery shall go into Nebraska, or other new territories, is not a matter of exclusive concern to the people who may go there. The whole nation is interested that the best use shall be made of these territories. We want them for the homes of free white people. This they cannot be, to

any considerable extent, if slavery shall be planted with them. Slave states are the places for poor white people to move from. . . . New free states are the places for poor people to go and better their condition.[45]

This idea—that the new territories were to become a whites-only preserve—defined the Republican Party's position on slavery in 1860. As Lincoln confidant and Secretary of State William Seward explained, "The motive of those who protested against the extension of slavery had always really been concern for the welfare of the white man, and not an *unnatural* sympathy for the Negro" (emphasis added).[46]

New York Tribune editor Horace Greeley, perhaps the most influential journalist of his day and a staunch Republican, expressed the Republican Party's stance most succinctly: "All the unoccupied territory . . . shall be preserved for the benefit of the white Caucasian race—a thing which cannot be except by the exclusion of slavery."[47]

Lyman Trumbull, a U.S. Senator from Illinois and Lincoln confidant, explained that "we, the Republican Party, are the white man's party. We are for the free white man, and for making white labor acceptable and honorable, which it can never be when Negro slave labor is brought into competition with it."[48] Trumbull pledged that he would never consent to "Negro equality" on any terms. "When we say that all men are created equal," Trumbull declared, "we do not mean that every man in organized society has the same rights. We don't tolerate that in Illinois."[49] He agreed with Lincoln that colonization was the best "solution" to the race problem.

Throughout the 1860 campaign, writes historian Eugene Berwanger, "Republicans made no pretense of being concerned with the fate of the Negro and insisted that theirs was a party of white labor. By introducing a note of white supremacy, they hoped to win the votes of the Negrophobes and the anti-abolitionists who were opposed to the extension of slavery."[50] Republican Party leaders—"especially from the Middle West"—"made it sufficiently clear that they had no intention of uplifting the Negro or equalizing his place in society."[51]

When Representative David Wilmot of Pennsylvania introduced his historic proviso to exclude slavery from the territories acquired after the Mexican War, he carefully explained that he had "no morbid sympathy for the slave" but "[pled] the cause and the rights of white freemen": "I would preserve to free white labor a fair country, a rich inheritance, where the sons of toil, of my own race and color, can live without the disgrace which association with Negro slavery brings upon free labor."[52]

There was a second political reason why Lincoln and the Republicans opposed the extension of slavery into the new territories: It would artificially inflate the congressional power of the Democratic Party. The three-fifths clause of the Constitution allowed every five slaves to account for three persons *for purposes of determining the number of congressional seats in each state,* which has always been a function of a state's population. This, Lincoln believed, was "manifestly unfair" to the Northern states that, in 1860, chose him as the first sectional presidential candidate in U.S. history. (He received no electoral votes from any Southern state in the election because he was perceived as representing only Northern interests.)

In his Peoria speech, Lincoln spoke of "the practical effect of this" by comparing Maine and South Carolina, each of which had six congressional representatives and eight electors, even though Maine had 581,813 white people and South Carolina had a mere 274,567. By Lincoln's accounting, the three-fifths clause gave each white male South Carolinian two votes in Congress for every one vote for a man from Maine because of the former state's 384,984 slaves. "This principle, in the aggregate, gives the slave States in the present Congress, twenty additional representatives."[53] The extension of slavery into the new territories would exacerbate this congressional imbalance in favor of the Democratic Party, which is why Lincoln led the Republican Party's opposition to it—it was opposition to slavery, but not on moral grounds.

NORTHERN ATTITUDES TOWARD RACE

THE MORE OR LESS "official" interpretation of the cause of the War between the States, as described in *The Complete Book of U.S. Presidents,* by historian William A. DeGregorio, asserts that the slavery issue "pitted abolitionists in the North who viewed it as a moral evil to be eradicated everywhere as soon as practicable against southern extremists who fostered the spread of slavery into the territories." Lincoln is posited as one of the moderates "who believed slavery to be wrong but nevertheless protected by the Constitution and who were content to contain it in the South."[54]

This may be the official interpretation, but myriad facts suggest that it is, at the least, an incomplete interpretation. There was indeed a vigorous abolitionist movement in parts of the North, but it was a very small movement—so small that politicians like Lincoln did not risk associating themselves with it. No abolitionist was ever elected to any major political office in any Northern state. The overwhelming majority of white Northerners cared little about the welfare of the slaves and treated the blacks who lived among them with contempt, ridicule, discrimination, and sometimes violence. As Eugene Berwanger wrote in *North of Slavery,* as of 1860,

> In virtually every phase of existence [in the North], Negroes found themselves systematically separated from whites. They were either excluded from railway cars, omnibuses, stagecoaches, and steamboats or assigned to special "Jim Crow" sections; they sat, when permitted, in secluded and remote corners of theaters and lecture halls; they could not enter most hotels, restaurants, and resorts, except as servants; they prayed in "Negro pews" in the white churches, and if partaking of the sacrament of the Lord's Supper, they waited until the whites had been served the bread and wine. Moreover, they were often educated in segregated schools, punished in segregated prisons, nursed in segregated hospitals, and buried in segregated cemeteries . . . racial prejudice haunts its victim wherever he goes.[55]

In *Democracy in America,* Tocqueville wrote that "the prejudice of race appears to be stronger in the states that have abolished slavery than in those where it still exists; and nowhere is it so intolerant as in those states where servitude has never been known."[56] Tocqueville found that in the North, if laws did not discriminate against blacks in virtually every area of their existence, "popular prejudices" did. Public opinion "did not permit" blacks to legally marry, vote, or utilize the judicial system.

Lincoln was the first "sectional" president in the sense that he owed his election exclusively to support from the Northern states. He won a four-man race with just under 40 percent of the popular vote and 180 of the 303 electoral votes. His electoral victory came from winning the electoral votes in eighteen states from the North and West: California, Connecticut, Illinois, Indiana, Iowa, Maine, Massachusetts, Michigan, Minnesota, New Hampshire, New Jersey, New York, Ohio, Oregon, Pennsylvania, Rhode Island, Vermont, and Wisconsin. He was thus the North's candidate in the election and, as such, could not have won had he diverged significantly from the views of mainstream Northerners on the issue of race.

Northerners discriminated against blacks in cruel and inhumane ways during the 1850s—raising serious questions about the notion that the majority of the population in the North elected Lincoln (primarily) because of his enlightened views on slavery. If his views were enlightened, they were sharply at odds with those of most Northern voters.

So-called Black Codes existed in the North decades before such discriminatory laws were enacted in the South after Reconstruction (1865–1877). The *Revised Code of Indiana,* for example, prohibited Negroes and mulattos from coming into the state; all contracts with Negroes were null and void; any white person (such as an employer) who encouraged blacks to enter the state was subject to a fine of up to $500; Negroes and mulattos were not allowed to vote; no Negro or mulatto having even one-eighth part of Negro blood could legally marry a white person—an act punishable by ten years' imprisonment and a fine of up to $5,000; any person counseling or encouraging interracial marriage was subject to a fine of up to $1,000; Negroes and mulattos were forbidden from testifying in court against white people, from sending their children to public schools, or from holding any political office.[57]

This meant that blacks could not earn a lawful living in any kind of business, would be subject to political plunder, since they had no voting rights, and could be subjected to criminal abuse by whites, since they had no right to defend themselves in court. They were denied, in other words, all of the most basic human freedoms, making a mockery of the notion that they were "free men."

Such discriminatory laws were common in virtually every Northern state as of 1860. In 1847 Ohioans prohibited the resettlement of the 518 emancipated slaves of the Virginia statesman John Randolph. An Ohio congressman threatened that if any blacks tried to cross the border into Ohio "the banks of the Ohio River . . . would be lined with men with muskets on their shoulders to keep off the emancipated slaves."[58]

The new territories either explicitly prohibited blacks from residing within their borders or required them to post a bond of up to $1,000 that could be forfeited for "bad behavior." To the extent that this was enforced, it made it impossible for black emigration to occur. If such fines were imposed but not paid, then blacks were subject to being whipped, hired out, or sold into slavery, according to an 1853 Illinois statute.[59]

The federal government required every new territory or state to deny voting rights to blacks all the way up to the 1860s. The only Northern states where blacks were permitted to vote were Massachusetts, New Hampshire, Vermont, and Maine; and even there they were often intimidated out of showing up at the polls. Only 6 percent of all the "free" blacks in the North lived in these states, however; 94 percent of all Northern blacks did not enjoy the right to vote as of 1860.[60]

New Jersey and Connecticut actually amended their constitutions in the 1840s to prohibit black suffrage; no such distinctions were made in their original constitutions.[61] Only Massachusetts permitted blacks to serve as jurors prior to the end of the War between the States.

Illinois, along with Indiana and Oregon, amended its state constitution to prohibit the emigration of blacks into the state. These amendments were approved by public referenda with a margin of more than two to one in Illinois, almost three to one in Indiana, and eight to one in Oregon.[62] Illinois Senator Lyman Trumbull explained that "there is a very great aversion in the West—I know it to be so in my State—against having free Negroes come among us. Our people want nothing to do with the Negro."[63]

With attitudes and laws like this in existence in all the new territories, it is easy to understand why Lincoln's (and the Republican Party's) stance against the extension of slavery into the new territories struck such a responsive chord among the white population.

Lincoln said he was in favor of extending basic protections of life, liberty, and the pursuit of happiness to freed blacks, but he contradicted himself by simultaneously opposing black citizenship. He reminded his constituents in 1858 that only states, not the federal government, could offer Negro citizenship and promised that if Illinois should entertain such a proposal he would oppose it.[64] A disenfranchised black man who could not testify in court in a case involving a white man and could not sit on a jury did not enjoy common legal protection. Thus, Lincoln's clever political position, which was quite popular, was to have the government protect Negro life and property, but deny blacks all rights to vote, to participate in the judicial system, and to enjoy any semblance of social equality, while promoting a plan to colonize them in Africa, Central America, Haiti—anywhere but America. He supported and voted for all the laws of his own state that denied blacks basic citizenship rights and economic freedoms and did not object to the constitutional prohibition of black emigration into the state.

Although New York State helped to elect Lincoln in 1860, it overwhelmingly rejected a proposal to allow Negro suffrage. As late as 1869, New York voters defeated equal-suffrage referenda; between 1849 and 1857 Michigan, Iowa, and Wisconsin also overwhelmingly rejected equal-suffrage referenda.[65]

Northern labor unions, attempting to become popular with the masses, did not accept black members and vigorously opposed abolition. Unions were at the forefront of political lobbying for laws and regulations that would prohibit blacks from competing for jobs held by whites in myriad trades. As one Connecticut union official warned, "Unless the legislature adopted appropriate entry restrictions . . . the sons of Connecticut would soon be driven from the state by the great influx of black porters, black truckmen, black sawyers, black mechanics, and black laborers of every description."[66] Every other Northern state legislature was petitioned to enact various Black Codes that would deprive blacks of economic liberties.

Stripped of most of their legal rights in Northern states, blacks were often the victims of mob violence. Irish immigrants were especially guilty of such abominations since they viewed free blacks as direct competitors for their jobs—more so, apparently, than did most other immigrant groups.

White supremacist attitudes were not only on display in the Northern Black Codes and other pieces of legislation but were enunciated in Northern newspapers as well. As the *Philadelphia Daily News* editorialized on November 22, 1860, "It is neither for the good of the colored race nor of our own that they should continue to dwell among us to any considerable extent. The two races can never exist in conjunction except as superior and inferior. . . . The African is naturally the inferior race."[67]

The Niles (Michigan) *Republican* wrote on March 30, 1861, that "this government was made for the benefit of the white race . . . and not for Negroes."[68] The *Daily Chicago Times* editorialized on December 7, 1860, that "evil and nothing but evil, has ever followed in the track of this hideous monster, Abolition." It continued, "Let [the slave] alone—send him back to his master where he belongs."[69]

On January 22, 1861, the *New York Times* announced that it opposed the abolition of slavery. Instead, it proposed that slaves should be allowed to legally marry and should be taught to read and to invest their money in savings accounts. Those actions should be taken "to ameliorate, rather than to abolish, the Slavery of the Southern States" and would thus permit slavery to become "a very tolerable system."[70]

"We have no more right to meddle with slavery in Georgia, than we have to meddle with monarchy in Europe," declared the *Providence Daily Post* on February 2, 1861.[71] The *Columbus* (Ohio) *Crisis* added five days later that "we are not Abolitionists nor in favor of Negro equality."[72] The *New York Herald,* which had the largest circulation in the country at the time, sang the praises of slavery on March 7, 1861: "The immense increase in the numbers [of slaves] within so short a time speaks for the good treatment and happy, contented lot of the slaves. They are comfortably fed, housed and clothed, and seldom or never overworked."[73]

The *Philadelphia Inquirer* endorsed Lincoln's colonization proposals on March 11, 1861, when it pointed out that "Hayti lies in the torrid zone, the proper residence of the Negro."[74] "The proposition that the Negro is equal by nature, physically and mentally, to the white man, seems to be so absurd and preposterous, that we cannot conceive how it can be entertained by any intelligent and rational white man," the *Concord* (New Hampshire) *Democrat Standard* editorialized on September 8, 1860.[75] To this the neighboring *Boston Daily Courier* added, on September 24, 1860, that "we believe the mulatto to be inferior in capacity, character, and organization to the full-blooded black, and still farther below the standard of the white races."[76]

The foregoing discussion calls into question the standard account that Northerners elected Lincoln in a fit of moral outrage spawned by their deep-seated concern for the welfare of black slaves in the deep South. Blacks in the North were treated horribly and were institutionally deprived of the most fundamental human freedoms by the myriad Black Codes and by discrimination and violence.

It is conceivable that many white supremacists in the North (which included most of the population) nevertheless abhorred the institution of slavery. However, given the attitudes of most Northerners toward blacks, it is doubtful that their abhorrence of slavery was sufficient motivation for hundreds of thousands of them to give their lives on bloody battlefields, as they did, during the war. It is one thing to proclaim one's disdain for slavery; it is quite another to die for it.

CHAPTER 3

WHY NOT PEACEFUL EMANCIPATION?

————— ◆ —————

Abraham Lincoln was not an abolitionist.
—DAVID DONALD, *LINCOLN RECONSIDERED*

WITH REGARD TO the slavery issue, Lincoln matched his deeds to his words. In the summer of 1861, he had several opportunities to liberate thousands of slaves, but he refused to do so. Union General John Frémont (the Republican Party presidential nominee in 1856, for whom Lincoln campaigned) was in charge of the Federal government's military efforts in Missouri, where a very effective guerilla warfare campaign was being waged by the Confederates. In an attempt to deter the guerillas, Frémont issued a proclamation on August 30, 1861, adopting martial law throughout the state and asserting that any persons resisting the occupying Federal army would have their property confiscated and their slaves declared freemen. Unionists were free to keep their slaves.[1]

When Lincoln learned of Frémont's proclamation, he ordered him to modify it so that no Federal troops could shoot civilians unless first given Lincoln's personal permission to do so. Furthermore, he not only nullified the emancipation part of the proclamation but also stripped Frémont of his command on November 2, 1861, despite a personal plea by Frémont's wife. A similar incident occurred in May 1862 when Union General David Hunter attempted to emancipate slaves in Union-held territory in Georgia, Florida, and South Carolina.[2]

Many slaves who ended up in the hands of the Federal army were not set free but were put to work doing the most unpleasant tasks in and around army encampments. Others were sent back to their owners. Congress passed several "confiscation acts" in the early years of the war that allowed Federal troops to confiscate the slaves (and other property) in conquered rebel territory. As one Illinois lieutenant wrote, "I have 11 Negroes in my company now. They do every particle of the dirty work. Two women among them do the washing for the company."[3]

Lincoln was excoriated by abolitionists for failing to take the opportunity to free some slaves and by Republican Party politicians for the way he treated Frémont. Senator Ben Wade of Ohio wrote "in bitter execration" that "the President don't object to General Frémont's taking the life of the owners of slaves, when found in rebellion, but to confiscate their property and emancipate their slaves he thinks monstrous."[4]

In a famous public letter to New York Tribune editor Horace Greeley in 1862, Lincoln explained that he wasn't particularly concerned about emancipation per se; forcing the secessionists to remain in the Union was his main objective:

> My paramount object in this struggle is to save the Union, and is *not* either to save or to destroy slavery. If I could save the Union without freeing *any* slave I would do it; and if I could save it by freeing some and leaving others alone I would also do that. What I do about slavery, and the colored race, I do because I believe it helps to save the Union.[5]

The letter to Greeley is notable because in it Lincoln contradicted the statements he made in his First Inaugural Address, some seventeen months earlier, that he had no constitutional authority to disturb slavery. He was now apparently willing to ignore the Constitution and assert more or less dictatorial powers.

At the same time, it is important to note that Lincoln's Emancipation Proclamation did not free a single slave. As described by James G. Randall and David Donald in their epic, *The Civil War and Reconstruction,* "The stereotyped picture of the emancipator suddenly striking the shackles from millions of slaves by a stroke of the presidential pen is altogether inaccurate."[6]

The Emancipation Proclamation applied only to *rebel* territory, even though at the time Federal armies occupied large parts of the South, including much of Tennessee and Virginia, where it would have been possible to emancipate thousands of slaves. Specifically exempted by name in the Proclamation were the federally occupied states of Maryland and Kentucky, as well as West Virginia and many counties of Virginia. The Federal army also occupied much of Louisiana at the time, and those areas were exempted as well. Exempted were the parishes of "St. Bernard, Plaquemines, Jefferson, St. John, St. Charles, St. James, Ascension, Assumption, Terrobonne, Lafourche, St. Mary, St. Martin, and Orleans."[7] Lincoln, one of the nation's preeminent lawyers, was careful to craft the proclamation in a way that would guarantee that it would not emancipate any slaves.

The Emancipation Proclamation was immediately excoriated throughout the North (and much of the world) as a political gimmick. The *New York World* newspaper sarcastically editorialized that

> The President has purposely made the proclamation inoperative in all places where we have gained a military footing which makes the slaves accessible. He has proclaimed emancipation only where he has notoriously no power to execute it. The exemption of the accessible parts of Louisiana, Tennessee, and Virginia renders the proclamation not merely futile, but ridiculous.[8]

As to the Proclamation's practical effect, wrote the *World,* "It has none . . . the freedom declared by this proclamation is a dormant, not an actual, freedom."[9]

Lincoln's own secretary of state, William Seward, mocked the Emancipation Proclamation by saying, "We show our sympathy with slavery by emancipating slaves where we cannot reach them and holding them in bondage where we can set them free."[10]

The *London Spectator* succinctly observed that "The principle [of the Proclamation] is not that a human being cannot justly own another, but that he cannot own him unless he is loyal to the United States."[11] That, of course, is exactly the position that Lincoln espoused in his letter to Horace Greeley. It should have been no surprise to anyone.

The British writer Earl Russell noted that "The Proclamation . . . professes to emancipate all slaves in places where the United States authorities cannot exercise any jurisdiction . . . but it does not decree emancipation. . . . There seems to be no declaration of a principle adverse to slavery in this proclamation."[12] The *Saturday Review*, an American magazine, denounced the Proclamation as a "crime" that will "precipitate the ruin of [Lincoln's] cause."[13]

Lincoln himself maintained that the Proclamation was merely a war measure, not an attempt at genuine emancipation. In a letter to his Treasury Secretary Salmon P. Chase, he admitted that the original proclamation had no legal justification, except as a military measure.[14] He apparently knew that it was unconstitutional as well, for he insisted on calling it a "war measure." In reality, the president at the time had no power to dictate such a thing to a state government. Today, of course, presidents routinely dictate thousands of laws and regulations and executive orders that state and local governments must comply with. It was Lincoln who let the genie out of the bottle with regard to the transformation of the states into mere subsidiaries of the federal government.

If the Emancipation Proclamation was a "war measure," what might have been its objectives as such? Most likely, Lincoln understood that the European powers, who had recently abolished slavery *peacefully*, would balk at trading with and otherwise supporting the Confederacy if he introduced emancipation as one purpose of the war. It is also likely that he entertained the notion that the Proclamation might incite a slave insurrection or at least the threat of one. There were very few white males left on the plantations—they were almost all off at war—and the Southern women were left in charge.

If this sounds desperate, it is because Lincoln was, in fact, in a desperate situation. After several smashing Confederate victories on the battlefield, he said he had reached "the end of our rope on the [military] plan of operation."[15] If England and France had at that point offered economic support to the Confederacy or offered to broker a peace deal, Lincoln might have been pressured to end the war. A few facts about the conduct of the first two years of the war will help explain why Lincoln believed that he was at the end of his rope militarily.

THE MILITARY CONTEXT

THE FIRST MAJOR BATTLE of the war was fought in Manassas, Virginia, in late July 1861 (known as the Battle of First Manassas in the South, the Battle of Bull Run in the North). The Federal army, under General Irvin Mc-Dowell, had amassed some 33,000 troops and attacked 22,000 Confederates thirty miles west of Washington, D.C. There was great optimism in Washington that the war would end on that day, July 16, 1861. Many Washingtonians rode out to Manassas Junction in their carriages with their packed lunches in hopes of watching the rebels surrender soon after the first shots were fired. General Mc-

Dowell himself was confident that he could end the war then and there.

It didn't turn out that way, for the Battle of First Manassas was a resounding Confederate victory in the sense that it thoroughly convinced the Federal government that it was not going to be easy to defeat the secessionists. The battle ended with a wild scramble of Federal troops and civilians retreating back to Washington, D.C. "The retreating army became a wild mob several miles long and a hundred yards wide as soldiers and civilians raced each other for whatever safety the Northern capital offered."[16] It was here that "Stonewall" Jackson earned his nickname by fearlessly turning back a seemingly overpowering Federal force. After the battle he approached Confederate President Jefferson Davis, who had just arrived on the battlefield, and said, "Give me ten thousand men and I will take Washington tomorrow!"[17] Davis refused, and he would speak of his regret over that decision for the rest of his life, considering it "one of the great mistakes of the war."[18]

In a single day, Lincoln (and most of Washington) must have moved from a belief in the possibility of immediately putting an end to the "rebellion" to a fear that the capital city (and Lincoln himself) could be captured by the Confederate army of General P. G. T. Beauregard and forced to sign a peace agreement.

A number of smaller battles ensued in early 1862, with Federal victories at Forts Henry and Donelson in Tennessee. Then both sides suffered horrible losses of manpower in the Battle of Shiloh in early April. The battle was considered to be a Federal victory even though Federal

casualties were 1,754 killed, 8,408 wounded, and 2,885 captured (total, 13,047), compared to Confederate casualties
of 1,723 killed, 8,012 wounded, and 959 missing (total,
10,694).[19] It would be all downhill from there for the Federal armies for the next fifteen months.

Stonewall Jackson's 16,000 troops defeated some 45,000
Federal troops in the Shenandoah Valley during the battles
of Kernstown, McDowell, Winchester, Cross Keys, and
Port Republic. The remarkable military successes of
"Mighty Stonewall" generated sheer panic in Washington,
D.C., which was filled with rumors that Jackson was on his
way to capture the capital. Jackson biographer James
Robertson described Jackson's operations in the Shenandoah Valley in 1862 as ranking among the most spectacular
military achievements of the nineteenth century. Writers
the world over began comparing Jackson to Napoleon for
his brilliance and daring.[20]

Together, Jackson and General Robert E. Lee outwitted
Lincoln, who had effectively taken over command of the
Federal army (from a distance), in the Peninsula Campaign
of 1862. In what came to be known as the Seven Days Battle, in July 1862, total casualties were even more shocking
than at Shiloh: 14,000 Federals and 12,500 Confederates.[21]
It was not a major victory for either side, but the Federal
army was forced to retreat back across the James River and
away from Richmond. Lincoln became even more dis-
tressed and depressed.

The armies returned to Manassas in late August of 1862
and engaged in the Battle of Second Manassas, which had
essentially the same outcome as the first. Once again the

Federal army, this time some 80,000 strong, was forced to vacate the Virginia countryside and return to Washington.

The Battle of Antietam, Maryland (Sharpsburg, to Southerners), in mid-September 1862, ended in a stalemate, with Robert E. Lee holding his Army of Northern Virginia on its battle lines for an entire day after the fighting had stopped to make the point that he was not giving up the field, despite horrific losses (September 17, 1862, is considered to be the date of the bloodiest battle ever fought on American soil). The battle was considered a defeat for both armies, or a stalemate.

The Battle of Fredericksburg, in December 1862, was the largest and most grandiose battle of the war up to that point. More than 121,000 Federal troops attacked 80,000 Confederates in thirteen charges across an open plain, but not one of them got as close as 50 yards to the Confederate battle line, which had been established over the preceding month. The Federal army, now under the leadership of General Ambrose Burnside, had suffered 12,653 casualties, compared to 5,309 for the Confederates; and once again the Federal army retreated—this time under cover of night during a violent winter storm.

With the stunning defeat at Fredericksburg, write historians James Randall and David Donald, "the nadir of Northern depression seemed to have been reached":

> Sorrow caused by the death or mutilation of thousands of brave men turned into rage as the people wondered how so fine a fighting instrument as the Army of the Potomac had been used with such stupid futility. The slump in public credit

was evident in the rise of gold to 134, involving the greatest depreciation of the greenback up to that date. Many urged that the South was ready for a reasonable peace.[22]

That is the military context in which the Emancipation Proclamation was issued. Lincoln was admittedly at the end of his rope militarily, and he feared that intervention by the European powers would lead to a military defeat for the North. But if his objective was to dissuade the English from assisting the Confederacy, he did not fool them. Although historians Randall and Donald selectively quoted a few British writers who approved of the Proclamation, Sheldon Vanauken did a more systematic study of British opinion; he concluded that the overwhelming majority of British opinion makers not only did not support the Proclamation but also believed that, at best, it was intended to incite a violent slave rebellion against the women and children who were left on the Southern plantations—a most odious thought to the British mind. They referred to it as "Lincoln's last card." As Vanauken explained, when Lincoln issued the official Emancipation Proclamation on January 1, 1863,

> The Confederate States were winning the war. Only a few days before, Lee had smashed Burnside at Fredericksburg. The Proclamation freed all the slaves *within* the Confederate lines, that is, the slaves which the Federal armies were manifestly unable to reach. These slaves were grouped on the isolated plantations, controlled for the most part by women since their gentlemen were off to the wars. The only possible effect of the Proclamation would be the dreaded servile insurrection. . . . Either a slave rising or nothing. So English-

men saw it. Lincoln's inconsistency was regarded as proven by two things: his earlier denial of any lawful right or wish to free the slaves; and, especially, his not freeing the slaves in "loyal" Kentucky and other United States areas or even in Confederate areas occupied by the United States troops, such as New Orleans.[23]

NORTHERN RESPONSE TO THE PROCLAMATION

MOST NORTHERNERS in 1863 were shocked and surprised by the Emancipation Proclamation because they had not been told by their government that they were fighting and dying by the tens of thousands for the well-being of black strangers in faraway states where most Northerners had never been. Hostile white immigrant mobs had assaulted blacks in Northern cities for decades, and in July 1863 there were race riots in New York City as whites protested the Emancipation Proclamation (January 1863) and Lincoln's new conscription law (March 1863) by randomly assaulting (and sometimes killing) any and all black people unlucky enough to cross their path. The conscription law applied only to whites, and those with sufficient money could buy their way out of the draft for $300. Those without sufficient funds were outraged and made up the rioting mobs. Lincoln ordered five regiments of troops from the recently concluded Battle of Gettysburg to New York City to quell the riots; the troops achieved this goal by shooting between 300 and 1,000 citizens (there are no hard data on the number of deaths).[24]

An eyewitness to the riots was Colonel Arthur Fremantle, the British emissary to the Confederacy. Fremantle had
been with Robert E. Lee's Army of Northern Virginia as an
observer during the Battle of Gettysburg and was preparing
to sail back to England. In the widely read memoirs of his
travels with Lee's army during the summer of 1863, entitled
Three Months in the Southern States, Fremantle wrote of
the riots:

> The reports of outrages, hangings, and murder, were now
> most alarming, the terror and anxiety were universal. All
> shops were shut: all carriages and omnibuses had ceased run-
> ning. No colored man or woman was visible or safe in the
> streets, or even in his own dwelling. Telegraphs were cut, and
> railroad tracks torn up. The draft was suspended, and the
> mob evidently had the upper hand.
>
> The people who can't pay $300 naturally hate being
> forced to fight in order to liberate the very race who they are
> most anxious should be slaves. It is their direct interest not
> only that all slaves should remain slaves, but that the free
> Northern Negroes who compete with them for labor should
> be sent to the South also.[25]

When Fremantle "inquired of a bystander what the Negroes had done that they should want to kill them," the bystander replied, "Oh sir, they hate them here; they are the
innocent cause of all these troubles."[26]

The New York City draft riots apparently occurred
when they did—four months after the conscription law was
announced—because "not until the weekend of July 11 did
New Yorkers fully realize that Democratic officials would
fail to shelter them from the draft."[27] Violent mobs roamed

the streets for days, viciously attacking police, affluent Republicans, and blacks. "Rioters tore through expensive Republican homes on Lexington Avenue and took—or more often destroyed—pictures with gilt frames, elegant pier glasses, sofas, chairs, clocks, furniture of every kind."[28] The mob set fire to an orphanage for black children and "began attacking black men and boys in the tenement district along the downtown waterfront." Furthermore, "anti-Republicanism remained the refrain of the violence as crowds returned to [Horace] Greeley's *Tribune* office."[29] The building that housed Greeley's *New York Tribune* was set on fire. The mob then hanged a black man named William Jones and burned his body. Many other racially inspired and unspeakably violent murders occurred for the better part of a week.

The Emancipation Proclamation also caused a desertion crisis in the U.S. army. At least 200,000 Federal soldiers deserted; another 120,000 evaded conscription; and at least 90,000 Northern men fled to Canada to avoid conscription while thousands more hid out in the mountains of central Pennsylvania to place themselves beyond the reach of enrollment officers.[30]

Enlistment rates plummeted, as did subscriptions to war bonds, whose price declined sharply. "Plenty of soldiers believed that the proclamation had changed the purpose of the war," writes James McPherson. "They professed to feel betrayed. They were willing to risk their lives for the Union, they said, but not for black freedom."[31]

McPherson writes of a "backlash of anti-emancipation sentiment" in the Federal army and quotes various officers as saying things like, "If emancipation is to be the policy of this war . . . I do not care how quick the country goes to pot."[32] A Massachusetts sergeant wrote in a letter that "if anyone thinks that this army is fighting to free the Negro . . . they are terribly mistaken." Another officer declared that "I don't want to fire another shot for the Negroes and I wish that all the abolitionists were in hell. . . . I do not fight or want to fight for Lincoln's Negro proclamation one day longer."[33]

These attitudes must have reflected the majority opinion in the Federal armies in light of the discussion in chapter 2 of how horribly Northerners treated the small number of free blacks who resided within their own states. The average white Northerner had about the same attitude toward blacks as did the average white Southerner. Indeed, Tocqueville even believed that racism was actually worse in the Northern states than it was in the South.

The abolitionists were a very small group in terms of the general population. There were in fact hundreds of small abolition societies in the North that claimed a total membership of about 200,000. The total population of the Northern states was about 20 million. If half were adults, that would mean that abolitionists constituted about 2 percent of the adult population. It is reasonable to assume that this is also the approximate representation of abolitionists among the rank and file of the Federal army.

The abolitionists' numbers were not very impressive, but among them were such extraordinarily effective spokesmen as William Lloyd Garrison. Thanks in part to newly invented publishing technology, activists like Garrison were influential far beyond the strength of their mere numbers.

EMANCIPATION AROUND THE WORLD

SLAVERY EXISTED virtually without criticism for some three thousand years before abolitionist movements around the world began criticizing it in the late eighteenth century. The first substantial abolitionist movement was organized in England on the eve of the American Revolution (1774), and by 1888 the last bastion of slavery in the Americas—Brazil—had achieved emancipation. Thus, an institution that was a normal state of affairs in most countries of the world for three thousand years was eliminated within the course of a century (although chattel slavery has been resurrected in the Sudan and elsewhere in contemporary Africa).

Abolition of slavery throughout the world occurred for religious, philosophical, and economic reasons. The Quakers were among the first abolitionists because of their belief that slavery was an offense against God. The philosophy of the Enlightenment, which championed individual rights and the idea of equality under the law, added fuel to the argument that all human beings have natural rights to life, liberty, and property and ought to be treated equally under the law.

The advent of the industrial revolution added economic pressures as well, for slave labor is inherently inefficient compared to free labor. Slaves have very few, if any, incentives to work productively, to acquire new skills, and to improve their productivity levels, since they do not stand to benefit from doing so. Furthermore, capital-intensive agriculture and industry began to render labor-intensive production, including slave labor, uncompetitive. As the economist Ludwig von Mises wrote, "Servile labor disappeared because it could not stand the competition of free labor; its profitability sealed its doom in the market economy."[34]

With the development of capitalism, slavery all over the world became uneconomical, with the result being manumission—the willingness of slave owners to allow their slaves to purchase their freedom—and other forms of peaceful emancipation.[35]

Dozens of countries, including the possessions of the British, French, and Spanish empires, ended slavery *peacefully* during the late eighteenth and nineteenth centuries. Only in the United States was warfare associated with emancipation. There was violence in some other countries during the abolition of slavery, but as Fogel and Engerman point out, "In countries such as Colombia and Venezuela the emancipation of slaves became an instrument of the revolutionaries who sought state power"; it was not motivated by a desire for emancipation per se.[36]

The next several chapters will show that this was also the main reason for Lincoln's reluctant endorsement of the abolitionist agenda. As he stated over and over, his concern with the issue of slavery was motivated by a desire to use the issue to "save the Union," which was a euphemistic way of saying that he wanted to consolidate governmental power in Washington, D.C. In this regard Lincoln's motivations were identical to those of the Central American revolutionaries who invoked violence in the fight against slavery as a tool to gain or expand state power. Of course, the violence and bloodshed that occurred in the United States was many orders of magnitude greater than in the small skirmishes that occurred in Central America and elsewhere.

In virtually every other country of the world, slavery ended through either manumission or some form of compensated emancipation. This usually involved freeing the children of slaves born on some date after an emancipation law was enacted. The freeing of the slave children was delayed until their eighteenth, twenty-first, or, in some cases, twenty-eighth birthday. Fogel and Engerman explain the economic logic behind such plans:

> Under such arrangements, slaveholders suffered no loss on existing male slaves or on female slaves who were already past their childbearing years. Having control over the services of a newly-born child until his or her twenty-first or twenty-eighth birthday meant that most, if not all, of the costs of rearing such slaves would be covered by the income they earned between the onset of their productive years and the date of their emancipation. . . . In other words, gradual abolition imposed an average cost on slaveholders . . . quite close to zero.[37]

In the British Empire, emancipation was not so gradual: It was completed in just six years, and the British government compensated slaveowners an amount that was estimated at 40 percent of the value of their slaves.[38] By 1840 all the slaves in the British Empire had been freed. Table 3.1 lists countries of the world where peaceful emancipation occurred during the nineteenth century prior to the War between the States.

Emancipation was also achieved during and after the War between the States in the Dutch colonies (1863), Brazil (1871–1878), Puerto Rico (1873), and Cuba (1886). The only violent slave uprising occurred in Haiti in 1794.[39]

TABLE 3.1   Peaceful Emancipation, 1813–1854

Country/Region	Year of Emancipation
Argentina	1813
Colombia	1814
Chile	1823
Central America	1824
Mexico	1829
Bolivia	1831
Uruguay	1842
French and Danish Colonies	1848
Ecuador	1851
Peru	1854
Venezuela	1854

Source: Robert Fogel and Stanley Engerman, *Time on the Cross: The Economics of American Negro Slavery* (New York: Norton, 1974), pp. 33–34.

In the War between the States, the explicit monetary cost alone was approximately $6.6 billion, about evenly divided between the two sides. The North's share would have been more than enough to purchase the freedom of every slave (and give each 40 acres of land and a mule).[40] The lesson that should have been learned from the peaceful emancipation that took place everywhere but in the United States was that slavery cannot last if the slaves have freedom within arm's reach. The underground railroad was a potential escape hatch for thousands of slaves in the border states—about a thousand slaves per year were escaping through that route as of 1861. Slavery as an institution was artificially propped up by the Fugitive Slave Law (which Lincoln supported), the legal prohibition of manumission, and myriad other laws and regulations that kept slavery alive. If it weren't for the Fugitive Slave Law, many more thousands of slaves would have escaped through the underground railroad, quickening the institution's demise. Lincoln's support of the Fugitive Slave Law was such that he made sure that the Republican Party convention of 1860 did not even consider it seriously. He was fearful that it would destroy the party—and his own political future.

In fact, these *political* support structures for slavery were breaking down in 1860. Slavery was already in sharp decline in the border states and the upper South generally, mostly for economic reasons, which made it more and more enticing for slaves in the deep South to attempt to escape.

Indeed, there is evidence that there was growing political support within the border states for gradual, peaceful emancipation that would have ended slavery there. As early as 1849, 10 percent of the participants in a Kentucky political convention expressed support for gradual emancipation in that state. Such support was gradually increasing in the border states, just as it had in the New England states decades earlier. The enforcement costs of slavery would have increased dramatically as a result of such an action.[41] Slavery was on its way out: Delaware, Maryland, Kentucky, Missouri, and much of Virginia had seen the proportion of slaves out of their total populations steadily dwindle during the three decades prior to the war. Lincoln could have put in motion a process to end slavery much more expeditiously—and peacefully—as more than twenty other slaveowning societies had done in the previous sixty years. But he chose instead to wage a long and devastating war in which the victims were not just slaveowners but every Southern citizen. Less than one-fourth of

Southern adults owned slaves; most existed on large plantations. The average Southerner was not a slaveowner but a yeoman farmer or merchant who had no special interest in slavery. Slavery could have been ended peacefully and at much less cost and toil.

Lincoln did pay lip service to various compensated emancipation plans, and he even proposed a compensated emancipation bill (combined with colonization) in 1862. But the man whom historians would later describe as one of the master politicians of all time failed to use his legendary political skills and his rhetorical gifts to do what every other country of the world where slavery once existed had done: end it peacefully, without resort to warfare. That would have been the course taken by a genuine statesman. Even though he assumed dictatorial powers to raise armies and wage war during the first year of his administration, he did not use them to spend tax dollars on compensated emancipation in even a few states.

Given the enormous costs of the war, including 620,000 military deaths, thousands of civilian deaths in the Southern states, hundreds of thousands of men crippled for life, the near destruction of nearly 40 percent of the nation's economy, and the direct costs of the war itself, most Americans would likely have chosen compensated emancipation, which would have cost them a tiny, almost trivial, fraction of the cost of the alternative: total war. Lincoln never seriously offered the nation the opportunity.

To gain a better understanding of the cost of the war in human lives alone, consider that 620,000 battlefield-related deaths out of a national population of 30 million, if standardized for today's population of some 280 million, would be the equivalent of roughly 5 million battlefield deaths—almost 100 times the number of Americans killed in the ten-year Vietnam conflict. That does not count the thousands of civilians who were killed in Southern states as Federal armies bombarded cities and towns, from Vicksburg, Mississippi, to Charleston, South Carolina, and Atlanta, Georgia.

One out of four Southern white males between 20 and 40 perished during the war. With a population of 10 million, that amounted to about 3 percent of the population. Three percent of the current national population would be a horrific 8.4 million deaths. This is perhaps why the Confederate government made several proposals for peace conferences during the war, all of which Lincoln ignored. He never gave peaceful emancipation a chance.

Perhaps the answer to the question of why Lincoln did not take the path to emancipation taken during the nineteenth century by every other nation on earth where slavery once existed lies in his own words—namely, that he was not particularly supportive of emancipation. He viewed it only as a tool to be used in achieving his real objective: the consolidation of state power, something that many Americans had dreaded from the time of the founding.

Ever the master of rhetoric, Lincoln sugarcoated the centralization of governmental power by repeatedly referring to it as "saving the Union." But the union could only be "saved," according to Lincoln's definition, by *destroying* the highly decentralized, *voluntary* union of states that was established by the founding fathers at the constitutional convention and replacing it with a coercive union that was kept in place, literally, at gunpoint. That was Lincoln's real agenda and is the subject of the next several chapters.

CHAPTER 4

LINCOLN'S
REAL AGENDA

*I presume you all know who I am. I am humble Abraham Lincoln. I
have been solicited by many friends to become a candidate for the
legislature. My politics are short and sweet, like the old woman's
dance. I am in favor of a national bank . . . in favor of the internal
improvements system and a high protective tariff.*
—ABRAHAM LINCOLN, 1832

LINCOLN'S STATEMENT of support for internal improvements and a high tariff, made when he first ran for
public office in 1832, succinctly summarizes the focus of
his twenty-eight-year political career before he was elected
president. The statement also offers a definition of the
Whig Party's political agenda. Lincoln was always a Whig
and was almost single-mindedly devoted to the Whig
agenda—protectionism, government control of the money
supply through a nationalized banking system, and government subsidies for railroad, shipping, and canal-building
businesses ("internal improvements").

Roy Basler, the editor of Lincoln's *Collected Works*,
commented that Lincoln barely mentioned slavery before

1854."[1] What Lincoln *did* speak about with great conviction for twenty-eight years was the Whig economic agenda, which was named the "American System" by Lincoln's political idol, Henry Clay.

In his 1,248-page treatise on the history of the Whig Party in American politics, historian Michael F. Holt noted that Lincoln served as a presidential elector for the Whig Party during the 1840 and 1844 presidential elections and "crisscrossed the state ardently and eloquently defending specific Whig economic programs like a national bank, a protectionist tariff, and distribution of federal land revenues to the states" to subsidize "internal improvements."[2] "Few people in the [Whig] party were so committed to its economic agenda as Lincoln," writes Holt.

And indeed he was. In 1859 Lincoln announced that he was "always a Whig in politics."[3] His in-laws were personal friends of the Clays of Kentucky. "One could hardly read any paragraph" in the eulogy to Clay, wrote Basler, "without feeling that Lincoln was, consciously or unconsciously, inviting comparison and contrast of himself with Clay" and setting himself up to be Clay's heir apparent in the Whig Party.[4]

"From the moment Lincoln first entered political life as a candidate for the state legislature," writes historian Robert Johannsen, "he had demonstrated an unswerving fidelity to the party of Henry Clay and to Clay's American System, the program of internal improvements, protective tariff, and centralized banking."[5]

When the Whig Party imploded in the mid-1850s, Lincoln switched to the Republican Party but assured his Illinois constituents that there was no difference between the two. As Johannsen explains, "Lincoln had labored for twenty-five years in behalf of Henry Clay's American System, the program that tied economic development to strong centralized national authority, and he was not prepared to give up that investment."[6] In this regard the Lincoln–Douglas debates were really "the contest all over again between the 'one consolidated empire' of the Federalists and Whigs, and the 'confederacy of sovereign and equal states' of Jefferson and Jackson."[7] As Stephen Douglas himself described it, "Lincoln goes for consolidation and uniformity in our government while I go for maintaining the confederation of the sovereign states."[8]

Economists have a different word for the combination of policies known as the American System—namely, *mercantilism*. As defined by economist Murray Rothbard, mercantilism, "which reached its height in the Europe of the seventeenth and eighteenth centuries," was "a system of statism which employed economic fallacy to build up a structure of imperial state power, as well as special subsidy and monopolistic privilege to individuals or groups favored by the state."[9] More specifically, protectionism (legal protection from international competition through trade tariffs and quotas) was a means by which a government could dispense favors to well-connected (and well-financed) special interest groups, which in turn provided financial and other support for the politicians dispensing the favors. It benefits both those industries that are protected from competition and the politicians, but it harms everyone else. Consumers pay higher prices because of the reduced competition, and they also have fewer choices. Potential competitors are kept out of the market, which means a loss of jobs. Protectionism always reduces the wealth of nations—which is why Adam Smith gave his magnum opus that very name.

The special interest groups that benefit from protectionism have always employed small armies of intellectuals and publicists whose job is primarily to confuse the public about their true intentions. They have always attempted to convince the public that economic policies that in reality only benefit a small special interest group are good for "the nation." That's what Murray Rothbard meant when he wrote that mercantilism always relies on "economic fallacy." The public must be intentionally miseducated in economics in order for mercantilism to survive.

The same can be said for another element of mercantilism—tax-funded subsidies to politically well connected businesses and industries. These subsidies generally benefit only those businesses that are lucky enough to get them, at the expense of the taxpayers generally. Much of the public has finally caught on to this fact; today, the progressive-sounding phrase, "internal improvement subsidies" is usually denigrated (and rightly so) as "corporate welfare" or "welfare for the well-to-do."

Nationalized banking was always part and parcel of the mercantilist agenda as well, for mercantilists have always advocated having the government simply print paper money in order to finance their special-interest subsidies. That way, the costs of the subsidies can be more easily hidden from the public. If taxes must be raised to finance the subsidies, the taxpaying public pays a direct cost and may well object. But if the subsidies are financed by printing money, the economic cost becomes the inflation that is caused by printing money. More often than not, politicians then blame the inflation on "greedy corporations" who are supposedly raising their prices too much rather than the real culprits, governments themselves.

Obviously, mercantilism has the potential for generating a great deal of political corruption, as is always the case with any system in which governments are empowered to dispense taxpayers' revenues to special-interest groups, rather than being restricted to spending money only on things that benefit the public as a whole. But it is exactly this potential for corruption, and the ability to literally buy votes and political support with taxpayers' funds, that attracts power-hungry politicians to mercantilism. It may be bad for the economy, but it has great potential for advancing one's political career. The Whigs always understood this perfectly clearly, which is why they made mercantilism, euphemistically referred to as "the American System," their top policy goal.

Edgar Lee Masters, the Illinois poet, playwright (author of *The Spoon River Anthology*), and onetime law partner of Clarence Darrow, provided a definition of the Whig Party economic agenda that was not very flattering, but that had more than a grain of truth to it (which is undoubtedly why there was so much opposition to the definition for over three decades):

> [Henry] Clay was the champion of that political system which doles favors to the strong in order to win and to keep their adherence to the government. His system offered shelter to devious schemes and corrupt enterprises. . . . He was the beloved son [figuratively speaking] of Alexander Hamilton

with his corrupt funding schemes, his superstitions concerning the advantage of a public debt, and a people taxed to make profits for enterprises that cannot stand alone. His example and his doctrines led to the creation of a party that had no platform to announce, because its principles were plunder and nothing else.[10]

Protectionism is an indirect subsidy to politically influential businesses that comes at the expense of consumers (who pay higher prices) and potential competitors. Because government never has the resources to subsidize all businesses, so-called internal improvement subsidies could never have amounted to anything but selective subsidies to politically favored businesses. And a nationalized banking system, which was finally adopted by Lincoln and the Republican Party during the War between the States, has always been used as a means of printing money (and thereby creating inflation) to pay for even more selective special-interest subsidies.

All of these policies tend to generate a centralization of governmental power as well, which is why they were the focus of American political debate from the time of the founding until the 1860s. At that point the debate was ended; the consolidators, led by Lincoln and the Republican Party, had won the debate, literally, by force of arms.

The American System, in other words, was the framework for a giant political patronage system. Politicians who could control such a system could use it to maintain and enhance their own power and wealth almost indefinitely, as the Republican Party eventually did. It was not an example of "capitalism," as James McPherson incorrectly stated in *Abraham Lincoln and the Second American Revolution*,[11] but quite the opposite: It was mercantilism, the very system that Adam Smith railed against in his epic defense of capitalism, *The Wealth of Nations*.[12]

Historian Gabor Boritt makes this same mistake in "Lincoln and the Economics of the American Dream," an essay in which he implausibly argues that Lincoln's economic policies were designed to improve "everyone's" standard of living.[13] Quite the opposite is true. The American System was (and is) the worst sort of special-interest, pork-barrel politics. Boritt is accustomed to performing literary somersaults to lionize Lincoln, but in this case his arguments just don't hold any water at all.

McPherson is equally confused on this point. He approvingly writes of an "astonishing blitz of laws, most of them passed within the span of less than one year" during the Lincoln administration, as creating a "capitalist revolution" and a "blueprint for modern America" of which "Lincoln was one of the principal architects."[14] "During the Civil War," writes Clay biographer Maurice Baxter, "Lincoln and the Republican party implemented much of the American System."[15]

It may have been a "blueprint" for economic policy, and Lincoln was undoubtedly one of the principal architects (as we'll see more fully in later chapters), but it most definitely was not a capitalist revolution. Capitalism is a system of free, voluntary exchange, not monopolistic privilege created by protectionism. It is a system in which capital markets finance those investment projects that are most likely to serve the largest number of consumers, not a system whereby capital investments depend on political connections, as with "internal improvement" subsidies.

One of the great defenders of capitalism during the twentieth century was the Nobel Prize–winning economist Friedrich Hayek, best known for his 1944 critique of socialism, *The Road to Serfdom*. Far from advocating the nationalization of the money supply as essential to a "capitalist revolution," Hayek entitled one of his better known books *The Denationalization of Money*, which he believed was essential to the development of a capitalist economy. Socializing the money supply, according to Hayek and other prominent capitalist intellectuals, is a dire mistake. McPherson, Boritt, and others who argue that the Lincoln/Whig mercantilist economic policy agenda advanced "capitalism" could not be more off base. If there was an economic policy "revolution" during the Lincoln administration, it was a mercantilist revolution.

The "blitz of laws" that McPherson refers to was decidedly anticapitalistic. Such laws thwart rather than enhance economic development, as economist David Osterfeld eloquently illustrated in *Planning versus Prosperity*.[16] What they do achieve is a further politicization of economic decision making and a greater centralization of political power. If there is any one lesson that we should have learned from the twentieth century, it is that the more politicized an economy becomes, the less economic opportunity it produces for ordinary citizens. This is true of all forms of statism, from mercantilism to full-blown socialism.

HENRY CLAY AND THE WHIGS

AN OVERVIEW OF some of Henry Clay's beliefs and political achievements will be useful in explaining just what Lincoln was so infatuated with and devoted to for more than thirty years of his adult life.

When Henry Clay entered national politics in 1811 as a member of Congress, on the eve of the War of 1812 one of his first acts was to try to convince his colleagues to invade Canada, which they did, three times. He waged a thirty-year political battle with the likes of James Madison, James Monroe, John C. Calhoun, John Randolph, Andrew Jackson, and the other defenders of the Jeffersonian philosophy of limited, decentralized, constitutional government. Clay was the political heir to Alexander Hamilton and so championed centralized governmental power driven by political patronage for the benefit of what U.S. Senator John Taylor of Virginia called the "monied aristocracy."[17]

Like Lincoln, Clay spent a large part of his career lobbying for government subsidies for corporations in the name of "internal improvements." Presidents Madison and Monroe both vetoed internal improvement bills that were sponsored by Clay on the grounds that the Constitution provided no basis for such an expenditure of tax dollars.[18] As Taylor saw it, Clay and his political compatriots (including Lincoln in later years) sought to bring the British mercantilist system to America, "along with its national debt, political corruption, and Court party."[19]

Clay was the fiercest proponent of protectionism in Congress from 1811 until his death in 1852. Northern manufacturers who wanted to be protected from foreign competition with high tariffs made him their man in Congress: Lincoln aspired to take over his mantle and eventually did. Clay's protectionist advocacy brought him into periodic conflict with a number of Southern politicians. By the 1840s the majority of U.S. exports came out of the South. Because the South's economy was almost exclusively an agrarian one, high tariffs meant that Southerners would have to pay more for manufactured goods whether they came from Europe or the Northern states.

Since the 1820s such political figures as John C. Calhoun had ritually condemned the tariff as an unconstitutional tool of plunder whereby Southerners were burdened with the lion's share of the cost of government (there was no federal income tax), while most of the expenditures financed by tariff revenue took place in the North.

Thus, when Clay proposed a sharp tariff increase in 1824 (which became law), Southern members of Congress immediately opposed it. Undeterred by the opposition, Clay then became the chief proponent and sponsor of what became known as the 1828 "Tariff of Abominations," which raised tariffs even higher. The higher rates were supposedly necessary, Clay argued, because the 1824 rates "fell short of what many of my friends wished."[20]

Clay's Tariff of Abominations almost precipitated a secession crisis as a South Carolina political convention voted to nullify the tariff (that is, to refuse to collect it at Charleston harbor). The resistance finally forced the federal government to back down, reducing the rate in 1833.

Clay was infuriated by being forced to compromise and, in a speech on the floor of the House of Representatives, promised that he would someday "defy the South, the president, and the devil," if necessary, to raise tariff rates once again.[21]

Clay was also a powerful proponent of a nationalized banking system. He fought a pitched political battle with Andrew Jackson (which Jackson eventually won) over the rechartering of the Bank of the United States.

As speaker of the House of Representatives, Clay personally demonstrated the usefulness of the Bank of the United States to politicians as ambitious as he was. He used his position to place his cronies from Kentucky on the bank's board of directors, enabling them to reward their political supporters with cheap credit. This was precisely the kind of political corruption that opponents of nationalized banking, such as Andrew Jackson, feared.

Jackson denounced the national bank as "dangerous to the liberty of the American people because it represented a fantastic centralization of economic and political power under private control."[22] He understood the implications of a politicized money supply as well as Clay and the Whigs did.

Having observed Clay's behavior as the major political string puller with the Bank of the United States, Jackson condemned the bank as "a vast electioneering engine" that had the "power to control the Government and change its character."[23] This, of course, is exactly what the Whigs wanted to do.

Jackson's Treasury Secretary, Roger B. Taney, who would later become the chief justice of the United States Supreme Court, also complained of the Bank's "corrupting influence," with "its patronage greater than that of the Government" and its ability to "influence elections" by essentially buying votes near election time through selective government expenditures financed by the bank.[24]

Further evidence that the concerns of Jackson and Taney were well founded lies in the behavior of Henry Clay himself from 1822 to 1824. Having incurred $40,000 in personal debt, Clay left Congress for two years in 1822 to serve as general counsel of the Bank of the United States. As Clay biographer Maurice Baxter explains,

> His income from this business apparently amounted to what he needed [to pay off his personal debt]: three thousand dollars a year from the bank as chief counsel; more for appearing in specific cases; and a sizable amount of real estate in Ohio and Kentucky in addition to the cash. . . . When he resigned to become Secretary of State in 1825, he was pleased with his compensation.[25]

Who wouldn't be pleased? In current dollars the amount of money Clay earned in just two years would be nearly a million dollars.

Another Whig, Daniel Webster, never even bothered to resign from Congress before collecting "compensation" from the bank. He simply demanded a "retainer" from the bank as a payoff for being one of the bank's chief spokespersons, along with Clay, in Congress. He once wrote to Nicholas Biddle, the bank's president, "I believe my retainer has not been renewed or *refreshed* as usual. If it be wished that my relation to the Bank should be continued, it may be well to send me the usual retainer."[26] It was this kind of political shakedown that Taney and Jackson were referring to when they spoke of the "corrupting influence" of a nationalized banking system.

By 1840 Clay and the Whigs thought they finally had a chance to break the constitutional logjam that stood in the way of their vaunted American System with the election of their presidential candidate, William Henry Harrison. Clay, a dominating influence in Congress, was at the pinnacle of his career. He was certain that the Congress would essentially rubber-stamp a rechartering of the Bank of the United States, enact radically higher tariff rates, and ladle out internal improvement subsidies to politically well connected corporations—and that Harrison would support what Congress did.

Unfortunately for the Whigs, Harrison died after exactly one month in office. His vice president, John Tyler of Virginia, turned out to be a Jeffersonian and an advocate of states' rights and limited, decentralized government. The Whig Party apparently paid little attention to Tyler's views before placing him on its presidential ticket. Tyler's biographer, Oliver Chitwood, wrote that "what little attention was paid to Tyler's role in the campaign was due primarily to the fact that 'Tyler Too' rhymed with 'Tippecanoe.'"[27] (Harrison, a former general, was the hero of the Battle of Tippecanoe in the War of 1812.)

Tyler vetoed Clay's bank bill by saying, "The power of Congress to create a national bank to operate per se over the Union has been a question of dispute from the origin of the Government . . . my own opinion has been uniformly proclaimed to be against the exercise of any such power by this Government."[28] Tyler was also opposed to protectionist tariffs and internal improvement subsidies.

The Whigs protested wildly, burning Tyler in effigy in front of the White House and expelling him from the Whig Party. The idea of a nationalized banking system and high protectionist tariffs to pay for a massive system of subsidies for corporations would lie dormant for another twenty years, until it finally came to fruition during the Lincoln administration.

Protectionism, a money supply that is controlled by the central government, and government subsidies to corporations were the keystones of what might be called the Hamilton/Clay/Lincoln American System. A fourth item would be the quest for empire, a goal that the founding fathers never intended to be the purpose of the new government they had created. In this regard Clay's attitude toward the American Indians is telling, for it is essentially the same attitude that informed government policy toward them under the Republican Party's monopolistic dominance of politics from 1865 to 1890. This was the time period in which all of the Plains Indians were either killed or placed on reservations.

One of Clay's first statements as the American secretary of state was that "there never was a full-blooded Indian who took to civilization," for "it was not in their nature." He "did not think them, as a race, worth preserving"; they were "inferior" to Anglo-Saxons; and their "breed could not be improved." "Their disappearance from the human family will be no great loss to the world."[29] Such statements are hard to reconcile with Lincoln's characterization of Clay as a champion of liberty and equality and a great humanitarian.

LINCOLN THE WHIG

FROM THE TIME he entered politics Lincoln was devoted to the American System. During the national election campaign of 1840, he made numerous speeches in favor of establishing a nationalized banking system. In a speech on banking policy delivered December 26, 1839, in Springfield, Illinois, Lincoln attacked Andrew Jackson and defended the alleged constitutionality of a national bank.[30]

During the 1848 presidential election campaign, when the Whig candidate was Zachary Taylor, Lincoln stumped for Taylor and promised that if Taylor was elected the country would once again have a national bank.[31]

Even when commenting on the Dred Scott decision on June 26, 1857, Lincoln apparently couldn't resist once again criticizing Andrew Jackson's refusal thirty years earlier to recharter the Bank of the United States, insinuating that Jackson had acted unconstitutionally; he tarred Stephen Douglas with the same criticism. He made the same arguments a month later in a response to Douglas.[32] Lincoln frequently made it a point to champion the nationalization of money and to demonize Jackson and the Democrats for their opposition to it. Of all the Whigs, Lincoln—next to Clay himself—was the fiercest advocate of a nationalized money supply.

If the Whigs could not have a federal government that printed paper money, they would settle for state government control of the currency as a second-best alternative. Thus, after Jackson refused to recharter the Bank of the United States, Lincoln and the Whigs in Illinois turned to championing paper currency issued by state government banks to help pay for their internal improvement projects.

As a leading member of the Illinois legislature, Lincoln repeatedly opposed proposals by Democratic legislators to audit the Illinois state bank.[33] In December 1840 the Democrats in the legislature wanted to require the bank to make payments in specie (that is, gold) instead of paper. The bank was authorized to continue its suspension of specie payment through the end of the year. Lincoln wanted desperately to avoid this move toward sounder, gold-based money, so in an attempt to stop the adjournment of the legislature, he and his fellow Whigs headed for the door, which was locked and guarded. Their objective was to leave the room so that there would be no quorum to vote for adjournment. Blocked from the door, Lincoln jumped out of the first-story window and was followed by his Whig compatriots; after this event, the Democrats began referring to "Lincoln and his flying brethren."[34]

Like Clay, Lincoln was an ardent protectionist for his entire political career and sought to pick up Clay's mantle as the chief political spokesman for Northern manufacturers who wanted a tariff to protect them from foreign competition. Like other mercantilists of his time, Lincoln ignored the well-known case for free trade that had been made in 1776 by Adam Smith and extended and elaborated on in the early nineteenth century by such prominent economic theorists as David Ricardo, John Baptiste Say, and Frederic Bastiat. He also ignored the economic logic of the commerce clause of the U.S. Constitution, which—in order to guarantee free interstate commerce—made it illegal for one state to impose a tariff on goods imported from another state. If free trade among states is a good idea—and it is—it is just as good an idea with regard to international trade. This was the thinking of the framers of the amendment as well. Jefferson and Washington, for example, were staunch advocates of free international commerce as well as interstate commerce.

The benefits of free trade were well known by the time Lincoln entered politics, especially so in America, since there had been so much controversy over it since the 1820s. It was well established that trade restrictions tend to reduce the wealth of nations, although they provide at least temporary financial benefits to those industries that are protected from competition. The benefits, of course, come primarily at the expense of ordinary consumers and working people whose choices are more limited and who must pay higher prices for their goods.

When President Jefferson imposed a trade embargo as a response to British piracy against U.S. ships, the New England Federalists opposed him bitterly and plotted for more than a decade to secede from the Union, so upset were they over the reduction in foreign trade. It was an accepted principle at the time that a primary means of harming one's enemy in wartime was to blockade its ports to inflict economic damage. Indeed, this was one of Lincoln's first acts of war—to inflict harm on the Southern economy by interfering with its commerce. It was (and is) self-evident that tariffs and other forms of protectionism can effectively achieve the same result.

The benefits of free trade were so well understood that in 1850 England repealed its Corn Laws, which meant that all tariffs on grain were eliminated. By 1860 the other major European power, France, had eliminated most of its tariffs as well, and free trade was spreading throughout the rest of Europe.

Protectionists have always made the case for their special-interest policies by producing a blizzard of plausible-sounding but incorrect economic theories designed to blur the public's knowledge about their true intentions. In order for the public to support protectionism, in other words, a large part of the public must be convinced that what is actually in the self-interest of a small special-interest group—that is, certain manufacturers—is really in "the public interest." Convincing consumers that higher prices are in reality in their best interest is an absurd proposition on its face, but clever protectionist propagandists have always taken advantage of the public's ignorance of economics to pull the wool over its eyes.

Like many other protectionists within the Whig Party, Lincoln familiarized himself not with the work of Smith, Ricardo, Say, or Bastiat but with a publicist for the Pennsylvania steel industry named Henry C. Carey, who earned a living by popularizing protectionist myths on behalf of the industry. Although Carey once admitted that he had "never devoted three days to the study of political economy," he nevertheless claimed to "expose the fallacies" of Adam Smith's *Wealth of Nations*.[35]

Lincoln commented frequently on the tariff issue throughout his career, and his arguments were perhaps best expressed in a December 1847 speech, just before he took a seat in the U.S. Congress. Relying on the work of Carey, Lincoln made the counterintuitive argument that encouraging competition through free trade would actually cause higher prices. His argument was that since the costs of transporting goods from one country to another constituted "useless labor," an increase in such labor would cause prices to rise.[36] According to this logic, the importation of agricultural products from Illinois to Ohio or from Springfield to Chicago, Illinois, for that matter, should also be prohibited because of the effects of "useless labor." Of course, such transportation costs and virtually all marketing costs serve to *enhance competition* and, as such, they *reduce* prices to the consumer.

Lincoln also espoused a crude version of the long-discredited Marxian labor theory of value, which held that all value is created by the labor used to produce a product. According to this theory, for example, "value" can be created by digging a hole in the middle of the Sahara desert. Free trade, according to Lincoln, created a system whereby "some have laboured, and others have, without labour, enjoyed a large portion of the fruits. . . . To secure to each labourer the whole product of his labour . . . is a most worthy object of any good government."[37]

This ignores the fact that consumer preferences are also important in determining economic value, as are entrepreneurship, investment, and risk taking, which drive the profitability of industry. But Lincoln went so far as to say that if he were given the power, he would totally prohibit most foreign competition, allowing only the importation of goods that were not produced in the United States. "I . . . would continue [trade] where it is *necessary*, and *discontinue* it, where it is not. As instance: I would continue commerce so far as it is employed in bringing us coffee, and I would discontinue it so far as it is employed in bringing us cotton goods."[38] In other words, he would appoint himself

economic dictator. Consumers may have preferred competition in the cotton goods markets and the wider choice
and lower prices that it would have brought, but Lincoln
the economic dictator would "discontinue" it in order to
curry political favor with certain domestic cotton goods
manufacturers. In a true capitalist economy, *consumers* ultimately decide with their patronage which businesses will
be continued and which will not; the decision is not made
by an economic central planner such as Lincoln apparently
envisioned himself to be.

Lincoln remained a staunch protectionist for his entire
political career. Indeed, as historian Richard Bensel noted,
the tariff was no less than the "centerpiece" of the Republican Party platform of 1860.[39]

The one element of the American System that seems to
have been Lincoln's very motivation for entering politics in
1832 was government subsidies for "internal improvements," or, in modern terminology, "corporate welfare." It
was the very first thing he mentioned in his 1832 introduc-
tory speech to the people of Sangamo County, Illinois, in
announcing that he was running for the legislature. After
announcing that he was about to represent his "sentiments
with regards to local affairs," he proclaimed, "Time and
experience have verified to a demonstration, the public util-
ity of internal improvements."[40] Most of the speech had to
do with his advocacy of state subsidies for railroad- and
canal-building corporations.

During his brief stint as a member of Congress, Lincoln
gave an impassioned speech on internal improvements
(June 20, 1848) in which he addressed every one of the

Democratic Party's objections to such subsidies (they would overwhelm the treasury, would be inequitable and unconstitutional, and are the prerogative of the states).[41]

In this speech, and in many others, Lincoln's support for federal subsidies for railroad- and canal-building companies was never tempered, despite the miserable experience of Illinois—and of dozens of other states—during the late 1830s, when he was a leading member of the Illinois state legislature. In 1837, with the help of Lincoln's leadership, the Whigs were finally able to get the state legislature to appropriate about $12 million for myriad "internal improvement" projects. This was perhaps the high-water mark for the Whigs in state politics, for similar projects were underway simultaneously in many other states as well.

But the program was a disaster. As described by Lincoln's law partner, William H. Herndon, the Illinois internal improvement program was "reckless and unwise":

> The gigantic and stupendous operations of the scheme dazzled the eyes of nearly everybody, but in the end it rolled up a debt so enormous as to impede the otherwise marvelous progress of Illinois. The burdens imposed by this Legislature under the guise of improvements became so monumental in size it is little wonder that at intervals for years afterward the monster of [debt] repudiation often showed its hideous face above the waves of popular indignation.[42]

George Nicolay and John Hay, who studied law in Lincoln's Springfield, Illinois, law offices and later served as his personal secretaries in the White House, described the internal improvement debacle as follows:

The market was glutted with Illinois bonds; one banker and one broker after another, to whose hands they had been recklessly confided in New York and London, failed, or made away with the proceeds of sales. The system had utterly failed; there was nothing to do but repeal it, stop work on the visionary roads, and endeavor to invent some means of paying the enormous debt. This work taxed the energies of the Legislature in 1839, and for some years after. It was a dismal and disheartening task. Blue Monday had come after these years of intoxication, and a crushing debt rested upon a people who had been deceiving themselves with the fallacy that it would somehow pay itself by acts of the legislature.[43]

And Lincoln was as responsible as anyone for convincing the public of that "fallacy." The Illinois legislature had allocated $12 million in 1838 for this series of boondoggles. What was promised by Lincoln and other supporters of the projects, wrote Herndon, was that "every river and stream . . . was to be widened, deepened, and made navigable. A canal to connect the Illinois River and Lake Michigan was to be dug, . . . cities were to spring up everywhere, . . . people were to come swarming in by colonies, until . . . Illinois was to outstrip all others, and herself become the Empire State of the Union."[44]

But after the $12 million had been spent, observed Nicolay and Hay, nothing was left of the "brilliant schemes" but "a load of debt that crippled for many years the energies of the people, a few miles of embankments that the grass hastened to cover, and a few abutments that stood for years by the sides of leafy rivers, waiting for their long delaying bridges and trains."⁴⁵ Herndon wrote that "the internal improvement system, the adoption of which Lincoln had played such a prominent part, had collapsed, with the result that Illinois was left with an enormous debt and an empty treasury."⁴⁶ When Illinois amended its constitution in 1848, it prohibited the expenditure of tax dollars on any kind of private business enterprise.

In his *History of the People of the United States,* John Bach McMaster noted that in every other state that had "gone recklessly" into funding internal improvements in the late 1830s, the results were the same; *no* works were finished (none!), little or no income was derived from them, and the accumulation of debt required onerous tax increases to pay for it all.⁴⁷ The Whig experiment with internal improvement subsidies at the state level had proved to be an unmitigated disaster for the states, but the Whigs— and Lincoln—seem to have been completely unfazed by this colossal failure since they continued to relentlessly advocate more of the same for decades.

Lincoln explained to a friend his motivation for being such a fierce proponent of corporate subsidies despite the Illinois debacle. His career ambition, he told the friend, was to become "the De Witt Clinton of Illinois."⁴⁸ De Witt Clinton, a governor of New York, is credited with having introduced the spoils system to America; he persuaded his state legislature to finance the Erie Canal, which to this day is held up by some historians as an example of a "successful" nineteenth-century internal improvement subsidy. Such "success" is debatable, however, in light of the fact that the canal became obsolete with the advent of railroad transportation.

INTERNAL IMPROVEMENTS IN HISTORICAL PERSPECTIVE

LINCOLN WAS an extraordinarily astute politician, and it was not just happenstance that caused him to choose internal improvements as his key issue when he entered politics in 1832. It was a central component in the most important political and economic debate of the first half of the nineteenth century, and Lincoln made sure that he weighed in on it. One cannot fully understand Lincoln's agenda without understanding this debate in historical perspective and Lincoln's role in it.

From the time of the founding there was a sharp political divide between those who advocated centralized governmental power and those who supported decentralized governmental power. The Federalists battled the anti-Federalists (or, the Hamiltonians battled the Jeffersonians), with U.S. Treasury Secretary Alexander Hamilton being the foremost proponent of centralization. Hamilton advocated a powerful central government that would be engaged in economic interventionism, whereas the Jeffersonians were highly skeptical, if not alarmed, at such a prospect.

At the constitutional convention, Hamilton, the "great centralizer," proposed an alternative constitution that concentrated all political power in the central government, especially the executive branch, with virtually no role at all for the states. He also proposed a "permanent president" who would have absolute veto power over all legislation and who would also have the power to appoint all state governors. He did not believe in the divided sovereignty of federalism that was adopted by the other founding fathers.

By the 1820s this debate over the fundamental purposes of government became a debate over an economic policy agenda put forth by the political heirs of the Federalists, mostly Northern politicians. As historian F. Thornton Miller has described it, there was "a group of Northerners determined to use the federal government to bring about its economic goals. Its means were national banks, internal improvements, and tariffs."[49]

The advocates of centralized government had effectively adopted British-style mercantilism as their economic agenda, and this was the agenda on which Lincoln would eventually base his entire political career. Jefferson and his disciples were so opposed to that agenda because they were well aware of its results: government-sanctioned favors for the politically well connected at the expense of the general public, oppressive taxation, socially harmful inequities, economic monopoly, political corruption, and the monopolization of political power by a group of men who would orchestrate the unholy alliance between government and business. In fact, it was just such a system, with the oppressive taxation that it created, that drove many British citizens to flee their own country and settle in the American colonies.

Senator John Taylor of Virginia described the British mercantilist system as "undoubtedly the best which has ever appeared for extracting money from the people; and commercial restrictions [that is, tariffs] . . . are its most effectual means for accomplishing this object. No equal mode of enriching the party of government, and impoverishing the party of the people, has ever been discovered."[50]

By the 1830s the Hamiltonian/mercantilist mantle had been adopted by the men who formed the Whig Party. They would battle mightily, but with only modest success, until the demise of the Whig Party in 1856. At that point the agenda was adopted by the Republican Party, and in 1860 Abraham Lincoln became its standard bearer. Later chapters will demonstrate that Lincoln's election—and the North's victory in the war—represented the final victory of the Federalist/Hamiltonian wing of American politics.

Hamilton first proposed government subsidies for internal improvements in his 1791 *Report on Manufactures* because of his belief that private capital markets would not be sufficient to adequately support such projects.[51] But Jefferson's Treasury Secretary, Albert Gallatin, was the first to present a detailed central plan, the "Gallatin Plan," for extensive taxpayer funding of internal improvements. Proposed to Congress in 1806, the Gallatin Plan was a ten-year program of federally financed canal and road building that Gallatin believed would supposedly offer "protection against storms and enemies."[52]

Very little came of Gallatin's plan, however, because of constitutional issues raised by Jefferson, who believed that the Constitution would need to be amended to permit such an expenditure of funds.

President John Quincy Adams (1825–1829) was the second most prominent champion of internal improvement subsidies, but had no success in getting such funds appropriated. In a private letter after he left the presidency, Adams opined that "the great effort of my administration was to mature into a permanent and regular system the application of all the superfluous revenue of the Union to internal improvement" so that "the whole surface of the nation would have been checkered over with Rail Roads and Canals."[53] Adams bitterly complained that his grandiose plans were foiled by the constitutional arguments of James Monroe, who had been afflicted by "Jefferson's blighting breath."[54] He also castigated South Carolina Senator John C. Calhoun (whom he called the "Sable Genius of the South") for the fact that "the great object of my life . . . as applied to the administration of government has *failed*."[55]

After Adams was defeated by Andrew Jackson in the 1828 election, Henry Clay became the preeminent champion of Hamilton's vision. And a young Abraham Lincoln, thinking of getting involved in politics, jumped on the internal improvement bandwagon, carrying also the other elements of Whig/Hamiltonian centralization; at this time, he began rhapsodizing about the greatness of Henry Clay and his economic policy ideas.

James Madison, the "father" of the Constitution, made the most powerful constitutional argument against using federal tax dollars for internal improvements. When the Bank of the United States was rechartered in 1816, Henry Clay placed in the bill a $1.5 million appropriation for canal- and road-building subsidies. On his very last day in office Madison vetoed the bill. He decided that

> it was time to teach the nation a lesson in constitutionalism. . . . The bill, he said, failed to take into account the fact that Congress had enumerated powers under section eight of the first article of the Constitution, "and it does not appear that the power proposed to be exercised in the bill is among the enumerated powers, or that it falls by any just interpretation

within the power to make the laws necessary and proper" for carrying out other constitutional powers into execution.[56]

Madison warned Congress that the general welfare clause of the Constitution was never intended to become a Pandora's box for special-interest legislation.

Some sixteen years later, Andrew Jackson vetoed numerous internal improvement bills, referring to such bills, most of which were sponsored by Henry Clay, as "saddling upon the government the losses of unsuccessful private speculation." In his Farewell Address, Jackson boasted that he had "finally overthrown . . . this plan of unconstitutional expenditure for the purpose of corrupt influence."[57]

This was not just a debate over the building of canals, roads, and railroads. It was a debate over the very meaning of the Constitution and the form the United States government would take.

WASTE, FRAUD, AND CORRUPTION

BEGINNING WITH Alexander Hamilton, the proponents of government subsidies for internal improvements argued that private capital markets would not provide sufficient resources. But economist Daniel Klein has shown that privately funded roads proliferated throughout the early nineteenth century. As early as 1800 there were sixty-nine privately financed road-building companies in the United States. Over the next forty years more than 400 private roads (which were called "turnpikes") were built.[58]

Railroad entrepreneur James J. Hill even built a transcontinental railroad (the Great Northern) without a dime of government subsidy; New Hampshire and Vermont gave no aid at all to railroads, yet privately built lines crisscrossed the two states; and the Mormons built several privately funded railroads in Utah. After the Illinois debacle of 1837, Chicago went on to become the railroad center of the United States without any government subsidies.

Local merchants and town residents invested heavily in private road and canal building because they understood that it would be helpful to their businesses and their communities. There were significant social pressures to invest for the good of the community. State and local governments did get involved in subsidizing internal improvements, however; and in virtually every single case the result was a financial calamity not unlike the debacle in Illinois in the late 1830s.

Ohio was one of the most active states in subsidizing internal improvements, but there was so much waste and corruption, writes economic historian Carter Goodrich, that Ohio "stood as one of the chief examples of the revulsion of feeling against governmental promotion of internal improvement."[59] In 1851 Ohio followed Illinois in amending its constitution to prohibit government subsidies to private corporations. Indiana and Michigan were even less successful than Illinois and Ohio, and in three short years, after spending millions on canal- and road-building projects, the projects were all bankrupt. These states also amended their constitutions to prohibit government subsidies for internal improvements.[60]

Subsidized internal improvements were such a universal disaster that when Wisconsin and Minnesota entered the Union in 1848 and 1858, their state constitutions prohibited grants and even loans to private companies. In Iowa the state courts held that local government aid to private companies was unconstitutional. By 1861 state subsidies for internal improvements were forbidden *by constitutional amendment* in Maine, New York, Pennsylvania, Maryland, Minnesota, Iowa, Kentucky, Kansas, California, and Oregon. West Virginia, Nevada, and Nebraska entered the Union in the 1860s with similar prohibitions. By 1875 Massachusetts was the only state that still permitted state subsidies for internal improvements.[61]

What this all suggests is that the Hamilton/Clay/Lincoln agenda of government subsidies for road building and railroad corporations was wildly unpopular throughout the nation and had been an abysmal failure in every instance. None of these experiences seem to have fazed Lincoln, however, for he continued to promote even bigger and more grandiose internal improvement projects throughout his political career. Indeed, even during the first year of the war, when the fortunes of the Federal army were on the decline, the Lincoln administration diverted millions of dollars to railroad-building projects in California.

Most of the opposition to internal improvement subsidies at the federal level of government came from Southerners, who were "the most consistent opponents of federal aid," wrote Carter Goodrich.[62] Southerners were so opposed to it, in fact, that the Confederate Constitution of 1861, like most state constitutions at the time, outlawed internal improvement subsidies. Article I, Section 8, Clause 3 of the Confederate Constitution stated that "neither this, nor any other clause contained in the Constitution, shall ever be construed to delegate power to Congress to appropriate money for any internal improvement intended to facilitate commerce."[63]

This prohibition, and the opposition to protectionist tariffs and a nationalized banking system, was ended once and for all during the first two years of the Lincoln administration.

CHAPTER 5

THE MYTH OF
SECESSION AS "TREASON"

*Any people anywhere, being inclined and having the power, have
the right to rise up and shake off the existing government, and form
a new one that suits them better. This is a most valuable, a most
sacred right—a right which we hope and believe is to liberate the
world. Nor is this right confined to cases in which the whole people
of an existing government may choose to exercise it. Any portion of
such people, that can, may revolutionize, and make their own of so
much of the territory as they inhabit.*
—ABRAHAM LINCOLN, JANUARY 12, 1848

*To secure these rights [of Life, Liberty, and the Pursuit of Happi-
ness], Governments are instituted among Men, deriving their just
powers from the consent of the governed. . . . Whenever any Form of
Government becomes destructive of these ends, it is the Right of the
People to alter or to abolish it, and to institute new Government.*
—DECLARATION OF INDEPENDENCE, 1776

I N   T H E   E Y E S of the American founding fathers, the
most fundamental principle of political philosophy was the
right of secession. The Declaration of Independence was,

first and foremost, a declaration of secession from the British government of King George III, whom the founders believed was a tyrant. The United States were founded by secessionists and began with a document, the Declaration, that justified the secession of the American *states*. That is the language of the Declaration. When it mentions equality, it is equality of the people of the several states. The Declaration of Independence was the cornerstone of the states' rights doctrine embraced by the Southern secessionists of 1861 and was seen as the most important defense against the tyranny of centralized governmental power.

The Jeffersonian dictum that governments derive their just powers from the consent of the governed and that whenever a government becomes destructive of the rights of life, liberty, and property, citizens have a right to secede from that government and form a new one, was the basis of America's two wars of secession: 1776 and 1861.

Thomas Jefferson, the principal author of the Declaration, was a strong supporter of the Union, but he nevertheless defended the right of any state to secede from it. In his First Inaugural Address in 1801 he declared, "If there be any among us who would wish to dissolve this Union or to change its republican form, let them stand undisturbed as monuments of the safety with which error of opinion may be tolerated where reason is left free to combat it."[1] This statement is both a defense of freedom of speech and a defense of the right of secession. Some have argued that it is merely an expression of Jefferson's devotion to free speech, but this is clearly wrong. He says, "let them stand undisturbed" if they want to secede. The fact that he cites the sanctity of free speech as a reason for letting them "stand undisturbed" does not negate the fact that he was willing to tolerate secession, regardless of how impractical or unwise he may have thought it to be at the time. What he is saying is that even if he personally believed it to be foolish for any individual state to secede, he would still defend that state's right to do so. (It was Jefferson who also wrote to James Madison in 1787 that "a little rebellion now and then is a good thing, & as necessary in the political world as storms in the physical . . . a medicine necessary for the sound health of government."[2]

Fifteen years later, after the New England Federalists attempted to secede from the Union, Jefferson maintained his position that "If any state in the Union will declare that it prefers separation . . . to a continuance in union . . . I have no hesitation in saying, 'let us separate.'"[3] Nine years after that, in 1825, the author of the Declaration of Independence stuck to the same principle that while he hoped with all his being that the Union would survive, he maintained that the states had never yielded their rights to be sovereign over the federal government which they had created. Moreover, although actual secession would be a "calamity," such a "rupture," as he put it, would be necessary if, in the opinion of the citizens of a state, the federal government had become "one of unlimited powers"—that is, one which exceeded the express powers given it by the Constitution.[4]

John Quincy Adams was also a staunch Unionist, but in an 1839 speech celebrating the Jubilee of the Constitution, he also defended the basic American right of secession:

The indissoluble link of union between the people of the several states of this confederated nation is, after all, not in the *right* but in the *heart*. If the day should ever come (may Heaven avert it!) when the affections of the people of these States shall be alienated from each other; when the fraternal spirit shall give way to cold indifference, or collision of interests shall fester into hatred, the bands of political associations will not long hold together parties no longer attracted by the magnetism of conciliated interests and kindly sympathies; to part in friendship from each other, than to be held together by constraint. Then will be the time for reverting to the precedents which occurred at the formation and adoption of the Constitution, to form again a more perfect Union by dissolving that which could no longer bind, and to leave the separated parts to be reunited by the law of political gravitation to the center.[5]

Alexis de Tocqueville observed in *Democracy in America* that

The Union was formed by the voluntary agreement of the States; and in uniting together they have not forfeited their nationality, nor have they been reduced to the condition of one and the same people. If one of the states chooses to withdraw from the compact, it would be difficult to disprove its right of doing so, and the Federal Government would have no means of maintaining its claims directly either by force or right.[6]

Tocqueville was correct in his rendition of how the Constitution was formed, but he likely never dreamed that an American president would ever send an invading army to kill some 300,000 of his own citizens in order to destroy the right of secession, a right that all of America's founding fathers held as sacrosanct and that was at the very heart of the American system of government.

No member of the founding generation was associated more with the cause of centralized governmental power (or "consolidation," as it was called) than Alexander Hamilton. But Hamilton also adamantly opposed the use of military force to either force a state to perform some "duty" against its will or to stop it from seceding if it wanted to. In *The Federalist Papers* (number 81) he stated:

> It is inherent in the nature of sovereignty not to be amenable to the suit of any individual without its consent. This is the general sense and the general practice of mankind; and the exemption, as one of the attributes of sovereignty, is now enjoyed by the government of every State in the Union. . . . The contracts between a nation and individuals are only binding on the conscience of the sovereign, and have no pretensions to a compulsive force. They confer no right of action, independent of the sovereign will. To . . . authorize suits against States for the debts they owe . . . could not be done without waging war against the contracting State . . . , a power which would involve such a consequence, would be altogether forced and unwarranted.[7]

Hamilton here was addressing the issue of the federal government suing a state over unpaid debts. It would be unacceptable, he said, to use force against a state for this or for virtually any other reason, since sovereignty rests with the states, not the central government. Waging war against a state would be "altogether forced and unwarranted."

He went even further. At the constitutional convention he said, "To coerce the States is one of the maddest projects that was ever devised. . . . What picture does this idea present to our view? A complying State at war with a non-complying State: Congress marching the troops of one State into the bosom of another? Here is a nation at war with itself. Can any reasonable man be well disposed toward a government which makes war and carnage the only means of supporting itself—a government that can exist only by the sword?"[8] In the same speech Hamilton said that he could never "dream" that one state would ever coerce another state in that way. It would be "impossible."

John Marshall, the chief justice of the U.S. Supreme Court, is perhaps the second most renowned "consolidationist" of the founding generation, and he agreed with Hamilton that a state cannot be "called at the bar of the Federal court."[9] Even Daniel Webster, who took up the consolidationist mantle after the deaths of Hamilton and Marshall, said in 1851 that "if the Northern states refuse, willfully and deliberately, to carry into effect that part of the Constitution which respects the restoration of fugitive slaves, and Congress provide no remedy, the South would no longer be bound to observe the compact. A bargain can not be broken on one side, and still bind the other side."[10]

This was in fact one of the chief complaints of the states of the deep South before they seceded—that some of the Northern states were not fully enforcing the Fugitive Slave Act (which will be discussed further).

It is important to recall that at the outset of the American Revolution, each state declared its sovereignty and independence from Great Britain on its own. After the war, each state was individually recognized as sovereign by the defeated British government. These sovereign states then formed the "Articles of Confederation and Perpetual Union," which created the federal government as the agent of the states. The states then seceded from that document and dissolved the Union when the Constitution was adopted. The Union wasn't "perpetual" after all, and the words "perpetual Union" are nowhere to be found in the Constitution. No state agreed to enter a perpetual Union by ratifying the Constitution.

The new Constitution was adopted by vote of the states. Nine states out of thirteen were required for ratification. Many of the state voting margins were quite slim (89 to 79 in Virginia; 30 to 27 in New York; 34 to 32 in Rhode Island), and these three states declared in their ordinances of ratification that, being sovereign states, they reserved the right to secede from the Union. Virginia's convention, for example, affirmed that "the powers granted under the Constitution being derived from the People of the United States may be resumed by them whensoever the same shall be perverted to their injury or oppression."[11] They also asserted this right for the other states, which was unnecessary since it was self-evident to everyone at the time that no state could be forced to join or remain a part of the Union.

It is also important to note that at the time the term "United States" referred to the individual states united in forming a compact, as opposed to today's meaning of the phrase as a more or less monolithic state. The fact that these ordinances were accepted by all the other states indicates that this reservation was accepted without dissent.

From the very beginning, the right of secession was viewed by Americans as the last check on the potential abuse of power by the central government, powers that were enumerated and given to the central government by the states themselves for their mutual benefit. In *The Federalist Papers* (number 39) James Madison, the "father" of the Constitution, pointed out that the proposed Constitution would be subject to ratification by the people "not as individuals composing one entire nation, but as composing the distinct and independent States to which they respectively belong." To Madison the states were sovereign and the federal government was created by them to serve their purposes.

In the early nineteenth century one of the most prominent constitutional theorists was the Philadelphia lawyer William Rawle, who, in 1825, published a book, *A View of the Constitution,* that would become the text for the one course on the Constitution taught at West Point to virtually all the top military leaders who would later participate in the War between the States.[12] Rawle was a close friend of George Washington, and President Washington appointed him as the United States attorney for Pennsylvania in 1791. In 1792 Rawle joined the Maryland Society for Promoting the Abolition of Slavery; in 1818, he was elected president of that organization and remained in that position until his death in 1836.

In addition to being one of the most distinguished and prominent abolitionists of his time, Rawle was an articulate proponent of a *constitutional* right of secession. He believed that there was an implied right of secession in the Constitution and that this right should be enjoyed by the individual states. As he explained,

It depends on the state itself to retain or abolish the principle of representation, because it depends on itself whether it will continue a member of the Union. To deny this right would be inconsistent with the principle on which all our political systems are founded, which is, that the people have in all cases a right to determine how they will be governed. This right must be considered as an ingredient in the original composition of the general government, which, though not expressed, was mutually understood, and the doctrine heretofore presented to the reader in regard to the indefeasible nature of personal allegiance, is so far qualified in respect to allegiance to the United States. . . . The states, then, may wholly withdraw from the Union, but while they continue they must retain the character of representative republics.[13]

THE NEW ENGLAND SECESSIONISTS

MORE THAN A half century before the first shots were fired at Fort Sumter, three serious secession attempts were orchestrated by the New England Federalists, who believed that the policies of the Jefferson and Madison administrations (1801–1817), especially the 1803 Louisiana Purchase, the national trade embargo of 1807, and the War of 1812, were so disproportionately harmful to New England that they justified disunion. The New England Federalists, and the New England public, debated the wisdom of secession for fourteen years, but never was the inherent *right* of secession questioned.

When Thomas Jefferson was elected president in 1800, it was a calamity for the Federalist Party, which abhorred Jefferson and what he stood for (limited, decentralized government and the strict separation of church and state). New England clerics blamed Jefferson for a "moral putrefication" throughout the land and routinely denounced him with a most unholy hate. New England Federalists began condemning Jefferson for alleged "falsehood, fraud, and treachery" that would supposedly lead to "ruin among the nations."[14]

Massachusetts Senator Timothy Pickering led a movement to have the New England states secede from the Union. Pickering, who was George Washington's adjutant general and quartermaster general during the Revolutionary War and served as President Washington's secretary of state and secretary of war, announced in 1803 that with the peaceful secession of New England, "I will rather anticipate a new confederacy, exempt from the corrupt and corrupting influence of the aristocratic Democrats of the South."[15] "There will be a separation," Pickering wrote, and "the black and white populations will mark the boundary."[16]

Pickering's colleague, Senator James Hillhouse, agreed, saying "The Eastern States must and will dissolve the union and form a separate government."[17] "The Northern States must be governed by Virginia or must govern Virginia," warned Aaron Burr.[18] These and other New England secessionists were among the best-known Federalist politicians. Also included in their numbers were George Cabot, Elbridge Gerry, John Quincy Adams, Fisher Ames, Josiah Quincy, and Joseph Story, among others. Their cause was very similar to the cause of the Southern Confederacy a half century later: the principle of states' rights and self-government as opposed to an overbearing, tyrannical federal government. They believed that the South—especially Virginia—was gaining too much power and influence and that it was using that power in ways that would disadvantage New England. In 1861 the Southern Confederacy would make the exact same charges against the Northern-dominated Lincoln administration.

The New England secessionists were convinced that, with the election of Jefferson, the federal government "had fallen into the hands of infidel, anti-commercial, anti-New England Southerners," and they believed that there was a conspiracy among the "Virginia faction" to "govern and depress New England," in the words of Stephen Higgenson.[19]

John Lowell, Jr., expressed the strong states' rights sentiments of the New England secessionists when he announced that in any conflict between Massachusetts and the federal government, "it is our duty, our most solemn duty, to vindicate the rights, and support the interests of the state we represent."[20] This statement was strikingly similar to the response Robert E. Lee gave to General Winfield Scott after Scott, at the request of President Lincoln, offered Lee command of the Union army in 1861: "If the Union is disrupted I shall return to my native state and share the miseries of my people and save in defence will draw my sword on none."[21]

Governor Roger Griswold of Connecticut would anticipate the states' rights arguments made by John C. Calhoun in protesting the 1828 Tariff of Abominations. "The balance of power under the present government," Griswold said, "is decidedly in favor of the Southern States. . . . The extent and increasing population of those States must for ever secure to them the preponderance which they now possess." New Englanders believed they were "paying the principal part of the expenses of government" without receiving commensurate benefits, which led Griswold to conclude that "there can be no safety to the Northern States without a separation from the confederacy [that is, the Union]."[22] This is *exactly* the complaint made by Calhoun in the early 1830s and by various other Southern statesmen up through 1861, only with the words "North and South" transposed.

Jefferson's Louisiana Purchase infuriated the New England Federalists, who wanted America to remain as "ethnically pure" as possible. Most of them agreed with William Smith Shaw that "the grand cause of all our present difficulties may be traced . . . to so many *hordes of foreigners* immigrating to America."[23] Given such strong feelings about ethnic purity, for New Englanders the Louisiana Purchase, which encouraged the settlement of even more "hordes of foreigners" in the United States, was intolerable. Josiah Quincy was so outraged that he believed the only recourse for the New England states was secession. The Louisiana Purchase meant that "the bonds of this Union are virtually dissolved; that the States which compose it are free from their moral obligation; and that, as will be the right of all, so it will be the duty of some, to prepare definitely for a separation, amicably if they can, violently if they must."[24] (Note that Quincy only acknowledged a "moral," but not a legal or constitutional right to preserve the Union.)

Pickering spoke of the "depravity" of the Purchase and concluded that "the principles of our Revolution point to the remedy—a separation. That this can be accomplished, and without spilling one drop of blood, I have little doubt."[25] "The people of the East," Pickering further concluded, "cannot reconcile their habits, views, and interests with those of the South and West."[26]

It is telling that Timothy Pickering, George Washington's secretary of state, considered secession to be *the* principle of the American Revolution and that he expected no violent opposition to a principle that, he believed, virtually everyone believed in: the right of secession.

Pickering and the other New England secessionists did not want to be part of a political union with the Southern states, but they still wanted to maintain or even expand commercial relationships with them. They wanted to eliminate the political conflicts, but retain the benefits of trade and exchange between the two regions. In 1804 the New England Federalists began plotting their strategy in earnest. In a letter to Theodore Lyman, Pickering explained that Massachusetts would "take the lead" and secede first, at which time "Connecticut would instantly join," as would New Hampshire, Rhode Island, Vermont, New York, New Jersey, and Pennsylvania.[27]

Pickering believed that New York was the key to persuading all the New England states to secede as a block. The New England Federalists struck a deal with Aaron Burr: The party apparatus would do all it could to get Burr elected governor of New York, and, in return, a Governor Burr would see to it that New York promptly seceded. The election was very close, with Burr losing by only 7,000 votes. During the campaign Alexander Hamilton denounced Burr as dangerous, intemperate, profligate, dictatorial, and lacking integrity.[28] Burr demanded an apology after the election, but Hamilton declined. Burr then challenged Hamilton to a duel, which Burr won by killing Hamilton with one shot.

The entire nation mourned the death of one of its last surviving founding fathers, and Burr became a pariah. Because of Burr's association with the New England Federalists, the death of Hamilton discredited and temporarily stopped the New England secession movement. While this drama unfolded, however, no one questioned the *right* of the New England states to secede. The only arguments were over the wisdom of secession and whether it would be good or bad economically for the region.

When President Jefferson declared an embargo on all foreign trade in 1807, he rekindled the New England secession movement. At the time, Great Britain was at war with France and announced that she would "secure her own seamen wherever found," and "wherever" included U.S. ships. After a British warship captured the USS *Chesapeake* off Hampton Roads, Virginia, Jefferson imposed his temporary embargo.

The embargo was economically damaging to the entire country, as trade restrictions always are, but New England was harmed disproportionately because it was so trade-dependent. When Jefferson left office and his successor, James Madison, assumed the presidency, he imposed an

Enforcement Act that allowed for the seizure of goods on the mere suspicion that they were intended for export. This radicalized the New England secessionists, who publicly called for secession. They issued a public proclamation asserting that the Constitution was "a Treaty of Alliance and Confederation" among the states and that the central government was but an association of states. Consequently, "whenever its provisions are violated, or its original principles departed from by a majority of the states or their people, it is no longer an effective instrument, but that any state is at liberty by the spirit of that contract to withdraw itself from the Union."[29]

The Massachusetts legislature condemned the embargo, demanded that Congress repeal it, and nullified Madison's Enforcement Act, just as South Carolina would vote to nullify the Tariff of Abominations twenty years later. Madison carried only tiny Vermont of all the New England states in the 1808 presidential elections, after which he ended the embargo.

The Republican Party of the 1850s was not the first political party to recognize that the three-fifths clause of the Constitution artificially inflated the congressional representation of the Southern states (see chapter 3). As Josiah Quincy explained, "The slave representation clause is the cause of all the difficulties we labor under . . . the Southern states have an influence in our national counsils, altogether disproportionate to their wealth, strength, and resources."[30] "What the Federalists wanted," writes historian James Banner, "and what their assaults upon the three-fifths clause were designed to gain, was not the abolition of slavery but the abolition of Negro representation. . . . Freed, it appeared, the Negro was more of a political threat than enslaved."[31] Secession, according to Quincy, was the solution to this problem since he saw no prospect in his lifetime of the three-fifths clause being repealed.

The War of 1812 also outraged the New Englanders and added more fuel to the secessionist fire. They feared that another war with England would annihilate their commerce and also feared being taxed into poverty. Massachusetts refused to send troops to the war, effectively seceding from the Union temporarily. On August 24, 1813, the British captured Washington, D.C., and New England was in rebellion. The governor of Massachusetts announced that the federal government had failed to live up to the terms of the Constitution. The state legislature agreed and issued a decree that the Constitution "must be supplanted."[32]

In December 1814 the New England Federalists held a secession convention in Hartford, Connecticut, which was attended by politicians who were not quite so radical as the rank-and-file Federalists. These men feared that voting for secession would ruin any possibility they would have for a career in federal politics in the event that they didn't muster sufficient votes to actually secede, and so most of them voted against secession. The convention did call for an elimination of the three-fifths clause, a two-thirds vote from both houses of Congress to admit any new states, a sixty-day limit on trade embargoes, and a two-thirds vote requirement in Congress before any embargoes could be enacted. Pickering complained bitterly that the convention had been "captured" by "political careerists," but to no avail. Pickering and Governor Strong of Massachusetts nevertheless predicted that the Union would not last. When the war ended, so did the Federalist Party's efforts to have New England secede from the Union.

Throughout this whole ordeal no one ever made a principled argument against a state's right of secession. It was assumed by everyone that, as Pickering said, secession was *the* principle of the American Revolution, and there would be nothing so un-American as opposing the right of secession.

THE CENTRAL CONFEDERACY

PRIOR TO FORT SUMTER there was widespread sentiment *in the North* in favor of allowing the Southern states to peacefully secede. This sentiment was so pervasive, in fact, that there were individual secession movements in what at the time were called the "middle states"—New York, New Jersey, Pennsylvania, Delaware, and Maryland.[33] These states, which accounted for more than 40 percent of the country's gross national product, contained three types of secessionists: those who wanted to join the Southern Confederacy, those who wished to form their own "Central Confederacy," and those who simply preferred to allow the South to go in peace rather than essentially destroying the Union by holding it together by military force. One or the other of these secession movements had the support of the Democratic Party in every one of these states, and the cities of Baltimore, New York, and Philadelphia were hotbeds of secessionism. New Jersey had the largest secession movement, followed by New York City and New York State's Hudson Valley region.

Allowing the Southern states to go in peace was the most popular secessionist notion in the middle states. As explained by Edward Everett, who had run as the vice presidential candidate with John Bell on the Constitutional Union Party ticket in 1860, "To expect to hold fifteen States in the Union by force is preposterous. The idea of a civil war, accompanied as it would be, by a servile insurrection, is too monstrous to be entertained for a moment."[34]

The majority of Maryland's political leaders favored peaceful secession in 1861, not necessarily of Maryland but of the Southern Confederacy. However, they were all arrested by Federal soldiers under orders from President Lincoln, who had suspended the writ of habeas corpus, and were never permitted to assemble in the state legislature to even debate the issue of secession (see chapter 6).

United States Senator James Alfred Pearce of Maryland, who did not want Maryland to secede but who supported the peaceful secession of the Southern states, expressed the majority sentiment: "I have no idea that the Union can be maintained or restored by force. Nor do I believe in the value of a Union which can only be kept together by dint of a military force."[35] According to statements made by Maryland's political leaders at the time, most Marylanders, like so many other Northerners, believed that *forcing* a state at gunpoint to remain a part of the Union would destroy the concept of the Union as a voluntary association of states and preserve it only in a geographical sense. "Any attempt to preserve the Union between the States of this Confederacy by force," said Maryland Congressman Jacob M. Kunkel, "would be impracticable, and destructive of republican liberty."[36]

Nearly all the wealthy and influential citizens of Baltimore favored peaceful secession, as did four of Maryland's former governors. About half the men from Maryland who fought in the war fought on the side of the Confederacy. Among these men were the famous Confederate naval commander Raphael Semmes, the commander of the *Alabama*.

Most Maryland newspapers (none of which supported Lincoln in the 1860 election) also supported peaceful secession; some favored joining the Southern Confederacy and others the Central Confederacy, while the *Annapolis Gazette* proposed "making Maryland a government separate and distinct from all others."[37]

Secessionist sentiment was strong not only in border states like Maryland in 1860 but also in New York, Delaware, parts of Pennsylvania, and especially New Jersey. Fernando Wood, the mayor of New York City, wanted the city to secede from both the state of New York and the United States and become a free-trade zone. The state Democratic Party held a convention on January 31, 1861, to address the secession crisis and issued several resolutions condemning the use of military force to keep the Southern states in the Union. There were a few dissenters, including George W. Clinton, the son of former New York Governor De Witt Clinton, who advocated war to keep the South from seceding.

Horatio Seymour, a former governor who would be elected to that office again during the war, supported the idea of a Central Confederacy. "The middle states would be amply justified," he said, "before the world to posterity in casting their lot with their more southern brethren."[38] Like most other Democrats, Seymour believed that using force to hold the Union together perverted the very idea of a Union designed to preserve liberty. "Consent" at the barrel of a gun was viewed by these men as a sheer absurdity.

The leadership of the New York Republican Party also favored allowing the Southern states to secede in peace in early 1861. Thurlow Weed, a powerhouse in the party, urged Lincoln to reduce tariff rates and make less use of federal patronage powers—two things the Southerners were complaining bitterly about—which he hoped would moderate Southern opposition to the federal government. Henry J. Raymond, the editor of the *New York Times,* favored peaceful secession as well and recommended compensated emancipation. Horace Greeley, the editor of the *New York Tribune* and a prominent Republican, also favored peaceful secession, although he supported the Lincoln government once the war began.

Historian William C. Wright found that of the 101 New York newspapers that existed in 1861 and could be located, 46 advocated some form of secession, mostly peaceful separation of the Southern states.[39] None of them endorsed New York State's joining the Southern Confederacy; but some, such as the Albany *Atlas and Argus,* advocated joining the Central Confederacy. Three New York City newspapers (the *Morning Express, Day Book,* and *Daily News*) recommended that New York City secede. The largest group of secessionist newspapers, Wright determined, was in New York City. Every one of the Democratic congressional representatives from New York City supported peaceful secession.

Although Pennsylvania was a strong Republican state, primarily because the Republican Party championed protectionist tariffs that would benefit the state's steel and other manufacturing industries, there were many prominent secessionists. Robert Tyler, chairman of the state Democratic Party's executive committee, favored peaceful secession, as did the chief justice of the Pennsylvania Supreme Court, George W. Woodward, and several other prominent Pennsylvania politicians and businessmen.[40] "The leadership of the Democratic Party as well as most of its rank and file favored a policy of no coercion."[41]

About 75 percent of all the Democratic newspapers and 26 percent of all the Republican newspapers in the state supported some form of secession in early 1861, according to a survey by William Wright.[42]

Secessionist sentiment was much stronger in New Jersey than in either New York or Pennsylvania. Many of the leading "Copperheads"—Northerners who supported the right of secession—came from New Jersey. The state Democratic Party was firmly opposed to the use of military force, while the Republican Party was divided on the question. Some prominent New Jersey Republicans, such as Joseph P. Bradley, who would later become a justice of the United States Supreme Court, believed that "coercion is out of the question" because it would mean "we are then a broken and divided empire."[43] The New Jersey congressional delegation supported peaceful secession, as did a large majority of newspapers in the state. New Jersey, more than any of the other five Middle Atlantic states, supported the Central Confederacy.

The small state of Delaware also had a great deal of support for the Central Confederacy, but Lincoln ordered the Federal army to occupy the state and prevent the state legislature from discussing the issue, forcing the First State to "support" the Union cause under threat of bombardment.

SECESSION AND NORTHERN PUBLIC OPINION

THE HISTORIAN Howard Cecil Perkins compiled 495 editorials from Northern newspapers that were written from late 1860 to mid-1861 in an attempt to characterize public opinion in the North regarding the right of secession.[44] He found that "During the weeks following the [1860] election, editors of all parties assumed that secession as a constitutional right was not in question. . . . On the contrary, the southern claim to a right of peaceable withdrawal was countenanced out of reverence for the natural law principle of government by consent of the governed."[45] The "classic statement" of this doctrine came from none other than Horace Greeley, who on November 9, 1860, wrote, "We hope never to live in a republic whereof one section is pinned to the residue by bayonets."[46] As of that date, the large majority of *Northern* newspapers were opposed to the use of force against any state that might secede. Table 5.1 presents a sampling of some of these opinions.

There were editorials in favor of the use of force, but they were admittedly in the minority. What these examples of Northern public opinion show is that the right of secession, as espoused in the Declaration of Independence, was thought to be a cherished right of any free and sovereign people by the major opinion makers *of the North* on the eve of the war. Indeed, Northern abolitionists had been

TABLE 5.1 Selected Northern Editorials on Secession

Newspaper	Date	Editorial Statement
Albany Atlas and Argus	11/1/60	"We sympathize with and justify the South because their rights have been invaded to the extreme." If they wish to secede, "we would wish them God-Speed."
Chicago Daily Times	11/21/60	"Like it or not, the cotton states will secede," and Southerners will regain their "sense of independence and honor."
Concord Democratic Standard	11/24/60	Appealed for "concession of the just rights of our Southern brethren."
New York Journal of Commerce	11/26/60	Condemned the "meddlesome spirit" of Northerners who wanted to "seek to regulate and control people in other communities."
Bangor Daily Union	11/13/60	Union "depends for its continuance on the free consent and will of the sovereign people of each state, and when that consent and will is withdrawn on either part, their Union is gone." A state coerced to remain in the Union is "a subject province" and can never be "a co-equal member of the American Union."

(continues)

TABLE 5.1   Selected Northern Editorials on Secession (*continued*)

Newspaper	Date	Editorial Statement
Brooklyn Daily Eagle	11/13/60	"Any violation of the constitution by the general government, deliberately persisted in would relieve the state or states injured by such violation from all legal and moral obligations to remain in the union or yield obedience to the federal government . . . let them [the Southern states] go."
Cincinnati Daily Commercial	11/14/60	Southern states should be permitted to "work out their salvation or destruction in their own way" rather than to "attempt, through forcible coercion, to save them in spite of themselves."
Davenport (Iowa) Democrat and News	11/17/60	"The leading and most influential papers of the union believe that any State of the Union has a right to secede."
Providence Evening Press	11/17/60	Sovereignty "necessarily includes what we call the 'right of secession.' This right must be maintained" lest we establish a "colossal despotism" against which the founding fathers "uttered their solemn warnings."
Cincinnati Daily Press	11/21/60	"We believe that the right of any member of this Confederacy to dissolve its political relations with the others and assume an independent position is *absolute*."
New York Tribune	12/17/60	If tyranny and despotism justified the Revolution of 1776, then "we do not see why it would not justify the secession of Five Millions of Southrons from the Federal Union in 1861."

Source	Date	Quote
Kenosha (Wisconsin) Democrat	1/11/61	Secession is "the very germ of liberty . . . the right of secession inheres to the people of every sovereign state."
New York Journal of Commerce	1/12/61	Opposing secession changes the nature of government "from a voluntary one, in which the people are sovereigns, to a despotism where one part of the people are slaves."
New York Tribune	2/5/61	Lincoln's latest speech contained "the arguments of the tyrant—force, compulsion, and power." "Nine out of ten people of the North" are opposed to forcing South Carolina to remain in the Union. "The great principle embodied by Jefferson in the Declaration is . . . that governments derive their just power from the consent of the governed." Therefore, if the southern states want to secede, "they have a clear right to do so."
Detroit Free Press	2/19/61	"An attempt to subjugate the seceded States, even if successful, could produce nothing but evil—evil unmitigated in character and appalling in extent."
New York Times	3/21/61	"There is a growing sentiment throughout the North in favor of letting the Gulf States go."
Hartford Daily Courant	4/12/61	"Public opinion in the North seems to be gradually settling down in favor of recognition of the New Confederacy by the Federal Government."

Source: Howard Cecil Perkins, *Northern Editorials on Secession* (Gloucester, Mass.: Peter Smith, 1964).

arguing since the 1830s that the Northern states should secede from the Union and not be associated with slaveowning states. For seventeen years William Lloyd Garrison's
abolitionist newspaper, *The Liberator,* displayed the dis-
unionist slogan, "Covenant with Death." Garrison's advocacy of Northern secession was brilliant. The Northern
states would no longer have had the Fugitive Slave Law,
which would have dramatically increased the costs of returning runaway slaves, if indeed they could have been returned at all. Northern citizens would no longer have been
compelled to assist in returning runaway slaves, and Northern courts would not have had to condone doing so. Consequently, the underground railroad would probably have led
tens of thousands or more slaves to freedom per year, instead of just one thousand a year, and would have broken
the back of slavery.

LINCOLN'S "SPECTACULAR LIE"

THE UNION—that is, the government created by the
Constitution of 1789—was proposed by a convention that
was called by the states, it was ratified by the states, and
can only be amended by the states. Article VII of the
Constitution declares that "The Ratification of the Conventions of nine States, shall be sufficient for the Establishment of this Constitution between the States so ratifying
the Same." It then concludes, "Done in Convention by the
Unanimous Consent of the States present."

As we've seen, the Virginia, New York, and Rhode
Island state conventions explicitly reserved the right to se-

cede at some future point, and those reservations were accepted by everyone involved. U.S. Senators were elected by state legislatures from 1789 until 1914, during which time the legislatures took for granted their right to instruct their federal representatives how to vote on policy issues.

When Thomas Jefferson and James Madison authored the Virginia and Kentucky Resolutions of 1798, which declared the supremacy of the states in the federal system, they received little criticism. The Kentucky Resolution, for example, declared that "the several states composing the United States of America, are not united on the principle of unlimited submission to their general government; but that by a compact . . . they . . . delegated to [that government] certain definite powers, reserving . . . the residuary mass of right to their own self-government."[47] These resolutions announced the policy of nullification, whereby the states could nullify acts of the federal government which they believed to be unconstitutional.

The states were so instrumental in forming the federal government that even during the Revolutionary War, the Continental Congress was a standing committee *of the states* that coordinated the war effort. The colonial delegations awaited instructions from home before assenting to the Declaration of Independence, which itself proclaimed the colonies to be "Free and Independent States." The Articles of Confederation, which preceded the Constitution, reserved to each state "its sovereignty, freedom, and independence, and every Power, Jurisdiction, and right, which is not by this confederation expressly delegated to the United States, in Congress assembled."[48] The founding fathers, who had just fought a war against a highly centralized state, were not about to turn around and create one of their own.

There can be no doubt that the states created the Constitution and delegated certain powers to the federal government *as their agent,* while reserving the right to withdraw from that compact, as three states did explicitly. But this history—the true history of the founding—always stood in the way of the grandiose plans of those who advocated centralized governmental power (with themselves in charge, of course), for such power could not be exercised to its fullest extent with such a limited and decentralized state. That, of course, was the way the founding fathers wanted it. So the advocates of centralization, beginning with Lincoln's fellow Whig Daniel Webster, did what virtually all centralized governmental powers were to do in the late nineteenth and twentieth centuries: They rewrote history to suit their political purposes.

The history of the founding, some of the elements of which were just sketched out, went unchallenged for forty-four years after the Constitution was adopted. Then in 1833 the Whig Party, frustrated over losing political battles with Andrew Jackson over the bank issue and with South Carolinians over the tariff, apparently decided that a rewriting of history would aid its cause. Webster and Joseph Story fabricated the notion that the federal government somehow created the states. Webster used his legendary rhetorical skills to wax eloquently about the mystical "blessings to mankind" derived from the Union, claiming that it "strengthens the bonds that unite us" and began talking of a "perpetual" union.

This notion—that the federal Union preceded the states—is not only a lie, but a "spectacular lie," in the words of Emory University philosopher Donald W. Livingston.[49] It was this spectacular lie that Lincoln embraced as his main rationale for denying the right of secession to the Southern states.

Contradicting the views of Jefferson, Madison, and most of the founding fathers, the New England Federalists, the majority of Northern editorialists of his time, and, indeed, virtually all of American political history up to that point, Lincoln denounced the right of secession in a special message to Congress as "an ingenious sophism." He angrily denounced the alleged "sacred supremacy, pertaining to a State," even though no such supremacy was ever advocated by Jefferson or anyone else. This does sound, however, like a perfect description of Lincoln's view of the "sacred" Union and its purported supremacy.

Lincoln argued that secession would "destroy" the government, but such an argument was simply foolish. The federal government that was supposedly "destroyed" by the secession of the Southern states proceeded to field the largest and best-equipped army in the history of the world over the next four years.

It was equally absurd for Lincoln to argue that representative government would "perish from the earth" if the Southern states were permitted to secede peacefully. Representative government would have still existed in the Southern Confederacy as well as the Northern one. In the Gettysburg Address, Lincoln claimed that the war was being fought in defense of "government by consent," but in fact exactly the opposite was true: The Federal government under Lincoln sought to deny Southerners the right of government by consent, for they certainly did not consent to remaining in the Union. H. L. Mencken stated this point as clearly as it can be stated. Commenting on the Gettysburg Address fifty-seven years after the fact, he said of the address that

> It is poetry, not logic; beauty, not sense. Think of the argument in it. Put it into the cold words of everyday. The doctrine is simply this: that the Union soldiers who died at Gettysburg sacrificed their lives to the cause of self-determination—that government of the people, by the people, for the people, should not perish from the earth. It is difficult to imagine anything more untrue. The Union soldiers in the battle actually fought against self-determination; it was the Confederates who fought for the right of their people to govern themselves. The Confederates went into battle free; they came out with their freedom subject to the supervision of the rest of the country—and for nearly twenty years that veto was so efficient that they enjoyed scarcely more liberty, in the political sense, than so many convicts in the penitentiary.[50]

The advocates of secession always understood that it stood as a powerful check on the expansive proclivities of the federal government and that even the threat of secession or nullification could modify the federal government's inclination to overstep its constitutional bounds. A case can be made that secession would "destroy" such extra-constitutional abuses of power; perhaps that is what Lincoln had in mind when he used such language. The right to secede is not expressly prohibited by the Constitution. Moreover, at the constitutional convention, a proposal was made to allow the federal government to suppress a seceding state, but that proposal was rejected after James Madison said

> A Union of the States containing such an ingredient seemed to provide for its own destruction. The use of force against a State, would look more like a declaration of war, than an infliction of punishment, and would probably be considered by the party attacked as a dissolution of all previous compacts by which it might be bound.[51]

In defending the individual right to bear arms embodied in the Second Amendment to the Constitution, Madison invoked the right of armed secession. In warning against the dangers of a standing army controlled by the federal government that might invade a state (or states), Madison believed that with a well-armed populace, "the State governments, with the people on their side, would be able to repel the danger" because of the existence of "a militia amounting to near half a million of citizens with arms in their hands, officered by men chosen from among themselves, fighting for their common liberties."[52]

As legal scholar James Ostrowski has pointed out, if states have the right to protect themselves by force from federal tyranny, as Madison stated, then surely they would also have the right to do so by means of peaceful secession.[53] (Keep in mind that in 1861 no one—especially not Lincoln— was arguing that the federal government was launching an invasion of the South for the purpose of ending slavery.)

Ostrowski presents an ingenious thought experiment that illustrates the absurdity of the notion that Lincoln's suppression of the Southern secession (not the secession itself) was constitutional. In order for such acts to have been agreed upon by the attendees of the constitutional convention, which barely ratified the Constitution as it was, they would have had to have agreed to the following stipulations:

1. No state may ever secede from the Union for any reason.

2. If any state attempts to secede, the federal government shall invade such a state with sufficient military force to suppress the secession.

3. The federal government may require all states to raise militias to be used to suppress the seceding state (or states).

4. After suppressing the secession, the federal government may rule by martial law until such time as the state accepts permanent federal supremacy (as occurred during "Reconstruction").

5. After the secession is suppressed, the federal government may force the states to adopt new state constitutions imposed upon them by federal military authorities (as also occurred during "Reconstruction").

6. The president may, on his own authority and without consulting any other branch of government, suspend the Bill of Rights and the writ of habeas corpus (as Lincoln did in the first months of his presidency).[54]

This, Ostrowski says, is a fair summary of what Lincoln said the Constitution had to say about secession, and Ostrowski is right. It is inconceivable that such amendments would ever have had the remotest possibility of being adopted by the constitutional convention.

Lincoln offered two political arguments (in addition to legal ones) against secession: It would supposedly lead to "anarchy," and it violated the principle of majority rule. But his position on majority rule was in deep conflict with the understanding of the role of majority rule in a federal system held by Madison and other founders of the American system of government. These men understood that political decisions under majority rule are always more to the liking of the voters in a *smaller* political unit. In a federal system, composed of federal, state, and numerous local governments, people can "vote with their feet" and migrate to those governmental jurisdictions that best fit their tastes and preferences. In one consolidated system, the one-size-fits-all nature of majoritarian politics guarantees that at least half the voting-age population will always be losers on any policy issue. Majority rule is not "destroyed" by smaller political units. Quite the contrary; it is rendered more efficient in serving the taxpaying public. Majority rule voting will exist in smaller political units even more efficiently than in larger, more centralized ones. That's why Switzerland, with its highly decentralized system of government and with power vested in more than sixty cantons, is arguably the world's most peaceful and prosperous democracy.

Lincoln's other political argument—that allowing the Southern states to secede would lead to further secessions and produce anarchy—is equally untenable. First of all, it never happened. There were no other secessions and, in fact, that has been the case throughout the world. When Norway seceded from Sweden in 1905, for example, it did not set off a dangerous rash of secessions throughout Europe.[55]

Even if additional secessions would have occurred (a Central Confederacy, for example), the effect would have been to discourage the exploitation of the people of the states by the federal government—the principal reason why the right of secession has such a long history in the United States. If the federal government then behaved itself and remained within its constitutional bounds, many of the states would likely have returned to the Union. Jefferson himself firmly believed that this would be the case if secession were ever to occur.

If the political history of the past 150 years teaches us anything, it is that centralized governmental power creates conditions of anarchy, not the opposite. Lincoln's four years of attempted forced association through total war, followed by twelve more years of violence and lawlessness under military rule during "Reconstruction," is unarguably the worst episode of anarchy ever witnessed on American soil.

In the end, the only real argument that Lincoln could offer for a highly centralized Union was its alleged mystical value as a tool for achieving "national greatness" at some point in the future. His legal and political arguments may have been weak or nonsensical, but when he maneuvered the South Carolinians into firing the first shots at Fort Sumter, he quite intentionally created a national feeling of patriotism in the North, where, all of a sudden, preserving the mystical Union became a matter of national honor. And maneuver he did. In a letter to naval commander Gustavus Fox (May 1, 1861), Lincoln said, "You and I both anticipated that the cause of the country would be advanced by making the attempt to provision Fort Sumter even if it should fail; and it is no small consolation now to feel that our anticipation is justified by the results."[56]

Lincoln had been advised by his top military commander, General Winfield Scott, and most of his cabinet, to abandon Fort Sumter. The Confederate States of America would no more tolerate a Federal fort within their borders than the Colonials would have tolerated a British fort in Boston or New York harbor, and to these advisers it wasn't worth going to war over.

Lincoln promised over and over that he was not planning on reprovisioning Fort Sumter, which had almost run out of food, oil, and other provisions. He lied. He sent a naval force ostensibly to reprovision the fort, accompanied by heavily armed battleships. The historian Bruce Catton explains how Lincoln maneuvered Jefferson Davis into firing the first shot:

> Lincoln had been plainly warned by [his military advisers] that a ship taking provisions to Fort Sumter would be fired on. Now he was sending the ship, with advance notice to the men who had the guns. He was sending war ships and soldiers as well. . . . If there was going to be a war it would begin over a boat load of salt pork and crackers. . . . Not for nothing did Captain Fox remark afterward that it seemed very important to Lincoln that South Carolina "should stand before the civilized world as having fired upon bread."[57]

Shelby Foote, author of *The Civil War*, concurred, writing that, "Lincoln had maneuvered [the Confederates] into the position of having either to back down on their threats or else to fire the first shot of the war. What was worse, in the eyes of the world, that first shot would be fired for the immediate purpose of keeping food from hungry men."[58]

Quite a few *Northern* newspapers recognized that Lincoln wanted a war and that he had maneuvered the South into firing the first shot. On April 16, 1861, the *Buffalo Daily Courier* editorialized that "The affair at Fort Sumter . . . has been planned as a means by which the war feeling at the North should be intensified."[59]

The *New York Evening Day Book* wrote on April 17, 1861, that the event at Fort Sumter was "a cunningly devised scheme" contrived "to arouse, and, if possible, exasperate the northern people against the South."[60] "Look at the facts," the *Providence Daily Post* implored its readers on April 13, 1861. "For three weeks the administration newspapers have been assuring us that Fort Sumter would be abandoned," but "Mr Lincoln saw an opportunity to inaugurate civil war without appearing in the character of an aggressor," and so he did just that.[61] The *Jersey City American Standard* wrote on April 12, 1861, that "there is a madness and ruthlessness" in Lincoln's behavior "which is astounding. . . . this unarmed vessell . . . is a mere decoy to draw the first fire from the people of the South, which act by the pre-determination of the government is to be the pretext for letting loose the horrors of war."[62]

Lincoln's personal secretaries, John Nicolay and John Hay, also concurred that Lincoln maneuvered the South into firing the first shot of the war. "Abstractly it was enough that the Government was in the right. But to make the issue sure, [Lincoln] determined that in addition the rebellion should be put in 'the wrong.'"[63]

The Confederates fired upon Fort Sumter for thirty-six hours, damaging the fort but injuring no one. During this time Federal warships arrived but did not return fire—not even one shot—which suggests that their mission had already been accomplished: The South was goaded into firing the first shot. Nothing would have stopped the Federal warships from returning fire eventually, which they certainly did not hesitate to do for the remainder of the war.

Lincoln hoped that he could goad the South Carolinians into firing at Fort Sumter, and his hopes were realized. He was determined to start a war, which he seems to have believed would last only a short time, after which the secessionists would be brought to heel. In a speech to Congress on July 4, 1861, Lincoln had the audacity to say, with regard to the Fort Sumter incident, that "having thus chosen our course *without guile and with pure purpose,* let us renew our trust in God, and go forward without fear and with manly hearts" (emphasis added).[64]

Jefferson Davis appointed a number of peace commissioners, in conformity with a resolution of the Confederate Congress, whose mission was to travel to Washington, D.C., in March 1861, *before* the attack on Fort Sumter, and offer to pay for any Federal property on Southern soil as well as the Southern portion of the national debt. Lincoln refused to even see them or acknowledge their existence. Napoleon III of France offered to mediate the dispute but was also rebuffed by Lincoln, who refused to meet with him.[65]

One of the few Southern statesmen who understood what the master politician and experienced trial lawyer from Illinois was up to was Confederate Secretary of State Robert Toombs, who, before Fort Sumter, warned that firing on the fort "is suicide, murder, and you will lose every friend at the North."[66] Toombs was right. The bombardment of Fort Sumter, even though it injured no one, helped to end the secession movements in the middle states as well as the support for secession among many Northern opinion makers. But that wasn't the only reason for the reduction in support for peaceful secession. The Lincoln administration imprisoned without trial literally thousands of war opponents and shut down or destroyed dozens of newspapers that opposed his war policies (see chapter 6). This demolition of civil liberties went a long way toward quieting public support for the right of secession.

AMERICA'S SECOND SECESSION

A CRUSADE AGAINST SLAVERY would have offered a compelling case for Lincoln's war, but he never made that case. Until the day he died, he insisted that the war was being fought to deny Southerners the right of secession that virtually all the founding fathers believed was fundamental. Slavery, according to Lincoln, was only incidental to the real cause of the war: "saving the Union." Lincoln called up 75,000 troops to suppress a rebellion, not to free the slaves. Indeed, the official name of the war is "War of the Rebellion." Lincoln and the Republican Party did use the slavery issue brilliantly, however, to advance their real objective: establishing a consolidated federal government and essentially destroying state sovereignty.

Whether the Southern states had a constitutional reason to secede (they did) is not the vital issue. The vital issue is whether Lincoln was justified in having the Federal army kill 300,000 fellow citizens, cripple tens of thousands more for life, destroy their economy, burn entire Southern towns to the ground, abolish civil liberties in the North, and inflict all the other costs of war (to be discussed in later chapters) to prevent them from leaving the Union. It is hard to make that case in light of all the historic support for the right of secession in American history.

In 1861 Southern slavery was secure, although not perfectly so. The 1857 Dred Scott decision had just ruled that slavery was constitutional and that the document would have to be amended in order to end slavery. Lincoln announced in his First Inaugural Address that he had no intention to disturb Southern slavery, and that, even if he did, there would be no constitutional basis for his doing so. And he was correct about that.

"Slavery" was the main reason why the seven states of the deep South were the first to secede, but to this day it is not entirely clear whether they genuinely believed that Lincoln's election as a Northern sectional president was a direct threat to slavery. What they were concerned with was not so much an act of emancipation, which the federal government at the time did not have the power to do, short of amending the Constitution (which no one was proposing to do), but a slave insurrection, encouraged by the increasingly prolific, albeit small, abolitionist movement in the North. Jefferson Davis himself, after the war, explained that what concerned the states of the deep South most was the prospect of "domestic insurrections among us."[67] Since Lincoln was a Northern, sectional candidate who had no support from any Southern state, wrote Davis, Southerners were fearful that the Northern public would pressure his administration to ignore the Fugitive Slave Law and even encourage abolitionist pamphleteering.

Southerners were not very alarmed about the moral condemnation by the small abolitionist movement, but they were concerned that *any* anti-slavery agitation might lead to a servile insurrection. There had already been several such insurrections, including Nat Turner's bloody rampage through Southampton County, Virginia, and many Southerners were paranoid about the prospect of further insurrections.

"The South" was not monolithic in the context of the secession movement. The states of the deep South might have left the Union because of slavery, but the upper South—Arkansas, North Carolina, Tennessee, and Virginia—did not. They remained loyal to the Union until Lincoln decided to wage an invasion of their neighbors to keep them from peacefully seceding. Lincoln was perfectly happy to have these four slave states in the Union. Without his invasion they most likely would have remained there. The Virginia legislature originally voted to remain in the Union and then reversed itself only after Lincoln launched his military invasion.

Lincoln waged war in order to create a consolidated, centralized state or empire. The South seceded for numerous reasons, but perhaps the most important one was that it wanted no part in such a system. As Confederate vice president Alexander Stephens explained in his postwar book, *A Constitutional View of the Late War between the States,* since the Northern abolitionist movement was so minuscule in numbers, and since everyone knew that the federal government was powerless to put an end to slavery at the time, it is likely that "not one in ten thousand" Northerners who voted for Lincoln did so because they thought he would end Southern slavery. It is much more likely that they joined the "Party which had virtually hoisted the banner of Consolidation":

> The contest . . . which ended in the War, was, indeed, a contest between opposing principles; but not such as bore upon the policy of African subordination. They were principles deeply underlying all consideration of that sort. They involved the very nature and organic Structure of the Government itself. The conflict, on this question of Slavery, in the Federal Councils, from the beginning, was not a contest between the advocates or opponents of that peculiar Institution, but a contest, as stated before, between the supporters of a strictly Federative [i.e., decentralized] Government, on the one side, and a thoroughly National one, on the other.[68]

Many Southerners believed that the federal government had been acting in an unconstitutional manner for many years, particularly with regard to its fiscal and trade policies, and that these policies were imposing disproportionate harm on the South.

These policies were primarily benefiting Northern businesses and laborers at the expense of the South. Now that there was a president who owed everything to Northern supporters and nothing to the South, they feared that the government's economic policy would be one of massive plunder at the South's expense.

In particular (and as will be discussed in greater detail in chapter 9), at the time the primary source of federal revenue was tariff revenue. Since the South had only a tiny manufacturing base, it purchased most of its manufactured goods from the North or from Europe. Since they were so dependent on trade, by 1860 the Southern states were pay-ing in excess of 80 percent of all tariffs, while they believed that most of the revenue from the tariffs was being spent in the North. In short, they believed they were being fleeced and plundered. With Lincoln promising even higher tariffs, they were convinced that the plunder was about to get much worse. Moreover, this system of financial plunder through discriminatory tariff taxation was patently uncon-stitutional, since the Constitution mandates that all taxes are to be uniform.

In a November 1860 speech before the Georgia legisla-ture, U.S. Senator Robert Toombs explained why Southern-ers were complaining of unconstitutional fiscal plunder by the federal government and why they believed it was about to get much, much worse with the election of Lincoln. In recent years, Toombs explained, the Northern states had succeeded in having Congress give them a legal monopoly in the shipbuilding business, prohibiting the sale of foreign-made ships in the United States. This increased the cost of shipping to the trade-dependent South.

Other laws prohibited foreign shippers from offering lower prices than American shippers. Special taxes were assessed on the citizens of Southern coastal areas to pay for lighthouses and harbors that primarily benefited the Northern shipping industry. "Even the fishermen of Massa-chusetts and New England," Toombs complained, "de-mand and receive from the public treasury about half a million dollars per annum as a pure bounty on their busi-ness of catching codfish."[69]

Northern manufacturers also enjoyed trade protection with tariffs and import quotas "for every trade, craft, and calling which they pursue," with tariffs ranging "from fifteen to two hundred percent," most of which end up being paid by Southerners.[70] "No wonder they cry out for glorious Union," Toombs said sarcastically, for "by it they got their wealth."[71]

On the eve of the South's secession, Toombs then railed against the proposed Morrill Tariff bill, which proposed raising the tariff rate by as much as 250 percent on some items. With this tariff bill, Northerners were "united in a joint raid against the South."[72] Because the federal government, largely under the influence of Northern politicians, had overridden its bounds of constitutionality with regard to public spending, the Treasury had become a "perpetual fertilizing stream to [Northern businesses and laborers] and a suction-pump to drain away our substance and parch up our lands."[73]

This theme of unconstitutional fiscal plunder by an increasingly centralized government was repeated throughout the South. The *Vicksburg Daily Whig* wrote on January 18, 1860, that "The North has been aggrandised, in a most astonishing degree, at the expense of the South . . . taxing us at every step—and depleting us as extensively as possible without actually destroying us."[74] The effective tripling of the average tariff rate that Lincoln and the Republicans were then proposing was deemed to be intolerable.

Congressman John H. Reagan of Texas reiterated these themes in a speech on the floor of the House of Representatives on January 15, 1861, when he protested "the vast millions of tribute" that Southern taxpayers were paying to Northern businesses, along with "navigation laws and fishing bounties." And most of this money was not being spent in proportion to who was contributing it, but, rather, was spent building up Northern cities, railroads, and canals.[75]

Northern opinion makers did not dispute these claims. On March 18, 1861, the *Boston Transcript* newspaper wrote that "it does not require extraordinary sagacity to perceive that trade is perhaps the controlling motive operating to prevent the return of the seceding States to the Union." The paper spoke of "alleged" grievances about slavery, but believed that "the mask has been thrown off, and it is apparent that the people of the principal seceding States are now for commercial independence."

The Confederate Constitution had outlawed protectionist tariffs altogether, so the Boston paper warned that if free trade were permitted to exist in the Southern states, then the merchants of New Orleans, Charleston, and Savannah would take most of the trade from Boston, New York, and other Northern ports. Consequently, "the entire Northwest must find it to their advantage to purchase their imported goods at New Orleans rather than at New York."[76] That, the Boston paper maintained, was why secession must not be permitted. As we'll see in chapter 9, many other Northern and Republican Party-affiliated newspapers echoed this view that the battle between the free-trade South and the protectionist North was a major impetus for the war.

To a very large extent, the secession of the Southern states in late 1860 and early 1861 was a culmination of the decades-long feud, beginning with the 1828 Tariff of Abominations, over the proper economic role of the central government. Lincoln and the consolidationists wanted to construct a massive mercantilist state, whereas it was primarily Southern statesmen who always stood in their way. These statesmen apparently believed that secession was their trump card. No one anticipated the enormous costs of Lincoln's war against the right of secession.

CHAPTER 6

WAS LINCOLN
A DICTATOR?

———◆———

*Dictatorship played a decisive role in the North's successful effort
to maintain the Union by force of arms. . . . one man was the
government of the United States. . . . Lincoln was a great dictator.
. . . This great constitutional dictator was self appointed.*
—CLINTON ROSSITER, CONSTITUTIONAL DICTATORSHIP

*You will take possession by military force, of the printing estab-
lishments of the* New York World *and* Journal of Commerce . . .
*and prohibit any further publication thereof. . . . you are therefore
commanded forthwith to arrest and imprison . . . the editors,
proprietors and publishers of the aforesaid newspapers.*
—ORDER FROM ABRAHAM LINCOLN
TO GENERAL JOHN DIX, MAY 18, 1864

THE FOUNDING FATHERS were so protective of the
strict construction of the Constitution that President James
Madison vetoed a $1.5 million internal improvement appro-
priation because such expenditures were not explicitly mentioned anywhere in the Constitution. Thomas Jefferson was

not opposed to internal improvement expenditures, but he argued that the Constitution should be amended if they were to be permitted. He also believed that allowing a state (or states) to secede would be an exemplary act that would illustrate the devotion the nation maintained to the First Amendment guarantee of free speech.

All during the New England secession crisis, the New England Federalists openly threatened secession; Federalist newspapers and clergy demanded it; and the Hartford Convention proceeded without any interference from the federal government. To the founding generation, free speech, freedom of association, and the right of secession were all jealously protected rights. For example, the Alien and Sedition Acts, which permitted the prosecution of individuals who were critical of the government during the Adams administration, were quickly abandoned as a gross interference with free speech and led to the collapse of the Federalist Party. New England effectively seceded from the War of 1812 by refusing to send militia when requested by President Madison, while the Federalists continued to agitate for secession.

All of these events illustrate the devotion that the founding generation had to constitutional liberty, even when facing the very real threat of disunion. Not so with Abraham Lincoln. Even though the large majority of Americans, North and South, believed in a right of secession as of 1861, upon taking office Lincoln implemented a series of unconstitutional acts, including launching an invasion of the South without consulting Congress, as required by the Constitution; declaring martial law; blockading the Southern ports;

suspending the writ of habeas corpus for the duration of his administration; imprisoning without trial thousands of *Northern* citizens; arresting and imprisoning newspaper publishers who were critical of him; censoring all telegraph communication; nationalizing the railroads; creating several new states without the consent of the citizens of those states; ordering Federal troops to interfere with elections in the North by intimidating Democratic voters; deporting a member of Congress, Clement L. Vallandigham of Ohio, for criticizing the administration's income tax proposal at a Democratic Party rally; confiscating private property; confiscating firearms in violation of the Second Amendment; and effectively gutting the Ninth and Tenth amendments to the Constitution, among other things.

"This amazing disregard for the . . . Constitution," wrote historian Clinton Rossiter, "was considered by nobody as legal."[1] Rossiter generally praised Lincoln, however, as a "great dictator" and a "true democrat," two phrases that are not normally considered to be consistent with one another.

Having suspended habeas corpus, Lincoln ordered the arrest and imprisonment of virtually anyone who disagreed with his views—views that were new, radical, and not yet subject to any debate by the people's representatives in Congress or by the judiciary. In retrospect, no man who had the least bit of respect for constitutional liberty could ever have done such things. It would have been simply unthinkable to Jefferson, Madison, or Washington.

Lincoln rationalized this suspension of constitutional liberties—at least in his own mind—with the rhetorical tool of falsely equating the Constitution with the Union.

But the Constitution makes no mention of any "perpetual" union, and one of the most distinguished constitutional scholars of the first half of the nineteenth century, William Rawle, forcefully argued that the Constitution contained an implicit recognition of the right of secession (see chapter 5). That was certainly the belief of most Americans at the time. In the end, it was Lincoln's willingness to use brute military force, not his legal reasoning or his rhetorical talents, that allowed him to get away with such a radical assault on constitutional liberties.

Historians have long referred to Lincoln as a "dictator," but they usually refer to him as a "good" or even "great" dictator, as Clinton Rossiter has done. In 1900 James Ford Rhodes, who was quite worshipful of Lincoln, wrote that "never had the power of a dictator fallen into safer and nobler hands."[2] "If Lincoln was a dictator, it must be admitted that he was a benevolent dictator," declared James G. Randall.[3]

Dean Sprague wrote a 340-page book about the suppression of constitutional liberty in the North during the Lincoln administration, inappropriately titled *Freedom under Lincoln*, in which he oddly labeled the last chapter, "Lincoln the Humanitarian."[4] The thousands of citizens of the Northern states who were imprisoned without trial, or without even being charged with a crime, would undoubtedly have disagreed with this characterization.

One victim of Lincoln's suppression of Northern newspapers was Francis Key Howard of Baltimore, the grandson of Francis Scott Key. Howard was imprisoned in Fort McHenry, the very spot where his grandfather composed "The Star Spangled Banner," after the newspaper he edited criticized Lincoln's decision to invade the South without the consent of Congress and his suppression of civil liberties in Maryland. After spending nearly two years in a military prison without being charged and without a trial of any kind, Howard wrote a book about his experiences titled *The American Bastille.*

Lincoln was extremely adept at swaying the masses with his rhetoric and was a successful trial lawyer, but his legal reasoning during the war often seemed bizarre, even to a layperson. He "justified" his unconstitutional power grab by "discovering" presidential powers in the Constitution that no previous president or, indeed, anyone at all, had ever noticed. Specifically, he claimed that the commander-in-chief clause of the Constitution, when combined with the duty of the president to "take care that the laws be faithfully executed," gave him carte blanche in ignoring any and all laws, and the Constitution itself, in the name of presidential "war powers."[5]

President James Madison, the father of the Constitution, had never noticed such powers during the War of 1812, nor did anyone else during the Mexican War in 1846. Lincoln invented the presidential "war powers" out of whole cloth.

SUSPENSION OF HABEAS CORPUS

THERE WAS A great deal of sympathy in the North for peaceful secession (see chapter 5); even some of the most ardent abolitionists favored secession because it would disassociate them from the slaveowning states. There was a great deal of opposition in the North to using military force to compel the Southern states to remain in the Union, and the Federal army's defeat in the Battle of First Manassas intensified that opposition. Lincoln turned the firing upon Fort Sumter to his advantage in rallying Northern support for an invasion of the South, but more was needed: He apparently decided that a severe crackdown on his political opposition was necessary, so he issued a declaration that he was suspending the writ of habeas corpus. This allowed him to order the military to arrest and imprison virtually anyone who voiced disagreement with his war policies and, as we shall see, even his domestic policies.

The writ of habeas corpus was embodied in England's charter of freedom, the Magna Carta, and allowed for a prisoner of the state to be released from prison by following established legal procedures. It is a most important ingredient of the rule of law in a free country that protects citizens from arbitrary arrest and imprisonment by the state for political reasons. American citizens accused of crimes have a constitutional right to a speedy public trial by an impartial jury, to be informed of the nature and cause of the accusation, to be confronted with witnesses against them, to bring witnesses in their favor, and to have the assistance of legal counsel. On April 27, 1861, Lincoln decided that such constitutional freedoms were no longer necessary and ordered the military to enforce his suspension of them. This suspension remained in effect for Lincoln's entire administration.

In England the suspension of habeas corpus was permitted only by an act of the legislature, and virtually every legal scholar in America assumed that the same was true there as well. Some years earlier the chief justice of the U.S. Supreme Court, John Marshall, had issued an opinion that "if . . . the public safety should require the suspension [of habeas corpus] it is for the legislature to say so."[6] Many other judges concurred with Marshall, including his successor, Roger B. Taney, who was chief justice at the outset of the Lincoln administration.

Chief Justice Taney responded to Lincoln's order suspending habeas corpus by issuing an opinion that the president had no lawful power to do so. He cited English and Colonial American precedents and pointed out that the provision regarding habeas corpus is in a section of the Constitution that pertains to legislative, not executive, powers. Taney argued that the Constitution was drawn up shortly after a long war was fought against the King of England and that the founders would never have given an American president "more regal and absolute power" over the personal liberties of the citizens than any king of England ever enjoyed.

Even if Congress supported the suspension of habeas corpus, Taney argued, that still would not justify holding a citizen indefinitely without trial, as Lincoln was doing. He cited Marshall as well as another Federalist icon, Joseph Story, as supporting that position and recommended that suspected treason should be dealt with by the normal judicial process. If not, then "the people of the United States are no longer living under a government of laws; but every citizen holds life, liberty and property at the will and pleasure of the army officer in whose military district he may happen to be found."[7] He then admonished Lincoln to see to it that the laws were faithfully executed and that the civil processes of the United States were respected and enforced. Taney's decision was delivered to Lincoln personally by courier, which apparently outraged him. After the suspension of habeas corpus had been an accomplished fact for some time, and thousands of arrests had been made, the Republican-controlled Congress finally got around to rubber-stamping the suspension. Taney had issued his opinion as part of his duties as a circuit court judge, a duty that Supreme Court justices had at the time. The Lincoln administration never bothered to appeal his decision to a higher court, but just ignored it.

The arbitrary arrests continued unabated, and, by 1862, the suspension of habeas corpus had been expanded to include anyone who "discouraged voluntary enlistments" in the army or who participated in any "disloyal practice," with the military given broad discretion in determining what constituted disloyalty. Martial law enabled the military to arrest and imprison thousands of citizens, sometimes on mere rumors. Northern citizens were subjected to the threat of arbitrary arrest by the military for the duration of the Lincoln administration.

James G. Randall's book, *Constitutional Problems under Lincoln,* is partly a defense or rationalization of Lincoln's unconstitutional actions, but even Randall admitted that "the weight of opinion would seem to incline to the view that Congress has the exclusive suspending [of habeas corpus] power. . . . this is the accepted American principle."[8]

In a book with the self-contradictory title, *Constitutional Dictatorship,* Clinton Rossiter excuses Lincoln's behavior with regard to the suspension of constitutional liberties by calling them "an illustrious precedent for constitutional dictatorship." But even he admits that the suspension of habeas corpus "was done by the President in the face of almost unanimous opinion that the constitutional clause regulating the suspension of the writ of habeas corpus was directed to Congress alone."[9]

During the Lincoln administration, the suspension of habeas corpus and the declaration of martial law in the North led to the imprisonment of thousands of anti-war protesters, including myriad newspaper editors and owners and even priests and preachers. Secretary of State William Seward established a secret police force that made thousands of arrests on mere suspicion of "disloyalty," broadly defined as disagreement with Lincoln's war policies. Prisoners were not told why they were being arrested, no investigations of their alleged "crimes" were carried out, and no trials were held.[10] There was no legal process at all, and many Northern citizens were imprisoned for such alleged infractions as "being a noisy secessionist," selling Confederate trinkets, or "hurrahing for Jeff Davis."[11] An Episcopal minister in Alexandria, Virginia, was arrested for omitting a prayer for the President of the United States in his church services as required by the Lincoln administration.[12] A New Orleans man was *executed* by General Benjamin Butler for merely taking down a U.S. flag.[13]

In May 1861 a special election was held to fill ten empty seats in the Maryland House of Delegates. The men elected were all leading industrialists, physicians, judges, and lawyers from Baltimore. But because they were suspected of harboring secessionist sympathies, most of them were arrested (without being charged) and sent to military prison without trial, while a few of them fled. As Dean Sprague explains, "This was . . . perhaps the only election in American history in which every man who was nominated and elected . . . went to prison or into exile shortly afterward."[14]

Seward famously boasted to the British Ambassador, Lord Lyons, that he could "ring a bell" and have a man arrested in Ohio, New York, or any other state, and was apparently thrilled that he thus had even more power over the population than the Queen of England had.[15]

New York City was specially targeted by Seward's secret police. Because there were so many business relationships between New Yorkers and Southerners, there was little sympathy there for Lincoln's invasion of the South. Arbitrary arrests of New Yorkers occurred "during most of 1861," according to Dean Sprague. "Wall Street bankers, priests, merchants, policemen, and anyone else who expressed disloyal sentiments were subject to arrest."[16] Even the mayor of New York City, Fernando Wood, barely escaped arrest because of his proposal to make New York a "free city." The Lincoln administration also placed the entire states of Kansas and Kentucky under martial law.

The administration protected itself from criminal prosecution for depriving so many citizens of their constitutional rights by orchestrating the passage of an "indemnity act" in 1863 that placed the president, his cabinet, and the military above the law with regard to unconstitutional and arbitrary arrests. This law was at odds with the centuries-old principle that no man (especially a government official) is above the law. It was well established at the time

that official governmental conduct that deprived citizens
of their constitutional rights or caused them private injury
or harm was prosecutable under criminal law. The indemnity law (sponsored by Pennsylvania Senator Thaddeus
Stevens) never received enough votes from the U.S. Senate
to become law; the presiding officer of the Senate simply
declared the law valid, adjourned the Senate, and let the
dissenters voice their protests. The act was "vigorously denounced in a protest signed by thirty-seven Representatives," but to no avail.[17]

State and local courts were as outraged as these congressional protesters were, and near the end of the war
there were literally thousands of lawsuits against administration officials and military officers accused of denying
citizens of virtually every Northern state their constitutional liberties. But the law also made it a criminal act for
state judges to prosecute federal authorities for making unconstitutional, arbitrary arrests and permitted enforcement
by federal courts.[18] Intimidating local judges in this manner guaranteed that few, if any, of the lawsuits would go
forward. In cases such as this, it usually takes many years,
even many decades, for legal precedents or legislation to re-
store constitutional liberties.

Fort Lafayette in New York Harbor came to be known
as the "American Bastille" because it housed so many political prisoners during the Lincoln administration. (The con-
sensus among historians is that more than 13,000 political
prisoners were held in Lincoln's military prisons.) It served
as an effective warning to anyone who would publicly question Lincoln's war policies. Many citizens who had done
nothing more than wish for peace rather than war found

themselves arrested, roughed up by soldiers, and shipped off to Fort Lafayette without any due process at all. Upon arriving there, they were crowded into cells with iron beds and mattresses made of straw or moss. The food was horrendous: Breakfast consisted of "some discolored beverage, dignified by the name of coffee, a piece of fat pork, sometimes raw and sometimes half cooked, and coarse bread cut in large thick slices."[19] Some days the water that was served at meals "would contain a dozen tadpoles from one-quarter to one-half inch long." The guards were "insolent" and the commanding officer "took no apparent interest in the comfort of his prisoners."[20] Most of the Maryland legislature ended up in Fort Lafayette, as did many prominent businessmen from Maryland and elsewhere.

Dean Sprague correctly commented that this "policy of repression" had a long-term impact on the nation because it was an important step along the road to centralized governmental power, "laying the groundwork" for such unprecedented coercive measures as military conscription and federal income taxation both during the war and in the decades thereafter:

At the outbreak of the war, the federal government was not a real source of power. But when the arm of the Lincoln administration reached into Cooperstown, New York, and took away George Browne, when it slipped into Freedom, Maine, and spirited away Robert Elliot, when it proved powerful enough to send three citizens of North Branch, Michigan, to Fort Lafayette, and imprison, without any recourse to law, a man in Des Moines, Iowa, it was apparent that the federal executive . . . had real power. . . . the balance of power inexorably changed and . . . altered the fundamental workings of the American political system. . . . "Father Abraham" had been born to the American people.[21]

SUPPRESSION OF FREE ELECTIONS

BY SEPTEMBER 1861 Maryland was under complete military occupation. Lincoln was taking no chances that the Maryland legislature would convene to discuss secession—or even to vote to remain neutral in the conflict—and sought to prohibit it from doing so by military force. Because General Benjamin Butler was threatening to bombard Annapolis if the legislature met there, legislators decided to meet in Frederick, Maryland. Lincoln gave General Nathan P. Banks, a Massachusetts native, the assignment of allowing Unionist members of the legislature to travel to Frederick but not members of the Peace Party. Simon Cameron, Lincoln's secretary of war, instructed Banks: "If necessary, all or any part of the members [of the Maryland legislature] must be arrested."[22] All of the members of the legislature from the Baltimore area were arrested (without due process), as was the mayor of Baltimore and U.S. Congressman Henry May. All other state legislators who were even suspected of having secessionist sympathies were arrested, as were several newspaper editors and owners from Baltimore. Overall, twenty-one men, including state legislators, a member of Congress, the mayor, and newspaper editors and publishers, were arrested and imprisoned at Fort Lafayette and elsewhere. Others fled the state.

The entire town of Frederick was sealed off by the military, under Lincoln's orders, and a house-by-house search was made for legislators who were not friendly to the Lincoln administration. General Banks reported to Lincoln that every last advocate of peace in the Maryland legislature had been imprisoned.

The normal legislative elections were scheduled to occur in November 1861, and they were similarly suppressed. General Banks was ordered to send his troops to voting places to "protect Union voters" and to "arrest and hold in confinement till after the election all disunionists."[23] Election judges were instructed to disallow any votes for candidates who opposed Lincoln's war. In western Maryland at least one candidate for public office was imprisoned along with dozens of other citizens in order to put an end to their electioneering.

The Federal government placed posters at the polling booths instructing everyone to point out any "peace activists" to soldiers so that they could be arrested and prohibited from voting. "Mr. John T. Robinson of 22 North Howard Street had a busy day accusing his neighbors. He stood at one of the polling places and as they filed by to vote, he accused one man of helping to incite the riot of April 19; he accused another of bearing arms on April 20; he accused a third of insulting soldiers. All three were arrested."[24]

The ballots were made of different colors so that the soldiers could throw out the Peace Party votes. "Many who attempted to vote the Peace ticket in Baltimore were arrested for carrying a ballot of the wrong color. The charge against these men was simply 'polluting the ballot box.'"[25]

Not surprisingly, the Republican Party candidates won every single election. Thus "it was in Maryland," writes Sprague, that "the orgy of suppression [of civil liberties] reached its apex."[26] Similar suppression of free elections occurred in most other Northern states. "Under the protection of Federal bayonets," wrote David Donald, "New York went Republican by seven thousand votes" in the 1864 presidential election.[27]

Despite this suppression of free elections, on November 7, 1861, the Maryland legislature's House Committee on Federal Relations managed to issue a courageous proclamation declaring that "the war now waged by the government of the United States upon the people of the Confederate States is unconstitutional in its origin, purposes and conduct; repugnant to civilization and sound policy; subversive of the free principles upon which the Federal Union was founded, and certain to result in the hopeless and bloody overthrow of our existing institutions."[28] After further defending the Confederates' rights to "the great American principle of self-government," voicing a desire to avoid wanton bloodshed, and supporting the principle of a *voluntary* Union, the proclamation resolved that "the State of Maryland earnestly and anxiously desires the restoration of peace" and while remaining a loyal member of the Union, the state implored President Lincoln to consider "immediate recognition of the independence of the Confederate States."[29]

This was an eloquent but useless proclamation, for Lincoln continued to use the state of Maryland as a launching pad for his four-year invasion of the Southern states.

SUPPRESSION OF THE PRESS

LINCOLN SAW ENEMIES throughout the North, if by "enemy" is meant people who were not necessarily aiding the Confederates but who disagreed with his war policies. Lincoln saw anyone who disagreed with him as a possible "traitor." This included dozens of prominent newspaper editors and owners who, while in favor of the Union, were critical of Lincoln and his policies. That, of course, is why they were imprisoned. Lincoln's response to such dissent was to use military force to shut down dozens of newspapers and arrest and imprison their editors. On February 2, 1862, the Federal government began censoring all telegraph communication in the United States as well.

Lincoln's suppression of the press began with the New York City newspapers, which dominated much of the nation's news. Although such papers as Horace Greeley's *New York Tribune* supported the war, others, such as the *Journal of Commerce* and the *New York Daily News* did not. These two papers were the heart of the opposition press in the North, because their articles were reprinted in many other papers that were also critical of Lincoln's war policies.[30]

In May 1861 the *Journal of Commerce* published a list of more than a hundred Northern newspapers that had editorialized against going to war. The Lincoln administration responded by ordering the Postmaster General to deny these papers mail delivery. At that time, nearly all newspaper deliveries were made by mail, so this action put every one of the papers out of circulation. Some of them resumed publication after promising not to criticize the Lincoln government. For example, the founder of the *Journal of Commerce,* Gerard Hallock, "brought the wrath of the government down on his head" with his "peace editorials"—appeals not to treason or even secession, but to peace. Hallock had spent thirty years of his life building the paper to its position as one of the most prominent in America, and, rather than see it become extinct, he obeyed the government's demand that he sell his ownership in the paper and withdraw from its management. With the paper's peace editorials censored, the paper was permitted to use the mails once again.

The same technique—denying the use of the mails—was used by the Lincoln administration against the *New York Daily News, The Daybook, Brooklyn Eagle, Freeman's Journal,* and several other smaller New York newspapers. The editor of the *Daily News* was Ben Wood, the brother of New York City Mayor Fernando Wood, who had denounced Lincoln as an "unscrupulous Chief magistrate" whose recent message to Congress was "an ocean of falsehood and deceit."[31] After being denied the use of the mails, Wood hired private express couriers and delivery boys to deliver his papers. The administration responded by ordering Federal marshals to confiscate the paper in cities throughout the Northern states. The paper then went into bankruptcy.

The *Brooklyn Eagle* promised not to write any more anti-Lincoln editorials and was therefore permitted to resume publication, but the *Freeman's Appeal* was censored after Lincoln ordered the arrest of the editor, James McMasters, who was sent to Fort Lafayette. By September of 1861 all of the opposition press in New York City was censored with the help of military force.

Among the other papers that suffered the same fate and were censored by Lincoln were the *Chicago Times, Dayton Empire, Louisville Courier, Maryland News Sheet, Baltimore Gazette, Daily Baltimore Republican, Baltimore Bulletin, Philadelphia Evening Journal, New Orleans Advocate, New Orleans Courier, Baltimore Transcript, Thibodaux* (Louisiana) *Sentinel, Cambridge Democrat* (Maryland), *Wheeling Register, Memphis News, Baltimore Loyalist,* and *Louisville True Presbyterian.*[32] (The Louisiana papers mentioned here were in territory that was occupied by the Federal army at the time.)

Fort Lafayette was filled with newspaper editors from all over the country who had questioned the wisdom of Lincoln's military invasion and his war of conquest. Seward and his secret police scoured the countryside for the editors of any newspapers, large and small, that did not support the Lincoln administration's war policy and had them arrested and imprisoned. These actions certainly had a "chilling effect" on other newspaper editors who, at various times in the coming years, undoubtedly pulled their punches—if they threw any punches at all—when commenting on Lincoln's policies.

Although the military presence was pervasive in Northern cities in order to implement the Lincoln/Seward censorship policy, it looked the other way when mobs—at times mobs of Federal soldiers—ransacked the offices and destroyed the property of newspapers that were critical of Lincoln.

A mob of Federal soldiers demolished the offices of the *Democratic Standard* in Washington, D.C., after it editorialized about military blunders during the Battle of First

Manassas. The same thing happened to the *Bangor Democrat* when a Unionist mob completely destroyed the Maine paper's printing facilities and demanded the hanging of the editor.

As the fatalities from the war multiplied, the peace movement in the North grew stronger and stronger, and the repression of it by the federal government became more and more severe. The editor of the *Essex County Democrat* in Haverhill, Massachusetts, was tarred and feathered by a mob of Unionists who destroyed the paper's printing equipment. Virtually the same thing happened to the *Sentinel* in Easton, Pennsylvania; the *Jeffersonian* in West Chester, Pennsylvania; the Stark County, Ohio, *Democrat;* the Fairfield, Connecticut, *Farmer;* and other papers. All of these newspapers were known as "peace advocates." They simply editorialized in favor of ending all the bloodshed of the war and working out some kind of peaceful solution to the crisis, including compensated emancipation. Lincoln would have none of that, and so he allowed his military and his supporters to destroy paper after paper in the North. The Northern peace movement was intimidated, physically assaulted, and destroyed.

LINCOLN'S UNCONSTITUTIONAL SECESSION

LINCOLN WAS NOT opposed to secession if it served his political purposes. This fact was proven when he orchestrated the secession of western Virginia from the rest of the state and set up a puppet government of the new state of West Virginia in Alexandria, Virginia, right across the Potomac River from Washington, D.C. His own attorney general, Edward Bates, believed that this act was unconstitutional, arguing the obvious—that states must first exist before being accepted into the Union. Neither the president nor Congress had the constitutional authority to *create* states, for a truly free state can only be created by its people.[33]

This was another patently undemocratic or dictatorial act that, once again, Lincoln rationalized in the name of "saving democracy." Lincoln ignored the arguments of his attorney general as well as the words of the Constitution, but benefited politically in 1864 by additional electoral votes and congressional representation that was completely controlled by the Republican Party in Washington, not the people of western Virginia. Interestingly, the legislation establishing West Virginia allowed for the people of the new state to vote on a gradual emancipation policy. This was Stephen Douglas's position in the Lincoln–Douglas debates—that the new territories should be permitted to vote on whether or not they wanted slavery.

LINCOLN'S "TRAIN OF ABUSES"

IN THE Declaration of Independence Thomas Jefferson listed a "train of abuses" by King George III that the founding fathers believed were so egregious that they justified the colonies' secession from England. Looking over Jefferson's list of these abuses, one is hard-pressed to discover any of them that were not also perpetrated by Lincoln. Consider the following words of the Declaration:

He has dissolved Representative Houses repeatedly, for opposing with manly firmness his invasions on the rights of the
people. He has refused for a long time, after such dissolu-
tions, to cause others to be elected.

Lincoln imposed military rule on those parts of the
South that became conquered territory during the war, and
for twelve years after the war the Southern states were run
by military dictatorships appointed by the Republican Party.

He has made Judges dependent on his Will alone.

By suspending habeas corpus, ignoring U.S. Supreme
Court Chief Justice Roger B. Taney, and threatening to
prosecute state judges who allowed criminal prosecutions
of government officials to go forward, Lincoln effectively
trumped the judiciary and became a dictator, but a "good"
one in the words of such historians as Randall, Sprague,
and Rossiter.

He has erected a multitude of New Offices, and sent hither
swarms of Officers to harass our people, and eat out their
substance.

Myriad new bureaucracies were created to run the occupied states during and after the war. General Benjamin
Butler famously harassed the people of New Orleans during the war by issuing an order that any woman who did
not display proper respect for occupying Federal soldiers
would be considered a prostitute and treated accordingly.
Federal armies pillaged and plundered their way through
the Southern states for the duration of the war, and Lincoln supported several confiscation bills that allowed them
to plunder private property as they went.

He has kept among us, in times of peace, Standing Armies without the consent of our legislatures.

This was carried out by the "Party of Lincoln" during Reconstruction (1865–1877) and during the war in areas of the South and the border states that were under military occupation.

He has affected to render the Military independent of and superior to the Civil Power.

This was a consequence of Lincoln's four-year suspension of the writ of habeas corpus.

He has combined with others to subject us to a jurisdiction foreign to our constitution, and unacknowledged by our laws, giving his Assent to their Acts of pretended legislation.

Lincoln's assault on constitutional liberties in the North would be consistent with this statement, as would his unconstitutional naval blockade of the Southern ports, his starting a war without the consent of Congress, and myriad other acts that, as Clinton Rossiter stated, were "considered by nobody as legal."

For quartering large bodies of armed troops among us.

This is self-explanatory; Federal troops occupied parts of the South throughout the war and remained there for twelve years thereafter.

For cutting off our Trade with all parts of the world.

Lincoln imposed a naval blockade of the Southern ports even though he never referred to the Confederacy as a "foreign power" or the war as a war (it was a "rebellion" or "insurrection"). The Constitution permits such blockades only in time of war with a foreign power.

> For imposing Taxes on us without consent.

Southern protests over protectionist tariffs helped precipitate the war. During the war, when parts of the Southern states were under military occupation and the citizens there had no voting rights in the Union, they were nevertheless taxed severely, with the military using the most drastic tax collection measures. Despite all his lofty rhetoric about democracy and "government by the people, for the people," Lincoln did not hesitate for a moment to impose a regime of taxation without representation on the occupied South.

> For depriving us in many cases, of the right of Trial by jury.

Habeas corpus was abandoned in the North; civil rights were even more precarious in the federally occupied South. At times during the war, Southern men were executed for refusing to take a loyalty oath to the Lincoln government. Many others were imprisoned.

> For taking away our Charters, abolishing our most valuable Laws and altering fundamentally our own legislatures, and declaring themselves invested with power to legislate for us in all cases whatsoever.

This is a perfect description of the "Reconstruction" South and the occupied South during the war.

> He has abdicated Government here, by declaring us out of his Protection and waging War against us. He has plundered

our seas, ravaged our coast, burnt our towns, and destroyed the lives of our people. He is at this time transporting large Armies, of foreign Mercenaries to compleat the works of death, desolation and tyranny.

The first sentence was certainly true. Lincoln declared all secessionists and peace advocates to be "traitors" who were undeserving of the protection of federal laws. This definition also applied to virtually anyone in the North who opposed Lincoln on matters of policy, as discussed earlier in the chapter. As James Randall has written, in the occupied South during the war, summary arrests were made; newspapers were suppressed; land was condemned and confiscated; railroads were taken over; private homes were commandeered; banks were shut down; priests and ministers were apprehended and imprisoned; church services were closed; public assemblages were suppressed; citizens refusing to take a loyalty oath were deported or, in some cases, executed; and property was confiscated.[34]

Federal armies did plunder and burn Southern cities, as in the cases of Atlanta and Columbia, South Carolina, and the laying waste of the Shenandoah Valley of Virginia in 1864 (see chapter 7). Thousands of new immigrants from Europe were recruited into the Federal army ostensibly to teach the grandsons of Thomas Jefferson and Patrick Henry, who fought on the side of the Confederacy, what it meant to be an American. (Young Thomas Garland Jefferson was killed by Federal soldiers in the Battle of New Market.) This use of immigrant soldiers is described in the book, *Melting Pot Soldiers: The Union's Ethnic Regiments*, by William L. Burton.[35]

DEPORTING A POLITICAL OPPONENT

AT 2:30 A.M. on the morning of May 4, 1863, armed Federal soldiers under the command of General Ambrose Burnside knocked down the doors of the Dayton, Ohio, home of Congressman Clement L. Vallandigham and arrested him without a civil warrant; they then threw him into a military prison in Cincinnati, Ohio. Congressman Vallandigham was subsequently deported by Lincoln to the Southern states, and he then moved to Canada.

Vallandigham's "crime" was making a speech in response to Lincoln's State of the Union Address in which he criticized the president for his unconstitutional usurpation of power. For this he was declared a "traitor" by Lincoln and imprisoned without trial. The Democrats in Ohio (a loyal Union state and home to Generals Grant and Sherman) were so outraged that they nominated Vallandigham for the office of governor even though he had been deported.

In his speech Vallandigham expressed his principled devotion to both the Union and the Constitution, which is why he was so critical of Lincoln. He made the point that Congress alone has the power to borrow money, and yet Lincoln had usurped that power. He criticized Lincoln's First Inaugural Address as one that was "spoken with the forked tongue and crooked counsel of the New York politician leaving thirty millions of people in doubt whether it meant peace or war."[36] He denounced the keystone of the Republican Party platform of 1860, the Morrill tariff, as "obscure, ill-considered, ill-digested, and unstatesmanlike."[37]

After discussing the suppression of the press, the suspension of habeas corpus, the blockade of Southern ports, and other dictatorial acts, Vallandigham then condemned the Lincoln administration for its "persistent infractions of the *Constitution,* its high-minded usurpations of power, [which] formed any part of a deliberate conspiracy to overthrow the present form of Federal-republican government, and to establish a strong centralized Government in its stead."[38]

Lincoln's actions, Vallandigham stated, were "wicked" and "cunning" and constituted a "dangerous violation of that very *Constitution* which this civil war is professedly waged to support."[39] Starting a war without the consent of Congress, in Vallandigham's opinion, was the kind of dictatorial act that "would have cost any English sovereign his head at any time within the last two hundred years."[40] It is important to recall that in early 1861 Lincoln sent 75,000 troops to invade the South without the consent of Congress. The conflict was never declared to be a war but was called a "rebellion." Lincoln never did recognize the Confederate government as a legitimate government, because to have done so would have been to admit that secession was legitimate. If it were officially declared a war, then the blockade of the Southern ports would have been constitutional. But it was never declared as such, which rendered the blockades yet another violation of the Constitution that the war was purportedly fought to defend.

The congressman from Ohio then listed "other grave and dangerous infractions and usurpations of the President," including

the quartering of soldiers in private houses without the consent of the owners, and without any manner having been prescribed by law; to the subversion in a part, at least, of

Maryland of her own State Government and of the authorities under it; to the censorship over the telegraph, and the infringement, repeatedly, in one or more of the States, of the right of the people to keep and to bear arms for their defense. . . . free speech, too, has been repeatedly denied.[41]

He then got to the heart of the matter: The purpose of all these dictatorial acts was not to "free the slaves" or even "to save the Union," but

national banks, bankrupt laws, a vast and permanent public debt, high tariffs, heavy direct taxation, enormous expenditure, gigantic and stupendous peculation . . . and strong government . . . no more State lines, no more State governments, and a consolidated monarchy or vast centralized military despotism.[42]

In other words, Vallandigham was exposing Lincoln's real agenda: the American System. The war was being fought and the Constitution was being disregarded, said Vallandigham, for the sole purpose of finally adopting the mercantilist/Whig economic agenda. This is why both the federalist system and the Constitution created by the founding fathers had to be destroyed—so that Lincoln and the Republican Party could lord over the largest political patronage system ever created by any government on earth.

This, of course, was nothing but a recitation of the Jeffersonian side of the great American political debate that had gone on since the founding. But Lincoln had apparently had enough of that debate and enough of the constitutional restrictions on his party's ability to enact the American System. After Lincoln had already censored the press and the telegraphs, the deportation of Vallandigham sent the message to all opposing politicians that any further criticisms of the administration's policies could possibly lead to their banishment. Lincoln did not have to close down every last opposition newspaper or deport every last opposition politician; rough treatment of a select few sufficed to end virtually all public discussion and criticism of his policies.

THE LARGEST MASS EXECUTION IN AMERICAN HISTORY

IN 1851 THE Santee Sioux Indians in Minnesota sold 24 million acres of land to the federal government for $1,410,000. By August 1862 thousands of white settlers were pouring onto the Indian lands, but there was such corruption in the government that almost none of the money was paid to the Sioux. A crop failure that year meant that the Sioux were starving. The federal government refused to pay what it owed, breaking yet another Indian treaty, and the Sioux revolted. A short "war" ensued, with Lincoln putting General John Pope in charge. Pope told a subordinate, "It is my purpose to utterly exterminate the Sioux. . . . They are to be treated as maniacs or wild beasts, and by no means as people with whom treaties or compromises can be made."[43]

The Indians were overwhelmed by the Federal army by October, at which time the "war" was over and General Pope held hundreds of "prisoners of war," many of whom were women and children who had been herded into military forts. Military "trials" were held, each lasting ten to fifteen minutes, in which most of the male prisoners where found guilty and sentenced to death. The lack of hard evidence against the accused was manifest; many men were condemned to death just because they were present during a battle.

Three hundred and three Indians were sentenced to death, and Minnesota political authorities wanted to execute every one of them, something that Lincoln feared might incite one or more of the European powers to offer assistance to the Confederacy, as they were hinting they would do. So his administration pared the list of condemned men down to thirty-nine, with the promise to Minnesota's politicians that in due course the Federal army would remove every last Indian from Minnesota. This was the bargain: Lincoln would look bad if he allowed the execution of three hundred Indians, so he would execute only thirty-nine of them. But in return he would promise to have the Federal army murder or chase out of the state all the other Indians, in addition to sending the Minnesota treasury $2 million.

On December 26, 1862, Lincoln ordered the largest mass execution in American history—and yet the guilt of the executed could not be positively determined beyond reasonable doubt.

THE HISTORY PROFESSION'S CONSTITUTIONAL FLIP-FLOP

LINCOLN PURSUED the peculiar policy that it was necessary to destroy constitutional liberties in order to preserve the Constitution, redefining "the Constitution" to mean "the Union," which is not at all what the founders intended. That is one of the ways he rationalized his unconstitutional, dictatorial behavior. For decades, generations of historians repeated this mantra and helped perpetuate the notion that Lincoln was only "defending the Constitution" with his illegal and unconstitutional acts. They never denied that he abandoned the Constitution and often acted in a lawless manner. Their argument has essentially been that the ends justified the means.

Even the title of James Randall's book, *Constitutional Dictatorship,* is a contradiction in terms. Furthermore, the thinking of these historians is completely at odds with the constitutionalist perspective of James Madison and the founders. Madison famously stated that if men were "angels," then there would be no need for government at all, for we could all live in peace and harmony without it. Because good men or "angels" will not always be in positions of political power, constitutional restrictions on governmental power are necessary, reasoned Madison. Even an Abraham Lincoln is not to be trusted with dictatorial powers, for (1) even he may eventually become corrupted by such power, and (2) it establishes a dangerous set of precedents that will be taken advantage of in the future by less benevolent "dictators."

Nevertheless, some historians have toiled mightily to pretend that Lincoln's wanton destruction of constitutional liberties was somehow protective of those same liberties and in keeping with the wishes of the founding fathers. After describing Lincoln's numerous illegal acts, Rossiter praises Lincoln for being a "superlative example" of a "true democrat" whose actions really resulted in only "a little injustice." Overall, they were supposedly acts of "moderation" that established an "illustrious precedent."[44] "Freedom of speech and press flourished almost unchecked," Rossiter claimed.

Randall describes the smashing of constitutional liberty in the North by Lincoln as nothing more than a few minor constitutional "problems." In chapter after chapter of his 595-page book, *Constitutional Problems under Lincoln,* he dutifully describes not mere problems but the destruction of constitutional liberty. He concludes almost every chapter with a string of excuses. There are no solid records on the exact number of arbitrary arrests in the North, he says, but he is nevertheless sure that the numbers that are mentioned are "exaggerated." The establishment of a dictatorship was not the overthrowing of the Constitution but merely "out of keeping with the normal tenor of American law."[45] Nor were thousands of arbitrary arrests an example of tyranny, but only "unfortunate" and made, after all, with "the best of motives."[46]

The shutting down of dozens of newspapers and the destruction of printing presses by mobs of Federal soldiers was not an affront to free speech but simply "unfortunate." And it was unfortunate not because of the harm done to freedom of speech, but because there was often a public backlash against the Lincoln government for its heavy-handed treatment of law-abiding citizens.[47] This public backlash harmed Lincoln politically and *that* is what was "unfortunate," in Randall's opinion. To Randall the political career of Abraham Lincoln was more important than the constitutional liberties of the American people.

To Dean Sprague, the thousands of Northern newspaper editors, businessmen, legislators, and other citizens who were abruptly snatched from their families by heavily armed Federal soldiers without a warrant, without being charged, and without any due process of law, and who were then thrown into dreary, cold, and unhealthy political prisoner-of-war camps were not really inconvenienced very much. After all, says Sprague, "no political prisoner was put to death."[48]

To his credit Sprague described Lincoln's "obliteration of the traditional American system of due process of law" whereby "the entire judicial system was set aside":

> The laws were silent, indictments were not found, testimony was not taken, judges did not sit, juries were not impaneled, convictions were not obtained and sentences were not pronounced. The Anglo-Saxon concept of due process, perhaps the greatest political triumph of the ages and the best guardian of freedom, was abandoned.[49]

But then he turns around and labels these acts of tyranny a "political achievement" because they enabled one man, Abraham Lincoln, to succeed politically. The ends justify the means. Another "political achievement" was the pervasive censorship of the peace protesters in the North. As we've seen, the peace advocates in the press were beaten into submission—sometimes literally—with the iron fist of William Seward's secret police force. The result, Sprague approvingly explained, was that "States Rights, which prior to 1860 had been as important a part of northern political beliefs as southern, were overturned."[50]

In perhaps the most bizarre of all statements in this regard, Sprague concludes his book by approvingly quoting the *New York Times* as saying that Lincoln "was the most humane man that ever wielded such authority" and "He had no taste for tyranny."[51] In reality Lincoln was a glutton for tyranny, as his actions proved time and again during his entire administration.

Some prominent contemporary historians have abandoned the effort to portray Lincoln as someone who was devoted to preserving the Constitution. They now praise him for doing precisely the opposite: destroying by force of arms the constitutional system established by the founding fathers. The historian James McPherson, for example, writes approvingly in *Abraham Lincoln and the Second American Revolution* that Lincoln did indeed engineer a constitutional "revolution" in which his assault on traditional constitutional liberties, described in this chapter, played a crucial role. The essence of this "revolution" was the creation of a highly centralized system of government of the sort that Lincoln and the Whigs had been battling to establish for some thirty years. McPherson explains this revolution by quoting Republican Congressman George W. Julian of Indiana, who, in 1867, advocated treating the Southern states as conquered provinces ruled by a military dictatorship under the direction of the Republican Party (which was the essence of "Reconstruction"). "What these regions need above all things," declared Congressman Julian, "is not an easy and quick return to their forfeited rights in the Union, but government, the strong arm of power, outstretched from the central authority here in Washington."[52]

Another well-known left-of-center historian, Garry Wills, wrote in *Lincoln at Gettysburg* that Lincoln's rhetorical gimmickry (an "open air sleight of hand") and willingness to use military force to achieve his political ends were so successful that they "remade America."[53] Wills is obviously thrilled by this arbitrary reinvention of the purpose of American government since he believes that Lincoln's emphasis on the word equality in the Gettysburg Address redefined the primary purpose of American government as the pursuit of egalitarianism, which always requires a large, activist, centralized state.

The word "equality" does not appear in the Constitution, so Lincoln's insistence that this was the principal feature of the federal government really was revolutionary. Wills refers not merely to equality of treatment for the ex-slaves, but also to the whole twentieth-century socialist enterprise of using the powers of centralized government to attempt to force all types of "equality" on the population. Wills apparently hopes that the failed twentieth-century collectivist ideology can somehow be revived if Lincoln can be associated with it. (After *Lincoln at Gettysburg,* one of Wills's next books tried to discredit the Jeffersonian tradition of limited government.)

Columbia University law professor George P. Fletcher echoed Wills's theme more recently in *Our Secret Constitution: How Lincoln Redefined American Democracy.*[54] Like Wills, Fletcher applauds the fact that Lincoln altered the ostensible purpose of the war from "saving the Union" to "reinventing the United States." The result was nothing less than a new constitutional order that, unlike the first one, was not adopted through a constitutional convention where all the issues were argued and debated by representatives of the states and then put to a vote but, rather, by the brute force of war. As Fletcher writes,

> The Civil War called forth a new constitutional order. At the heart of this postbellum legal order lay the Reconstruction Amendments—the Thirteenth, Fourteenth, and Fifteenth Amendments, ratified in the years 1865 to 1870. The principles of this new legal regime are so radically different from our original Constitution, drafted in 1787, that they deserve to be recognized as a second American constitution.[55]

The fourteenth amendment will be discussed more fully in chapter 8, but for now it will suffice to mention that Fletcher approvingly describes its main premises as being nationalism, egalitarianism, and "democracy," or the politicization of life. Government became more militaristic and began a quest for empire; myriad socialistic income and wealth-transfer schemes were adopted (and are still being adopted); and the Jeffersonian notion that "that government is best which governs least" was abandoned in favor of today's philosophy that nothing—not even the rules of golf—should be beyond the control of the federal government.

Fletcher heartily applauds this result and claims that the policies of egalitarianism, nationalistic empire building, and the politicization of society whereby the federal government claims "authority" to regulate (or tax) virtually all aspects of our lives somehow reflect a "higher law" than the written Constitution, so that those who believe in such things "allow themselves to sidestep the rules."[56] And he points to Lincoln as the champion sidestepper of constitutional rules, the man who showed us how it could be done (in his case, with the backing of a large military). "Lincoln's casual attitude toward formal constitutional institutions, such as the writ of habeas corpus," is to be applauded, says Fletcher.[57]

This constitutional transformation did not happen all at once, of course; it began with wartime legislation (see chapter 9), was extended through the postwar constitutional amendments, and continues on today. The pursuit of collectivism and the thorough politicization of society that occurs in politics, the courts, the government-run schools, and elsewhere is all a manifestation of what Fletcher calls "the Secret Constitution."

Fletcher mentions as his intellectual inspirations the Marxist historian Eric Foner, the leftist historian Garry Wills, and liberal historian James McPherson, but takes them all to task for being insufficiently enthusiastic about how Lincoln laid the groundwork for this silent constitutional coup. "They overlook the consolidation of the United States as a nation in the mid-nineteenth-century European sense of the term."[58]

Indeed they do, but the present book does not. Fletcher is correct in his assessment, but as later chapters will argue, the effects of this silent coup have been the development of a warfare/welfare state that has resulted in the unnecessary death of hundreds of thousands of Americans at war and the building up of a central government that—along with its franchises or appendages, the state and local governments—confiscates nearly half of national income in taxes, more than was taken from medieval serfs. The consolidation of governmental power that Fletcher praises and credits Lincoln for has at times been disastrous.

James Randall wrote in *Constitutional Problems under Lincoln* that "great social purposes" are sometimes promoted by abandoning "constitutional barriers."[59] Randall was an early proponent of the "liberal" or "progressive" notion of a "living constitution." He wrote that one must "broaden" one's view of the Constitution and look at it as a "vehicle of life" and a "matter of growth, development, and interpretation."[60] A community "re-expresses from time to time its will concerning its government," which is surely true, so that the Constitution must be "gradually molded to fit the nation. . . . The Constitution is fortunately not a straight-jacket."[61] Nor, he said, should we endure "excessive reliance upon the political wisdom of a by-gone generation."[62] Randall was especially enthusiastic over the fact that the commerce clause of the Constitution has been perverted to justify virtually any kind of federal power grab under the guise of "regulating interstate commerce."[63]

In the foreword to his 1950 edition, Randall added one more excuse: Lincoln was not as bad as Hitler, Stalin, Mussolini, and Hirohito as far as his attack on civil liberties was concerned. Writing just after the conclusion of World War II, Randall noted that Lincoln's secret police may have been "deplorable," but "it was exceedingly mild by modern standards."[64] In fact, in the 1950 edition of his book, Randall praised Lincoln even more than he had in the earlier editions precisely because it had become apparent to him that Lincoln's precedent of ignoring the Constitution had led to a vastly expanded and more highly centralized government. No longer concerned about constitutional restrictions on internal improvement schemes, Randall praised Lincoln for "railroad promotion" and myriad other government spending programs, as well as the crushing of states' rights, which Randall euphemistically labeled "federal-state readjustment."[65]

Lincoln "believed in purposeful government," Randall said, and "if one looks back over American history he will find that practically all the Presidents regarded as outstanding or great were strong executives."[66] This is certainly true if one defines a "great" president as one who enlarges the size and scope of government beyond what is permitted in the Constitution. If one alternatively defines "greatness" in a president as one who adheres to and *obeys,* rather than undermines, the Constitution, then one reaches the opposite conclusion.[67]

It is certainly true that the public's attitudes toward government change, but altering the Constitution by executive fiat without explicitly amending it in the way proscribed in the Constitution itself is a recipe for tyranny. In his Farewell Address to the Nation, George Washington warned of attempts to alter the meaning of the Constitution by means other than the formal amendment process and condemned such subterfuges as acts of tyranny designed to overthrow the government by stealth:

> If in the opinion of the People, the distribution or modification of the Constitutional powers be in any particular wrong, let it be corrected by an amendment in the way which the Constitution designates. *But let there be no change by usurpation; for though this, in one instance, may be the instrument of good, it is the customary weapon by which free governments are destroyed.*[68] (emphasis added)

Of course, the Constitution was always *meant* to be a "straight-jacket" worn by enterprising politicians who, the founders understood, could never be entirely trustworthy in protecting the lives, liberties, and property of the people from the temptations of special-interest politics. Jefferson himself spoke of "binding" government in "the chains of the Constitution." Randall reveled in the fact that that philosophy was effectively overthrown by Lincoln. As David Donald has remarked, once Lincoln became a martyr, politicians of all parties began invoking his example as "justification" for more and more unconstitutional power grabs, often making the politically unanswerable argument that "Lincoln did it; how could anyone object?"

In *Fate of Liberty: Abraham Lincoln and Civil Rights*, Mark E. Neely, Jr., observed that as early as the 1840s Lincoln, one of the most ambitious politicians in American history, was seething with resentment over the fact that constitutional arguments stood in the way of the Whig economic program and his vaunted American System. At that time, writes Neely, "Lincoln appeared to be marching steadily toward a position of gruff and belittling impatience with constitutional arguments against the beleaguered Whig program."[69]

The Federalist/Whig program of protectionist tariffs, nationalized banking, and government subsidies for corporations was foiled for sixty years by strict constructionist interpretations of the Constitution (see chapter 4). Once he and the old Whigs were finally in power, Lincoln was not about to let the Constitution stand in his way.

In 1962 literary critic Edmund Wilson compared Lincoln to Lenin and Otto von Bismarck because Lincoln granted himself dictatorial powers in order to usher in a highly centralized state, just as the other two had done.[70] The nineteenth century was the century of governmental consolidation, especially in Germany, Russia, and the United States. As Wilson explained,

> The impulse to unification was strong in the nineteenth century . . . and if we would grasp the significance of the Civil War in relation to the history of our time, we should consider Abraham Lincoln in connection with the other leaders who have been engaged in similar tasks. The chief of these leaders have been Bismarck and Lenin. They with Lincoln have presided over the unifications of the three great new modern powers. . . . Each established a strong central government over hitherto loosely coordinated peoples. Lincoln kept the Union together by subordinating the South to the North; Bismarck imposed on the German states the cohesive hegemony of Prussia; Lenin . . . began the work of binding Russia . . . in a tight bureaucratic net.[71]

Wilson didn't contend that Lincoln was *exactly* like them, especially Lenin, but they were nevertheless all considered to be the patron saints of centralized governmental power in their respective countries. Each of these men, says Wilson, "became an uncompromising dictator" and was succeeded by newly formed government bureaucracies that continued to expand the power of government over their people so that "all the bad potentialities of the policies he had initiated were realized, after his removal, in the most undesirable way."[72]

When Wilson wrote those words (1961), he recognized that America hadn't suffered from the calamities of dictatorship that the German and Russian people had endured, but he nevertheless feared what relentless growth and centralization of governmental power meant for American liberty. This, of course, is the same fear that was expressed by the Jeffersonians from the beginning of the republic and has a long and honored past in American political history. But Wilson was excoriated by Neely for expressing this time-honored view. "The ultimate source" of Wilson's concern that the precedents established by Lincoln set off centralizing tendencies that would lead to dangerous exercises of governmental power was "Wilson's own extremist theories of individual freedom," Neely snarled.[73]

However, the Bill of Rights and other guarantors of individual liberty embodied in the Constitution are "extremist" only to those like Neely who applaud the fact that the Old Republic established by the U.S. Constitution has been effectively overthrown, with Lincoln leading the way. To many others, extremism in the defense of constitutional liberty is no vice. Indeed, in every American war since the War between the States, military recruits and draftees have been told by the state they are being asked to risk their lives to defend the constitutional liberties of the American people.

CHAPTER 7

WAGING WAR ON CIVILIANS

To the petulant and persistent secessionists, why, death is mercy.
—GENERAL WILLIAM T. SHERMAN,
JANUARY 31, 1864

GENERAL SHERMAN illustrates the complete disregard that Lincoln and his generals had for the time-honored tradition of the right of secession in America. Even to Alexander Hamilton, who would have fully supported Lincoln's consolidationist agenda, using military force to keep a state from seceding was unthinkable or, in his own words, "impossible." It quickly became the policy of the Lincoln administration to use deadly force against anyone, including civilians, in order to deny Americans the right of secession. Combating the issue of secession with mere reason had all of a sudden become a quaint memory, eliminated by the might of the Federal military arsenal.

Many historians have praised Lincoln for his micromanagement of the war effort. James McPherson, for example, called Lincoln's management of the war "brilliant" and the work of a "genius."[1] Lincoln repeatedly replaced his top generals until he found the "right" one, Ulysses S. Grant. One of the most famous photographs of the war, taken by Mathew Brady, shows Lincoln standing outside the field tent of General George B. McClellan and presumably giving the general his instructions. To a great extent, Lincoln left most nonmilitary legislation to the initiative of Congress while he concentrated day to day on the war effort and on squelching domestic opposition to his war policies in the North for the duration of the war.

Lincoln's military commanders frequently complained of his intimate involvement with management of the war—just as their successors would complain (in private) about President Lyndon B. Johnson's involvement a century later during the Vietnam War. Lincoln was always in direct contact with his military commanders in the field, especially the ones in and around Virginia, where so many of the major battles were waged. During his entire administration, writes McPherson, there was scarcely a day "in which Lincoln was not preoccupied with the war. . . . he spent more time in the War Department telegraph office than anywhere else except the White House itself."[2]

Indeed, Lincoln even spent many nights at the War Department telegraph office, and he left Washington to be with the Army of the Potomac eleven times. "Some of the most dramatic events in Lincoln's presidency grew out of his direct intervention in strategic command decisions," McPherson says.[3]

By the second year of the war, a war that Lincoln originally believed could be ended in weeks and certainly in a few months, things were not going well for the Federal army. The Emancipation Proclamation of January 1863 was an act of desperation on Lincoln's part after the North suffered several major military defeats and world opinion held that the South was winning the war (see chapter 3).

In a major strategy change, the government abandoned international law and its own military code to begin waging war on Southern civilians. Much has been written about the targeting of Southern civilians—mostly women, children, and old men who were too feeble to participate in the Confederate army. Many excuses have been made for Lincoln in this regard—that he was unaware of the atrocities that were occurring or that he stated his opposition to them once he learned of them. But since the attacks on civilians and their property persisted for virtually the entire war and were sharply escalated during the last two years of the war in a systematic way by Generals Sherman, Grant, Sheridan, and others, it is inconceivable that they were not part and parcel of the war planning of the commander in chief.

One cannot praise Lincoln for his pervasive intervention in war management on the one hand, while on the other hand claiming that he had no idea what was occurring on a massive scale for years. Indeed, some historians openly praise Lincoln for his abandonment of international law and the American military's own code of conduct. Stephen Oates, for one, described the "scorched earth warfare" against the "rebel economy" (that is, civilians) in the most glowing terms and concluded that "Lincoln fully endorsed Sheridan's burning of the Shenandoah Valley, Sherman's

brutal March to the Sea through Georgia, and the . . . destructive raid across Alabama" (which will be discussed
later in this chapter).[4]

THE RULES OF WAR

IN 1863 AN international convention met in Geneva,
Switzerland, to codify rules of warfare that had been in existence for more than a century. During the century prior to
the War between the States, nations agreed that it was a
war crime, punishable by imprisonment or death, for
armies to (1) attack defenseless cities and towns, (2) plunder and wantonly destroy civilian property, and (3) take
from the civilian population more than what was necessary
to feed and sustain an occupying army. The only just war,
moreover, was a defensive war. On this account, Lincoln's
invasion of the South surely makes him the aggressor.

American politicians and military officers relied on the
work of the Swiss jurist Emmerich de Vattel, author of *The
Law of Nations,* first published in 1798, as their source of
information on the rules of war.[5] These international
"laws" weren't the result of any international agreements
or treaties, but consisted of accumulated wisdom and customs handed down since classical times; they were based
on the assumption that certain moral ideas were self-evident and worthy of respect by all civilized people.

With regard to the conduct of war, Vattel exempted
women, children, feeble old men, the sick, and people who
make no resistance. War was to be carried out only by soldiers: "The people, the peasants, the citizens, take no part

in it, and generally have nothing to fear from the sword of the enemy," he wrote. As long as they refrain from hostilities, they "live in as perfect safety as if they were friends." Occupying soldiers who destroy property, farms, and livestock, Vattel wrote, should be regarded as "savage barbarians."[6] Enemy civilians were to be exempted, as much as possible, from the dangers of war.

As of 1861 one of the leading American experts in the conduct of war according to international law was San Francisco attorney Henry Halleck, a former army officer and West Point instructor who was appointed general in chief of the Union armies in July 1862. General Halleck was the author of *International Law,* which was used as a text at West Point and so had informed virtually all the top commanders in the Union army (and the Confederate army as well) of the proper conduct of war.[7] Halleck relied heavily on the work of Vattel and agreed with him that noncombatants should be spared, as far as possible. He wrote that not only the persons but also the property of civilians was to be protected and that private property should be taken only with compensation unless (1) the confiscation was a penalty for a military offense, (2) it was necessary to maintain civil order, or (3) it was necessary to feed the invading army. Vattel condemned making hostages of civilians and burning private homes, but Halleck did not in his book. These two practices were widely used in the South by the Union armies.[8]

On April 24, 1863, Lincoln issued General Order No. 100 regarding the proper conduct of the war. The order came to be known as the "Lieber Code" because it was drafted by Columbia University law professor Francis

Lieber, a German immigrant and a staunch Unionist. Lieber's views influenced Otto von Bismarck, who, like Lincoln in America, introduced a highly centralized state in Germany in 1870. Lieber denounced the kind of federalist system created by the American founding fathers for creating "confederacies of petty sovereigns" and dismissed the Jeffersonian philosophy as a collection of "obsolete ideas."[9] In his youth he was arrested several times for allegedly subversive and treasonous activities in Germany.

The Lieber Code reiterated the accepted wisdom of international law at the time—that civilians were to be spared from the dangers of combat as far as possible. Commentators in Europe and the United States who had not read the code very carefully praised it quite lavishly for its supposed expression of humanity and morality. But the Lieber Code contained a piece of Lincolnian rhetoric at the very end that permitted military commanders to completely ignore the code if the situation at hand deemed it necessary in the commander's opinion. In other words, the Lieber Code was a smokescreen creating the impression that the Federal army would abide by international law, but in reality it essentially exempted all Federal military commanders from doing so.

TARGETING CIVILIANS

AT THE OUTSET of the war Union military commanders worried that a pillaging and plundering army roaming throughout the South would harm the Union cause by destroying any latent Unionist sentiment that existed there.

Nevertheless, wanton pillaging of private property took place in the South almost from the very start of the war. The invading Federal armies "foraged" as they went, confiscating crops, livestock, and a variety of agricultural products. "As early as October 1861," General Louis Blenker's division "was already burning houses and public buildings in the towns along its line of march" in the Shenandoah Valley of Virginia.[10]

In *The Hard Hand of War,* Mark Grimsley noted that the Army of the Potomac "possessed its full quotient of thieves, freelance foragers, and officers willing to look the other way."[11] As early as the Battle of First Manassas, the movement of the Army of the Potomac was marked by "robbing hen roosts, killing hogs, slaughtering beef cattle, cows, the burning of a house or two and the plundering of others."[12]

Such plundering of the unarmed civilian population greatly bothered General George McClellan, who wrote Lincoln a letter on June 20, 1862, imploring him to ensure that the war was conducted according to "the highest principles known to Christian Civilization" and was directed only against "armed forces and organizations," not the Southern population.[13]

Lincoln is said to have politely accepted McClellan's letter, after which he abandoned any type of conciliatory policy toward the Southern civilian population by supporting a Confiscation Act that was perceived by Union soldiers (and Southerners) as "a green light to go after Southern property."[14] McClellan was replaced several months later (Lincoln was unhappy with his alleged slowness and indecisiveness) and went on to run against Lincoln as the Democratic candidate for president in 1864.

Another way in which war was waged on civilians was the policy, adopted almost from the very beginning, of retaliating against Confederate attacks by holding randomly chosen civilians as hostages, sometimes shooting them and sometimes burning their houses or their entire towns to the ground. It is hard to believe that Lincoln, whom some historians celebrate as a skilled micromanager of the war effort who maintained almost constant contact with his field commanders, did not know about these atrocities.

Union Colonel John Beatty warned the residents of Paint Rock, Alabama, that "Every time the telegraph wire was cut we would burn a house; every time a train was fired upon we would hang a man; and we would continue to do this until every house was burned and every man hanged between Decatur and Bridgeport."[15] Beatty ended up burning the entire town of Paint Rock to the ground while seizing three hostages.

There are many other accounts of similar assaults on Southern civilians and their property. After suffering repeated battlefield defeats in the Shenandoah Valley at the hands of Confederate General Thomas "Stonewall" Jackson, Union General John Pope responded by commanding his troops to essentially begin waging war on the civilian population of Virginia. Pope argued that since civilians were not giving the invading Federal armies enough information about Confederate troop movements or guerilla attacks, they should be held "collectively responsible" for any such attacks. Consequently, he instructed his troops to plunder at will, using the following euphemism: "All villages and neighborhoods . . . will be laid under contribution."[16] Moreover, his General Order No. 11, issued on July

23, 1862, specified that all male citizens who wished to remain behind Union lines—that is, in their homes—would
be required to take a Loyalty Oath to the U.S. government.
Anyone who took such an oath and was later suspected of
being "disloyal" would be shot and his property seized.[17]

McClellan and several other top Union generals harshly
criticized such actions, but Lincoln ignored their criticisms.
By the end of 1862 there was a large upsurge in "authorized
foraging," the Federal government's euphemism for the pillaging and plundering of civilian property in the South.
Lincoln wanted Southern civilians to suffer, which required
him to abandon international law and the U.S military's
own code as he began to wage total war. And it was total
war waged against fellow citizens—mostly women and
children and old men—not an invading army.

There was rampant vandalism everywhere the Federal
armies went, as has been documented by numerous eyewitness accounts. According to one typical account of the
looting of Fredericksburg, Virginia, by Federal soldiers,

> Boys came in . . . loaded with silver pitchers, silver spoons,
> silver lamps, and castors, etc. Great three-story houses fur-
> nished magnificently were broken into and their contents
> scattered over the floors and trampelled on by the muddy feet
> of the soldiers. Splendid alabaster vases and pieces of statu-
> ary were thrown at 6 and 700 dollar mirrors. Closets of the
> very finest china were broken into and their contents
> smashed onto the floor and stamped to pieces. Finest cut
> glass ware goblets were hurled at nice plate glass windows,
> beautifully embroidered window curtains torn down, rose-
> wood pianos piled in the street and burned or soldiers would

get on top of them and kick the key-board and internal machinery all to pieces.[18]

It is not an exaggeration to say that Lincoln's entire battle plan, from the very beginning, was to wage war on civilians as well as the armed rebels. His overall strategy, devised by General Winfield Scott, was called the "Anaconda Plan" because an important part of the strategy was to strangle the Southern economy by attempting to blockade all the coastal ports and inland waterways, such as the Mississippi River. Any naval blockade is necessarily a war on a country's civilian population as well as its armed forces. So severe was the blockade of Southern ports that even drugs and medicines were on Lincoln's list of items that could not be imported into the Southern states. To the extent that the Federal navy was successful in this endeavor, many civilians must have suffered or perished due to the lack of medicines.

Hundreds of Southern churches were put to the torch, and priests and ministers were imprisoned for not saying prayers for Abraham Lincoln.[19] The devastation of Southern churches was so pervasive that one gets the impression that the invasion of the South was, among other things, a kind of medieval holy war.

SHERMAN

FURTHER EVIDENCE that waging war on civilians was not just the result of a few out-of-control soldiers but the deliberate policy of the Lincoln administration is the fact that Lincoln's most trusted generals, such as Sherman, Grant, and Sheridan, excelled at such practices for years. In the autumn of 1862 Sherman and his army were attempting to bring Memphis, Tennessee, under Federal control, but their Mississippi River gunboats were being fired upon by Confederate snipers. Frustrated by his inability to hunt down and subdue the Confederate soldiers, Sherman took vengeance upon the local population by burning the entire town of Randolph, Tennessee, to the ground. He wrote General Halleck that he had decided to "hold the neighborhood fully responsible . . . all the people are now guerrillas."[20] He ordered a subordinate, Colonel C. C. Walcutt, to burn the entire town but leave one house standing to mark the place where a town once existed. His troops also beat to death a young man who was a suspected guerilla, but whose family turned out to be Unionists. Sherman obviously knew that he was harming innocent civilians, for in his order to Colonel Walcutt he stated that he was sure the Confederate snipers had left and "therefore you will find no one at Randolph, in which case you will destroy the place."[21]

Sherman freely admitted that he had no idea whether "all" the people were assisting the Confederate guerillas— he just asserted that they were in order to justify waging war on civilians. Indeed, if he did possess such knowledge of guerilla activity, he would not have needed to target innocent civilians at all.

Historian Mark Grimsley attempts to defend Sherman, saying that he is unfairly criticized as the "father" of total war but ends up inadvertently condemning virtually the entire Union high command and, by implication, Lincoln himself, as war criminals according to the prevailing morality and international law of the day. Grimsley "defends" Sherman by asserting that his holding civilian hostages and burning down entire towns was by no means unique to him but was common among Federal generals. Sherman "pursued a policy quite in keeping with that of other Union commanders from Missouri to Virginia."[22]

Grimsley also asserts that Sherman must have been certain that none of the residents of Randolph, Tennessee, whose homes were burned, were actually responsible for the firing at Sherman's gunboats. But Grimsley hesitates to criticize him, offering only the feeble remark that "it is possible to question the wisdom, and even the justice, of burning Randolph."[23] It certainly is: Sherman undoubtedly turned the citizens of Randolph, and probably of all of Memphis, into implacable foes with his actions, especially after a century of international law, as espoused by Sherman's superior officer, General Halleck, had declared such behavior as patently unjust.

Sherman declared that all the people of the South were "enemies" and "traitors" in an attempt at rationalizing waging war on civilians, and he was given Lincoln's blessing in doing so. By drawing no line at all between civilians and the Confederate military, he (and Lincoln) abandoned all the premises of international law that civilized countries at the time were attempting to live by.

Upon taking command in Memphis, Sherman described his ultimate purpose in the war to his wife: "extermination, not of soldiers alone, that is the least part of the trouble, but the people."[24] His loving wife responded by expressing her sincerest wish that the war would be a war "of extermination and that all [Southerners] would be driven like the Swine into the sea. May we carry fire and sword into their states till not one habitation is left standing."[25] "Sherman and his family," explains Sherman biographer John Marszalek, "saw everyone south of the Mason-Dixon Line as an implacable enemy."[26]

Sherman covered his historical tracks by issuing numerous orders that private property should be spared, while his army relentlessly destroyed private property. In this regard he could well have learned a thing or two from Lincoln, who was the master of denouncing the very actions that he was ardently pursuing (such as discarding the Constitution).

Some historians have attempted to defend Sherman (and Lincoln) by pointing not to his actions but to his written orders and spoken words. There is little doubt, however, that these orders were given with a big wink and that they were received as such by his junior officers and soldiers. Sherman's subordinate officers understood that he could not go on record ordering war crimes. The object was to go ahead and commit the crimes without leaving a paper trail or, better yet, leaving a false paper trail. There are many recorded instances of Sherman's standing by in silence while pillaging and plundering was going on all around him. His silence told his troops all they needed to know with regard to whether or not he approved of their behavior. Furthermore, whenever Sherman did order his troops to stop the looting and burning so that the army could move on, they did so with great discipline. As Grimsley notes repeatedly, his army was extraordinarily well disciplined, and it understood that in pillaging and plundering the South it was indeed fulfilling its commander's wishes.

Although Lincoln was elected with less than 40 percent of the popular vote in 1860, Sherman argued repeatedly that the war was a rebellion against "the National Will" and that, as such, "the people at large" of the South "should be made to feel . . . the existence of a strong government, capable of protecting as well as destroying."[27] He was never particularly successful as a tactician in battle, but Sherman's armies became extremely adept at pillage and plunder.

In Vicksburg, Mississippi, farms were stripped bare and houses burned. The objective was to totally destroy the Southern economy and starve out the population as much as possible. Sherman wrote of "absolutely stripping" the land of all crops and even houses. The city was so heavily bombed that the residents had to resort to living in caves and eating rats, dogs, and mules.

Upon entering Jackson, Mississippi, in the spring of 1863, Sherman ordered a systematic bombardment of the town every five minutes, day and night. Similar bombardments occurred in other Southern cities under the orders of Sherman and other Federal generals. After Jackson was all but demolished, Sherman's army entered the town, where

> the soldiery proceeded to sack the town completely. Pianos and articles of Furniture were dragged into the streets and demolished. The aroused soldiers entered residences, appropriating whatever appeared to be of value . . . those articles which they could not carry they broke. . . . They thrust their bayonets into pictures and knocked out windows and even removed doors from their hinges.[28]

Fires set by Sherman's soldiers destroyed the entire business district of Jackson, and the city was thoroughly sacked and destroyed. Federal soldiers under Sherman's watchful eye sacked all the finest plantations as well as the lowliest slave cabins. Federal soldiers routinely robbed citizens at gunpoint during the mayhem. When it was all over, Sherman boasted to General Grant, "The inhabitants are subjugated. They cry aloud for mercy. The land is devastated for 30 miles around."[29]

Sherman always blamed the citizens of the South for their fate and took no responsibility for the damage and death to civilians caused by his army. If they hadn't resisted the Lincoln administration, he would argue, they would not have found themselves in such a predicament. He also rationalized the pillaging, plundering, and destroying of cities with socialistic or egalitarian rhetoric, such as "a woman who has fifty loads of fine furniture deserves to lose it."[30]

Entire towns in Mississippi ceased to exist after Sherman's army passed through, with the women and children who had lived there rendered homeless and fearful of starvation. As Sherman described the total destruction of Meridian, Mississippi, long after there was any Confederate army presence near the town, "For five days, ten thousand of our men worked hard and with a will, in that work of destruction, with axes, sledges, crowbars, clawbars, and with fire, and I have no hesitation in pronouncing the work well done. Meridian . . . no longer exists."[31]

By this time Ulysses S. Grant had been chosen by Lincoln as his commanding general; as Grimsley writes, "Grant had approved the Meridian expedition, and it formed a good example of the sort of war he expected to conduct against the South."[32] In light of Lincoln's compulsion to be in contact by telegraph with his military commanders, it is safe to assume that he, too, approved of the type of "warfare" against unarmed women and children that had been waged throughout Mississippi. It was effective, and Lincoln repeatedly thanked Sherman and Grant for their service and rewarded them accordingly.

In the 1860s the bombardment of a city under siege was considered beyond the bounds of international law and morality, but that did not deter Sherman in his bombardment of Atlanta. By September 1864, when Sherman's army occupied Atlanta, he had been waging war on civilians in Southern towns and cities for more than two years, and his troops were well practiced. The city was bombed day and night until barely a house or building remained untouched. When Sherman's chief engineer, O. M. Poe, voiced his dismay at seeing so many corpses of women and young children in the streets of Atlanta, Sherman coldly told him that such scenes were "a beautiful sight" because they would bring the war to a quicker end.[33] Poe believed, moreover, that the bombardment of the city of Atlanta had no military purpose and did not advance the Federal army's move into the city by a single second. There are no accurate casualty accounts, but many eyewitness accounts tell of large numbers of civilians, including slaves, being killed and maimed.

After destroying much of the city, Sherman's army went on its usual binge of looting and burning. Even the cemeteries were looted, with graves dug up and carcasses stripped of jewelry and valuables.[34] There were approximately 4,000 private homes in the city of Atlanta before the bombardment, and about 400 were left standing. It has been estimated that more than 90 percent of the city was demolished, including many churches.

Once in Atlanta, Sherman decided to depopulate the city as well and ordered the remaining civilian inhabitants to vacate the city with whatever belongings they could carry. Thousands of women, children, and old men were made homeless just as the dead of winter was approaching. Again, Sherman blamed the people of the South for their "faulty reasoning" and accepted no responsibility at all for the suffering of thousands of defenseless women and children. Federal armies had plundered the farms of Georgia, so these unfortunate souls faced the very real prospect of starvation. As is typical of so many "court historians" who write about Lincoln, Grant, and Sherman, Grimsley downplays the suffering of the citizens of Atlanta by saying that "only" a few thousand of them were evicted from their homes.

It is a good bet, however, that if General Stonewall Jackson had invaded Philadelphia, bombed the city into smoldering ruins, and then forcefully removed the remaining 2,000 citizens just as winter arrived, historians like Grimsley would still be writing of it as one of the greatest war crimes in history.

There were still pockets of Confederate resistance in northern Georgia even after the Federal capture of Atlanta. In October 1864 Sherman gave up all pretense of legality when he ordered the murder of randomly chosen civilians in retaliation for attacks on his army by Confederate soldiers. He made the following suggestion to General Louis D. Watkins: "Cannot you send over about Fairmount and Adairsville, burn ten or twelve houses of known secessionists, *kill a few at random,* and let them know that it will be repeated every time a train is fired on from Resaca to Kingston?" (emphasis added).[35]

Although it is oddly missing from most histories of Sherman's March, many eyewitness accounts of rape by Federal soldiers have been recorded. Many accounts emphasize that black women suffered the most and that many black men, in response, became just as bitterly opposed to the Federal army as any secessionist was. Civilized people do not publicize the names of rape victims, so we will never know the extent to which Sherman's army committed acts of rape. But the University of South Carolina library in Columbia, South Carolina, contains a large collection of thousands of letters and diaries of South Carolinians who wrote of their experiences during the war and Reconstruction. This collection contains hundreds of personal accounts of rape at the hands of Sherman's army.

As Sherman biographer Lee Kennett found, in Sherman's army "the New York regiments were . . . filled with big city criminals and foreigners fresh from the jails of the Old World."[36] Just as Fidel Castro did in the 1980s, European governments in the early 1860s gladly emptied their jails so that the most hardened criminals could emigrate to the United States. It is unlikely that many of Castro's criminals ended up in the U.S. military, but such characters were heavily recruited by the Lincoln administration, which promised them—and other European immigrants—land grants in return for their military service. Thousands of these immigrants perished in General Grant's numerous frontal assaults on a well-entrenched Army of Northern Virginia under the command of General Robert E. Lee.

Civilian hostages were constantly being taken and traded for Union army prisoners captured by Confederates, and numerous Georgia towns were put to the torch. Rome and Marietta, Georgia, were destroyed. Slaves were usually treated as roughly as the whites. As Grimsley describes it, "With the utter disregard for blacks that was the norm among Union troops, the soldiers ransacked the slave cabins, taking whatever they liked."[37]

Sherman's army killed thousands upon thousands of horses, cattle, hogs, and dogs. Every horse in sight would be stolen; the officers would pick the healthiest ones; and the rest would be shot. It was not unusual for cavalry officers to have five or six horses, all of which were stolen from Southern civilians. Since Sherman's army believed that the dogs that lived on Southern farms and plantations were often used to help run down escaped Union prisoners, the pillaging and plundering included the shooting of every dog in sight as well. Much of the plunder was usually abandoned at the campsite since it would impede the army's progress.

A Mrs. Walton described the Federal army's methods of looting to her daughter:

> The Yankees broke up and split up two of my bureau drawers, split up one of my secretary doors, they opened up one of your bundles I don't know what was in it, took the things. They took all my meat, sugar, coffee, flour, knives and forks, spoons all they could get into. . . . They broke up my caster, carried off the pepper box top, stamped the caster and broke it. Tell Mary they took the ambrotype she gave me of Joe's, they took all my corn, hogs, killed the goats, took chickens, broke open every trunk I had in the house. . . . They took my homespun dress and one smarter one, took all my shoes and stockings, my scarf and the silk that was left of my dress. They got my needles, thimble, scissors and thread.[38]

Much of "Sherman's March" was apparently to the great benefit of ladies in New York, Massachusetts, and other Northern states in whose possession many of these dresses, women's shoes, pieces of jewelry, and the like must have ended up.

One of Sherman's soldiers wrote in his diary, "Never before have I witnessed so much wanton destruction as on this march. The soldiers are perfectly abandoned."[39] Captain Poe described the March to the Sea as an orgy of "robbing and plundering" and prayed to God that "it may never be my duty to see the like again."[40]

Sherman biographer Lee Kennett attempts to downplay the plundering and pillaging of Sherman's army by saying, "it appears the soldiers behaved no worse in 1864 than in 1862 or 1863 . . . there is precious little here to indicate that the war was degenerating into something more cruel and more frightful."[41] But they were already pillaging, plundering, and sacking Southern cities and executing civilians in 1861 and were essentially engaged in terrorizing the civilian population of the South. How much more degenerate could it get?

Sherman and his army reserved their special wrath for South Carolina, the birthplace of the Confederate secession movement. The pillaging, plundering, and sacking of cities that had occurred in Mississippi, Georgia, and elsewhere in the South was intensified as the army entered South Carolina and especially when it reached the state capitol of Columbia. "The army burned everything it came near in the State of South Carolina," wrote a Major Connolly in a letter to his wife.[42] "A majority of the Cities, towns, villages and county houses have been burnt to the ground," wrote one of Sherman's chaplains, James Stillwell.[43]

At least two thirds of Columbia was burned to the ground. In his typical fashion, Sherman blamed the Confederates "for starting the fire and . . . God for enlarging it."[44] "God Almighty started wind sufficient to carry that [burning] cotton wherever He would," Sherman announced.[45] (Interestingly, the winds somehow passed over the French Consulate's house and the house that was used as a Federal military headquarters building.) Sherman blamed Confederate General Wade Hampton, a native of Columbia, for the improbable act of setting fire to his own hometown. In later years Sherman would admit in his memoirs that he publicly blamed General Hampton in an attempt to ruin his reputation among his own people during the war. In his memoirs he boasted that he (not Hampton) had "utterly ruined Columbia."[46]

The slaves suffered as much as anyone else at the hands of Sherman's army. Slaves were frequently threatened with death if they did not reveal to the soldiers where the plantation owners' valuables were. A typical practice was to put a hangman's noose around the slave's neck and threaten to hang him unless he "confessed." In one instance, "a large group of soldiers were lounging about a railway station when a black man walked past them. One of the soldiers snatched the man's hat, whereupon he tried to take it back. Instantly, the nearest soldiers attacked the black man, many others joined in, and by the time officers could intervene the black man had received a fatal beating."[47]

Hundreds of half-starved blacks followed Sherman's army, although at one point "when the column came to a stream that had to be bridged, the army passed over but the pontoons were removed before the mass of blacks following behind could use them."[48] Some of the blacks that did

travel with Sherman's army were made the personal ser-
vants of officers.

In one personal testimony of the aftermath of Sherman's March, a Miss Andrews wrote in her diary,

> About three miles from Sparta we struck the "Burnt Coun-
> try," as it is well named by the natives, and then I could better
> understand the wrath and desperation of these poor people.
> There was hardly a fence left standing all the way from
> Sparta to Gordon. The fields were trampled down and the
> road was lined with the carcasses of horses, hogs, and cattle
> that the invaders, unable either to consume or to carry away
> with them, had wantonly shot down to starve out the people
> and prevent them from making their crops. The stench in
> some places was unbearable. . . . The dwellings that were
> standing all showed signs of pillage, and on every plantation
> we saw the charred remains of the [cotton] gin house and
> packing screw, where here and there lone chimney stacks,
> "Sherman's Sentinels," told of homes laid in ashes.[49]

In 1957 the Oxford University Press published the
wartime diaries of Emma LeConte of Columbia, South
Carolina, who was eighteen when Sherman burned her
city to the ground.[50] Although it was published almost a
century after the fact, the book was widely praised as a
rare picture of Sherman's March *from* the sea. Sherman's
army burned every town, no matter how small, in South
Carolina on the way to its real target, Columbia. Many
of these small towns were never rebuilt, and to this day
the only evidence of their existence is a single stone
marker.

Emma LeConte wrote that the morning Sherman's army entered Columbia was "the longest morning I ever lived through."[51] Although Sherman had promised "not to disturb private property," as soon as the troops entered the city LeConte noticed that they were all well equipped with matches, crowbars, and other tools of the arsonist and plunderer. "As soon as the bulk of the army entered, the work of pillage began," she wrote. "What a scene of pillage and terror was being enacted."[52]

> The fire on Main Street was now raging, and we anxiously watched its progress from the upper front windows. In a little while, however, the flames broke forth in every direction. The drunken devils roamed about, setting fire to every house the flames seemed likely to spare. They were fully equipped for the noble work they had in hand. Each soldier was furnished with combustibles compactly put up. They would enter houses and in the presence of helpless women and children, pour turpentine on the beds and set them on fire. Guards were rarely of any assistance—most generally they assisted in the pillaging and firing.[53]

When the women and old men of the town attempted to put out the fires, LeConte wrote, the soldiers cut the fire hoses with their bayonets. By midnight "the whole town was wrapped in one huge blaze."[54]

Further describing the scene of the burning of Columbia after all the Confederate soldiers had long gone, LeConte wrote,

> Imagine night turned into noonday, only with a blazing, scorching glare that was horrible—a copper colored sky

across which swept columns of black, rolling smoke glittering with sparks and flying embers, while all around us were falling thickly showers of burning flakes. Everywhere the palpitating blaze walling the streets with solid masses of flames as far as the eye could reach, filling the air with its horrible roar. On every side the rackling and devouring fire, while every instant came the crashing of timbers and the thunder of falling buildings. A quivering molten ocean seemed to fill the air and sky. The library building opposite us seemed framed by the gushing flames and smoke, while through the windows gleamed the liquid fire.[55]

The soldiers were "infuriated, cursing, screaming, exulting in their work," she wrote, while the women, children, and old men suffered from sheer terror and helplessness.[56]

Emma LeConte remained in Columbia long after Sherman's pillaging and burning army left and concluded that "there is not a house, I believe, in Columbia, that has not been pillaged—those that the flames spared were entered by brutal soldiery and everything wantonly destroyed."[57]

On March 27, 1865, after his March to (and from) the Sea was completed, Sherman met with Grant and Lincoln at City Point, on the James River, where he regaled them with his exploits. Sherman wrote in his personal memoirs that Lincoln wanted to know all about his marches, particularly enjoying stories about the bummers [as the looters were called] and their foraging activities.[58] Sherman had kept his word to Lincoln: He had famously promised the president that he would "make Georgia howl" with his March to the Sea.

SHERIDAN'S BURNING OF THE
SHENANDOAH VALLEY

FURTHER EVIDENCE that waging war on civilians was an integral part of Lincoln's war strategy lies in the burning of Virginia's Shenandoah Valley in late 1864. The Confederates had finally been pushed out of the valley by the overwhelming power of the Federal arsenal when General Grant ordered General Philip Sheridan to make one more trip down the valley, pillaging, plundering and burning everything in sight. "Carry off stock of all descriptions, and Negroes, so as to prevent further planting," Grant instructed Sheridan. Anything that could not be consumed by the army was to be destroyed. The land was to become so devastated, Grant ordered, that crows flying over it would need to pack their own lunches. "If this war is to last another year we want the Shenandoah Valley to remain a barren waste."[59]

The valley was to be turned into a "desert" and the residents rendered homeless. General Hunter had already started the job, having burned the Virginia Military Institute, among other things. Grant was careful to inform Sheridan of the *political* imperative of his mission: If his army were defeated in the Shenandoah Valley, the bad news could cause Lincoln to lose the 1864 election, and the Democratic Party was inclined to work out a peace agreement. That was to be avoided at all cost. As Sheridan put it, "The defeat of my army might be followed by the overthrow of the party in power" and lead "to the complete abandonment of all coercive measures."[60]

Sheridan and his 35,000 infantry troops, plus three divisions of cavalry, faced no military opposition at all and proceeded to terrorize the women, children, and old men of the Valley in Shermanesque fashion. Reporting from the town of Woodstock, Virginia, on October 6, 1864, Sheridan informed Grant that his army "had destroyed over 2200 barns filled with wheat, hay, and farming implements; over 70 mills filled with flour and wheat; have driven in front of the army over 4000 head of stock, and have killed and issued to the troops not less than 3000 sheep. . . . Tomorrow I will continue the destruction."[61] A Federal officer reported that in the aftermath of Sheridan's army,

> The atmosphere, from horizon to horizon, has been black with the smoke of a hundred conflagrations . . . and at night a gleam brighter and more lurid than sunset has shot from every verge. . . . The completeness of the devastation is awful. Hundreds of nearly starving people are going north. Our trains are crowded with them. They line the wayside. Hundreds more are coming . . . so stripped of food that I cannot imagine how they escaped starvation.[62]

Despite the horrors of such a scene, Mark Grimsley describes Sheridan's "razing of the Valley" as "one of the more controlled acts of destruction during the war's final year."[63] In letters home Sheridan's troops referred to themselves as "barn burners" and "destroyers of homes."[64] One soldier wrote home that he had personally burned more than sixty private homes to the ground and opined that "it was a hard looking sight to see the women and children turned out of doors at this season of the year."[65]

A sergeant in Sheridan's army, William T. Patterson, described the burning of Harrisonburg, Bridgewater, and Dayton, Virginia:

> The work of destruction is commencing in the suburbs of the town. . . . The whole country around is wrapped in flames, the heavens are aglow with the light thereof . . . such mourning, such lamentations, such crying and pleading for mercy I never saw nor never want to see again, some were wild, crazy, mad, some cry for help while others would throw their arms around yankee soldiers necks and implore mercy.[66]

Lincoln conveyed his personal thanks and "the thanks of the Nation" to Sheridan after his destruction of the Valley was completed. He believed that might makes right and that he could ignore the Constitution, international law, and common standards of morality and decency as long as he held the upper hand militarily and as long as he could continue to confuse the public with his well-honed rhetorical talents. His top generals, such as Grant, Sherman, and Sheridan, followed his lead by blaming their carefully planned war on the civilians themselves and even on God. Neither Lincoln nor his generals ever accepted any responsibility, nor should they have been expected to, since they were the victors in the war.

But as Lee Kennett has written, there is no doubt at all that Lincoln and his top generals violated international law for the duration of the war. Moreover,

> had the Confederates somehow won, had their victory put them in position to bring their chief opponents before some

sort of tribunal, they would have found themselves justified (as victors generally do) in stringing up President Lincoln and the entire Union high command for violation of the laws of war, specifically for waging war against noncombatants.[67]

There seems to be no limit to the extent to which the so-called Lincoln scholars will distort history in order to maintain a false image of Lincoln. In an essay on the topic of total war, Mark Neely concluded with the surreal comment that while total war "breaks down the distinction between soldiers and civilians," Sherman and Sheridan cannot be said to have been practitioners of that brand of warfare. Quite the contrary, according to Neely. Sherman and his "fellow generals waged war the same way most Victorian gentlemen did, and other Victorian gentlemen in the world knew it."[68] Total war, according to Neely, was just not Sherman's cup of tea. The editors of the book in which Neely's essay appeared couldn't help but remark that Neely seemed to be commenting on a different war from the one the other thirty-one authors in the volume were assessing. Sherman would have agreed with them.

The victors are never charged as war criminals, of course; only the losers are. This was true in 1865 and it is true today. Lincoln's abandonment of the internationally agreed upon rules of war as codified by the Geneva Convention of 1863 and his demolition of constitutional liberties as described in chapter 6 established precedents that would provide countless excuses and rationalizations for empire-building and war-mongering politicians throughout the world in the decades to come. Politicians of all parties would routinely invoke the name of the martyred Lincoln to "justify" their own schemes to run afoul of the Constitution, international law, and commonly accepted norms of morality.

CHAPTER 8

RECONSTRUCTING AMERICA: LINCOLN'S POLITICAL LEGACY

All Radical schemes to reconstruct the South entailed some more or less permanent expansion of central state activity and expenditures.
—RICHARD BENSEL, *YANKEE LEVIATHAN*

AN ENDURING MYTH of American history is that federal policy in the conquered South after the war was aimed at "binding the nation's wounds" and establishing a "just and lasting peace," as Lincoln said. In reality, Southerners became more and more embittered over being treated as second-class citizens, at best, while the Republican Party set up puppet governments that seemed to perpetually raise taxes with very little, if anything, to show for the taxes in terms of public benefits. The so-called Reconstruction only poured salt into "the nation's wounds," an inevitable consequence of the precedents established by Lincoln in disregarding constitutional liberties and international law for the sake of politics.

The postwar Republican Party was emboldened by Lincoln's blatant disregard for constitutional liberties in the North during the war. Because he had become a martyr, party members invoked his name to engage in more of the same kinds of conduct after the war. Lincoln laid the political groundwork for the disastrous Reconstruction policies of 1865–1877.

There was certainly a lasting peace, but few Southerners would have characterized it as "just." Shortly before his death in 1870, General Robert E. Lee told former Texas Governor Fletcher Stockdale that, in light of how the Republican Party was treating the people of the South, he never would have surrendered at Appomattox, but would rather have died there with his men in one final battle. "Governor, if I had foreseen the use those people designed to make of their victory, there would have been no surrender at Appomattox Courthouse; no sir, not by me. Had I foreseen these results of subjugation, I would have preferred to die at Appomattox with my brave men, my sword in my right hand."[1]

The primary effect, if not the intent, of the "Reconstruction" policies of 1865–1877 was to centralize and consolidate state power in Washington, D.C., and to establish Republican Party political hegemony that would last for some seventy years. Even when the Republican Party did not control the White House during those years, its mercantilist policies generally prevailed until the Franklin Roosevelt administration of the 1930s, at which time government became even more interventionist.

The federal government did not totally succeed in centralizing all power in Washington after the war, thanks to continued Southern political resistance and a still-vibrant support among the American people for constitutionally limited government. Nevertheless, by 1890 the federal government was vastly larger than the founders ever envisioned, and its purpose had changed from the protection of individual liberty to the quest for empire. This was all the inevitable consequence of the Lincoln administration and its policies. Indeed, we have seen, some historians *celebrate* this outcome.

THE REVISIONIST VIEW
OF RECONSTRUCTION

A GREAT DEAL of excellent scholarship on Reconstruction was published during the early twentieth century by such historians as Claude Bowers and the Columbia University historian William Archibald Dunning and his cadre of graduate students.[2] The historians James Ford Rhodes and James G. Randall painted a picture of Reconstruction as a vindictive, abusive, corrupt, political racket.[3] Dunning, Rhodes, Bowers, and Randall were Northerners who documented in great detail how the Republican Party—which is to say, the federal government, since the party enjoyed a political monopoly—ignored presidential vetoes and federal court rulings, disenfranchised white Southerners while giving the vote to ex-slaves (who were instructed to vote Republican), formed new state puppet governments run by Republican Party political operatives, and used the power gained from this to plunder the taxpayers of the South for more than a decade after the war ended.

Beginning in the 1930s, and especially since the 1960s, a group of "revisionist" historians have come to the forefront to challenge what has come to be known as the "Dunning School" of Reconstruction scholarship. This group of scholars, which, according to Kenneth M. Stampp, has been dominated by "Marxists of various degrees of orthodoxy," rarely disputes the facts that were set out by the Dunning School.[4] They acknowledge that much of what Dunning's disciples have said about Reconstruction is true. Facts are facts. Relying heavily on Marxian class analysis, however, these revisionists have painted a more "enlightened" picture of the era. (The most prominent contemporary historian of Reconstruction is the Marxist Eric Foner, who calls Reconstruction "America's unfinished revolution.")[5]

These Marxist and "liberal" revisionists argue that Reconstruction wasn't all *that* bad compared to, say, what happened after the Japanese invaded Nanking in the 1930s, or the Nazi occupation of Europe, or the deeds of the Russian army in Germany at the end of World War II. After all, Kenneth Stampp has argued, there were not even any mass executions of former Confederates after the war.[6] Southerners were indeed "lucky" in this regard, according to the revisionist view.

Because Dunning and his disciples provided accurate descriptions of the ex-slaves and their role in Southern politics shortly after the war, the Marxist/Liberal revisionists have sought to discredit the Dunning School's views by labeling them as racist.[7] Dunning and his students, for example, questioned the wisdom of immediately extending to uneducated and propertyless ex-slaves the right to vote without first providing at least a couple of years of education for them. The revisionist historians have deemed this "racist." As Kenneth Stampp remarked, "As ideas about race have changed, historians have become increasingly critical of the Dunning interpretation of Reconstruction."[8]

But the revisionists create a problem when they use this criterion (allegedly racist attitudes) in judging the credibility of Reconstruction scholarship. Every one of the revisionists virtually deifies Lincoln. The problem here is that Lincoln himself was a white supremacist all his life, a man who didn't believe that the two races should even mingle (see chapter 2). In their work, the Dunning School scholars, by contrast, never made the kinds of racially disparaging remarks that Lincoln did. They never proclaimed the white race to be the "superior" race as Lincoln did; they never advocated shipping all blacks back to Africa or to some other foreign land; and they never pontificated in their writing about the alleged evils of interracial marriage, as Lincoln did.

If the revisionists are to dismiss Dunning's interpretation of Reconstruction on the grounds that he and his students were insensitive to blacks, then to be consistent they should be just as skeptical of what has been written about Lincoln over the past 100 years and even reevaluate much of their own scholarship.

THE POLITICS OF RECONSTRUCTION

THE SOUTHERN ECONOMY was almost completely destroyed by the Federal army and navy during the war. As described in the *Documentary History of Reconstruction,* "Never had a completer ruin fallen upon any city than fell upon Charleston."⁹ In 1870, five years after the war had ended, the Tennessee Valley consisted "for the most part of plantations in a state of semi-ruin," with many others "of which the ruin is . . . total and complete." "The trail of war is visible throughout the valley in burnt up [cotton] gin-houses, ruined bridges, mills, and factories . . . and large tracts of once cultivated land stripped of every vestige of fencing."

In Virginia, "from Harpers Ferry to New Market . . . the country was almost a desert. . . . The barns were all burned; a great many of the private dwellings were burned; chimneys standing without houses, and houses standing without roofs."¹⁰ Southern soldiers returning from the war found their homesteads destroyed, their farms devastated, and their communities on the brink of starvation. The roads and railroad beds were mostly destroyed, and in North Georgia there was "a degree of destitution that would draw pity from a stone."¹¹ Many Southern women, fearful that their small children would starve, traded sex for food with the hated Federal soldiers who remained in the South as an occupying army.

President Andrew Johnson's wise abolition of all restrictions on interstate trade helped to reestablish commercial relationships between all the states, but it nevertheless took an entire century for the Southern economy to regain the proportional relationship to the North that existed in 1861.

For the most part, Southern state governments were run by military dictatorships in the form of federally appointed U.S. Army generals. Those sitting governors of the Southern states whom the Federal army was able to capture at the end of the war were imprisoned without trial.¹²

The first order of business for these puppet governments was to convene "kangaroo" constitutional conventions that declared the ordinances of secession passed in 1860 and 1861 invalid. Jefferson Davis, who at the time was in a military prison, never had a trial and so never was able to make the case for secession; Republican Party political operatives simply declared the right of secession to be illegitimate.

Having just waged a four-year war to destroy the right of secession, the Republican Party was not about to allow the possibility that the concept could be revived by a ruling in Jefferson Davis's favor in a court of law. Author Charles Adams has persuasively argued, in fact, that Jefferson Davis would have had a very good chance of winning such a trial: One of the most famous trial lawyers of the era, Charles O'Conor of New York, had volunteered to defend Davis; the trial would have taken place in Virginia; and criminal intent on Davis's part would have had to be proven—a virtual impossibility in light of the long history of the right of secession in America.[13]

Lincoln never admitted that secession was legitimate or that the seceded states had ever actually left the Union. But the fact that the Republican Party believed that it was necessary to alter the Southern constitutions in order to denounce secession gives the lie to Lincoln's position: If there never was a right of secession, why would it be necessary to repudiate a right that supposedly never existed in the first place?

President Johnson vetoed the Civil Rights bill of 1866 on March 27 of that year on the grounds that it federalized law enforcement and was therefore unconstitutional. "The bill embodied an unheard-of intrusion of the Federal government within the sphere of the states, and was a stride toward centralization," explained Dunning.[14] Moreover,

> Never before had Congress been known to arrogate to itself the power to regulate the civil status of the inhabitants of a state. The proposition that United States courts should assume jurisdiction of disputes relating to property and contracts, and even of criminal actions down to common assault and battery, seemed like a complete revelation of that diabolical spirit of centralization, of which only the cloven hoof had been manifested heretofore.[15]

Congress overrode the president's veto, declared political war on Johnson, and almost succeeded in impeaching him. Johnson gave a sound constitutional reason for vetoing the Civil Rights bill, but the contemporary revisionist historians continue to denounce him as a "racist" on the grounds that he opposed a law with the words "civil rights" in it. But Johnson did not say that he was opposed to "civil rights," only to the federalization of the judiciary, which he feared would be harmful to *everyone's* civil rights.

Congress blackmailed the Southern states into passing the Fourteenth Amendment to the Constitution by prohibiting congressional representation by those states unless they ratified the amendment. In doing this the federal government effectively seceded from the Union—a Union that Lincoln never admitted had been broken in the first place. That is, after waging a war to force the Southern states back into the Union, they refused to allow those same states to be a part of that Union by denying them congressional representation in it. This action, in effect, broke up the union of states that they claimed to cherish so highly.

Every Southern state except Tennessee voted against ratifying the amendment. Southern legislators objected to (1) the fact that all high-ranking former Confederates were forbidden from running for public office, (2) the fact that the amendment would lead to a strong centralization of power in Washington, and (3) "the contention that, if the communities which the legislatures represented were really states of the Union, the presence of their members in Congress was essential to the validity of the amendment; while if those communities were not states, their ratification of the amendment was unnecessary."[16]

Congress responded to the South's rejection of the Fourteenth Amendment by passing the Reconstruction Act of 1867, which established a comprehensive military dictatorship to run the governments of each of the ten states that were not yet restored to the Union. Passed under the false pretense that there was little or no protection of life and property in the South, the law required passage of the Fourteenth Amendment before military rule would end in a state. And it was indeed a false pretense, since the courts had been operating normally in the South since the end of the war.

Great resources were expended on registering the adult male ex-slaves to vote, while a law denying the franchise to anyone involved in the late "rebellion" disenfranchised most Southern white men. So rigorous were the restrictions placed on white Southern males that anyone who even organized contributions of food and clothing for family and friends serving in the Confederate army was disenfranchised, as were all those who purchased bonds from the Confederate government.[17] Even if one did not participate in the war effort, voter registration required one to *publicly* proclaim that one's sympathies were with the Federal armies during the war, something that very few white Southerners would have dared to do.

The federally funded "Union Leagues" were run by Republican Party operatives and administered voter registration of the ex-slaves. This, too, was a dramatic change in the nation's political life, for tax dollars taken from taxpayers of all political parties were being used to register only Republican voters. The ex-slaves were promised many things, including the property of white Southerners, if they registered and voted Republican and, at times, were threatened or intimidated if they dared to register Democrat. All of this was funded with federal tax dollars. This was yet another repudiation of the Jeffersonian vision of government, for it was Jefferson who wrote in the Virginia Declaration of Religious Liberty that "to compel a man to contribute to a cause with which he disagrees is sinful and tyrannical." For years, these men, along with government bureaucrats associated with the "Freedmen's Bureau," promised blacks that if they voted Republican they would be given the property of the white population (and, of course, they never were).

Missionaries and many other people assisted the ex-slaves in integrating into society, but the primary concern of the Party of Lincoln was to get them registered to vote Republican, not to educate them, feed them, or help them find employment. The result was that by 1868 ten of the fourteen southern U.S. senators, twenty of the thirty-five representatives, and four of the seven governors were Northern Republicans who had never met their constituents until after the war.[18] Political office-holding was initially the exclusive pre-rogative of a small number of white men who professed alle-giance to the Republican Party. After several years, blacks were permitted to serve in public office.

If Northerners in general and the Republican Party in particular wanted blacks to be given the vote because of their concern for social equality, then one has to wonder why voters in Ohio, Michigan, Minnesota, and Kansas re-fused to extend the right to vote to blacks in 1867 and 1868. Women were not given the right to vote until 1920; and there was little agitation by Northern Republicans in the 1860s and 1870s to extend the franchise to women. If voting was such an overwhelmingly important civil right, one has to wonder why Republican politicians thought that illiterate and propertyless ex-slaves deserved voting rights but that even the most highly educated and accom-plished women, of which there were many, did not. One plausible answer is that extending the franchise to women would not necessarily give the Republican Party any spe-cial advantage, since the distribution of female votes might be expected to be quite diverse. In contrast, the ex-slaves could be counted on to be a uniformly Republican voting block.

Any local public officials who did not strictly adhere to the Republican Party programs were purged from office by the military. In May 1868 "the mayor, chief of police and other municipal officers of Mobile [Alabama] were sum-marily removed, and their places were filled with 'efficient Union [i.e., Republican Party] men.'"[19] Before Reconstruc-tion ended in 1877, the federal military authorities restaffed the municipal governments of every Southern city of any size. The rule of law meant next to nothing, for it could be superseded by military order at any time.

After being ruled by military dictatorships for a number of years, the Southern states finally acquiesced in the Fourteenth Amendment. But at that point New Jersey and Ohio, disgusted by Republican Party tyranny, voted to revoke their previous ratifications of the amendment. Congress failed to secure the constitutionally required three-fourths majority of the states, but simply issued a "joint resolution" declaring the Amendment valid anyway. To this day, the Fourteenth Amendment has not been properly ratified.

Some historians would argue that none of this has much to do with Lincoln, since it occurred after his death. But Lincoln showed his Republican Party compatriots the way with regard to the abandonment of constitutional principles and the use of the military to bully one's political opponents. The Party of Lincoln was following in its martyred leader's political footsteps.

Lincoln was a consummate political opportunist. If he had lived, it is very likely that he would have condoned or even championed the Reconstruction policies of the Republican Party. These policies, after all, created a monopoly of power for the party, an achievement that no political opportunist could walk away from.

POLITICAL PLUNDERING OF THE SOUTH

WHAT DID the Republican Party do with its monopolistic political power? First, it plundered Southern taxpayers by greatly expanding state and local governmental budgets.

Little of this governmental expansion benefited the general public; the main beneficiaries were the thousands of "carpetbaggers" (and a few "scalawags") who populated the newly bloated governmental bureaucracies and who benefited from government contracts. A few crumbs were shared with the ex-slaves in order to solidify their political support. As Dunning observed,

> The expenses of the governments were largely increased; offices were multiplied in all departments; salaries were made more worthy of the now regenerated and progressive commonwealths; costly enterprises were undertaken. . . . The result of all this was promptly seen in an expansion of state debts and an increase of taxation that to the property-owning class were appalling and ruinous.[20]

One of John C. Calhoun's great fears, that democracy would evolve into a class-warfare system whereby the taxpaying class would become outnumbered and perpetually looted by the tax-consuming class, was enshrined as national policy toward the South.[21] As Dunning further remarked, the property-owning class, which paid most of the taxes, "was sharply divided politically from that which levied them, and was by the whole radical theory of the reconstruction to be indefinitely excluded from a determining voice in the government."[22] It was a far worse situation than Calhoun ever imagined. The taxpaying "class" was not just outvoted by the tax-consuming class but was disenfranchised altogether for a number of years.

This expansion of state and local government provided for tax-funded government schooling, influenced heavily by the federal government. Consequently, generations of

Southerners (and Northerners) have been taught a politically correct version of history (and of many other subjects) in the federalized, government-run schools. This is one reason why most Americans are completely unaware of the long, distinguished history of the right of secession in America. To this day, the government-run school system reiterates Lincoln's "spectacular lie" that secession is an act of treason. Thousands of school districts in dozens of states require students to recite a pledge of allegiance to the central government, "one nation, indivisible. . . ." (Interestingly, the Pledge of Allegiance was written by the early-twentieth-century writer Walter Bellamy, an avowed socialist and outspoken advocate of centralized governmental power.)

The biggest item on the agenda of the Republicans was government subsidies to the corporations that bankrolled the Republican Party. The Confederate Constitution outlawed such corporate welfare, but with the defeat of the Confederate armies there was no longer any opposition to it.[23]

From 1866 to 1872 the eleven southern states amassed nearly $132 million in state debt for railroad subsidies alone.[24] In countless instances bonds were issued but were backed by no property of any value. In many states bonds were sold before work began on railroads, and "dishonest promoters sold these bonds for what they could get and never built the roads."[25]

Not surprisingly, "railways that had been owned in whole or in part by the states were grossly mismanaged, and were exploited for the profit of politicians."[26] And to no one's surprise, "the progressive depletion of the public treasuries was accompanied by great private prosperity among [Republican] politicians of high and low degree. . . .

Bribery became the indispensable adjunct of legislation, and fraud a common feature in the execution of the laws."[27]

The federal government established a "Land Commission" that was ostensibly set up to buy property and turn it into homesteads for the ex-slaves. Instead, most of the land was handed out to those with good connections to the Republican Party, including the Republican puppet governor of South Carolina, Robert K. Scott.[28] Many recipients of land grants were paid "front men" for mining and timber companies.

Many of the Republican Party operatives who dominated Southern state legislatures during Reconstruction literally sold their votes for cash on a daily basis: The going rate was just under $300 per vote. In Florida during the latter years of Reconstruction, black state legislators were being "discriminated" against—the bribes they were being offered to vote for railroad subsidies and the like were smaller than the bribes paid to white legislators. They convened a Black Caucus in which they fixed the price of their bribes at roughly the same price being charged by the white legislators. The expansion of government provided myriad opportunities for bribery, and Republican Party opportunists took great advantage of them.[29]

Railroad companies bribed legislators to sell state railroad holdings to them for next to nothing. In Alabama, General James H. Clanton observed that "in the statehouse and out of it, bribes were offered and accepted at noonday, and without hesitation or shame," and the effect was "to drive the capital from the state, paralyze industry, demoralize labor, and force our best citizens to flee Alabama as a pestilence."[30]

The revisionist historians do not dispute any of this. Foner wrote of how "every Southern state extended munificent aid to railroad corporations," which had to be abandoned, however, by the early 1870s due to gross mismanagement and the fact that the subsidies "opened the door to widespread corruption."[31]

The railroad debacle was a replay of the Whig/Republican pipe dream of creating prosperity through mercantilism rather than free markets. It was a replay because the same thing had happened on a national scale when the same political coalition had last exerted national influence, in the late 1830s (see chapter 4). This influence was eventually regained by the late 1850s with the political ascendancy of Lincoln and the Republican Party.

The historian E. Merton Coulter catalogued myriad ways in which Republican Party operatives figured out how to loot Southern taxpayers:[32]

- By 1870 the cost of printing alone to the government of Florida exceeded the entire state budget for 1860. The legislature sold to its friends (and to itself) over a million acres in public land for five cents an acre.

- The South Carolina legislature paid supporters $75,000 to take a state census in 1869, although the federal government was to do the same thing a year later for $43,000. It also paid the House Speaker an extra $1,000 in compensation after he lost $1,000 on a horse race.

- Before the war a session of the Louisiana legislature cost about $100,000 to run; after the war the cost exceeded $1 million because of lavish spending on lunches, alcohol, women's apparel, and even coffins. The Louisiana legislature also purchased a hotel for $250,000 that had just sold for $84,000 and chartered a navigation company and purchased $100,000 in stock even though the company never came into being. The chief justice of the state supreme court and his business partners purchased a railroad from the state for $50,000 after the state had spent more than $2 million on it.

- Taxes on property were increased by intolerable amounts so that the governmental agents could then confiscate the property for "unpaid taxes." As explained by a South Carolina politician, "Land in South Carolina is cheap! We like to put on the taxes, so as to make it cheap!"[33] In Mississippi at one point, about one fifth of the entire state was for sale. In Arkansas, a 228-page book was needed to advertise all the tax-delinquent land sales there. By 1872 property taxes in the South were, on average, about four times what they were in 1860. In South Carolina, the birthplace of the secession movement, they were thirty times higher.[34] This was devastating to the Southern economy and makes a mockery of the very term "Reconstruction."

The tax collectors stole much of this money. More than half a million dollars in taxes collected in 1872 were never turned into the Florida treasury.[35] Since very few of the ex-slaves had the resources with which to purchase significant tracts of land, one can reasonably assume that the main beneficiaries of these tax sales were carpetbaggers and scalawags. Once the ex-slaves began advancing economically and owning property, many of them joined with Southern whites to form Tax-Resisting Associations that sought tax relief.

Although the South was economically destitute, a punitive five cents per pound federal tax was placed on cotton, making it difficult, if not impossible, for many cotton growers to stay in business. A military order stated that anyone who had sold cotton to the Confederate government must give up his cotton to the U.S. government. Hundreds of U.S. Treasury agents swarmed over the South, confiscating cotton with the backing of armed U.S. troops. Little money was raised for the U.S. Treasury, however, for the Treasury agents embezzled much of it (probably putting it to better use than the financing of more counterproductive or corrupt government programs). As described by Sherrard Clemens, an investigator employed by President Andrew Johnson, "The local Agent divides these proceeds [from selling confiscated cotton] with the sub-Agents, or fails to make any return to the Treasury Department at all," so that the agents all "share the unlawful plunder."[36] In many instances the Treasury agents were simply shakedown artists and con men who "would propose to seize a man's property in the name of the United States, but abandon the claim on the payment of heavy bribes."[37]

In order to help keep this corrupt system running, the Republican-controlled governments subsidized pro-Republican newspapers to the tune of tens of thousands of dollars annually and, in some cases, granted them legal monopolies in the newspaper business in particular towns. In effect, the Republicans were extending Lincoln's policy of censoring or shutting down opposition newspapers in the North during the war.

One can get an idea of how wealthy some Republican politicians became through this racket by the example of

Illinois native Henry Clay Warmoth, the governor of Louisiana, who, on an $8,000 per year salary, "accumulated" more than $1 million in wealth in four years.[38]

By the mid-1870s even Republican Party newspapers in the North were denouncing the corruption and plundering of what was left to plunder in the South. The *New York Times* denounced the Republican puppet government of South Carolina, for example, as "a gang of thieves."[39]

Thirty years before the war, Tocqueville had observed that race relations seemed to be even worse in the North than in the South. But that changed during Reconstruction as the ex-slaves were used as political pawns by Northern Republicans. They helped the Republican Party loot and plunder its way through the state and local governments of the South for twelve years in return for a pittance in bribes and political patronage. Southerners reacted to this plunder by venting their frustrations on the ex-slaves. The creation of the Ku Klux Klan was an attempt to intimidate the ex-slaves so that they didn't vote and was a direct response to the activities of the federally funded Union Leagues. Had the Republican Party not been so determined to recruit the ex-slaves as political pawns in its crusade to loot the taxpayers of the South, the Ku Klux Klan might never even have come into existence.

General Donn Piatt, a close personal friend of Lincoln's who became a Washington, D.C., newspaper editor after the war, went so far as to say that "all race antagonism [in the South] came from the carpetbaggers using the Negro votes to get their fingers into the Treasury."[40] Republican Reconstruction policies so poisoned race relations in the South that their divisive effects are still felt today.

MONOPOLY GOVERNMENT

ONCE THE REPUBLICAN PARTY established itself as a political monopolist during Reconstruction, it immediately went to work expanding all the planks of the old Whig platform. It is important to recall that protectionist tariffs and corporate subsidies were outlawed by the Confederate Constitution and that it was a Southerner, Andrew Jackson of Tennessee, who abolished the Bank of the United States and temporarily put an end to central banking.

With the Confederate army out of the way and virtually no one making principled, constitutional arguments against such vast expansions of state power, the Republicans began creating a highly centralized, mercantilist state that they hoped would keep them in power indefinitely. They were also imperialists, in the tradition of the party's political inspiration, Henry Clay.[41]

By the middle of 1865, General Ulysses S. Grant was itching to invade Mexico. Just one month after General Lee surrendered at Appomattox, Grant sent General Philip Sheridan to Texas with orders to "assemble a large force on the Rio Grande" for a possible invasion of Mexico to expel the French from that country. The planned invasion never materialized.[42]

The U.S. government next began antagonizing the British, who had traded with the Confederate government during the war. Led by Massachusetts Senator Charles Sumner, the government began demanding "reparations" for the damage to the Union that such trade supposedly caused. On July 26, 1866, Congress modified the neutrality laws to permit warships and military expeditions to be fitted out against friendly powers, such as England.[43] Several bands of Irish Americans, with the implicit approval of the U.S. government, invaded Canada but were quickly driven back, further antagonizing the British. It is fortunate that a third war with England was averted.[44]

President Grant proposed the annexation of Santo Domingo, another expansionist venture that ultimately failed. Before being elected president, and while still commander of the U.S. Army, Grant gave General Sherman the assignment, in July of 1865, of conducting a campaign of ethnic genocide against the Plains Indians to make way for the government-subsidized railroads. "We are not going to let a few thieving, ragged Indians check and stop the progress of the railroads," Sherman wrote to Grant in 1866. "We must act with vindictive earnestness against the Sioux, even to their extermination, men women and children."[45]

The eradication of the Plains Indians was yet another subsidy to the railroad industry, albeit an indirect one. Rather than paying for rights of way across Indian lands, as James J. Hill's nonsubsidized Great Northern Railroad did, the government-subsidized Union Pacific and Central Pacific Railroads got the government to either kill or place on reservations every last Indian by 1890.

Sherman instructed his army that "During an assault [on an Indian village] the soldiers can not pause to distinguish between male and female, or even discriminate as to age. As long as resistance is made, death must be meted out."[46] As Sherman biographer John Marszalek wrote, "Sherman viewed Indians as he viewed recalcitrant Southerners during the war and newly freed people after: resisters to the legitimate forces of an orderly society."[47] Of course, the chaos of entire Indian villages, women and children included, being wiped out by federal artillery fire is hardly an "orderly" scene. There was "order" in the totalitarian societies of the twentieth century, too, but no freedom. Lincoln, Grant, and Sherman provided an ominous precedent for the totalitarian rulers of the twentieth century with their willingness to mass-murder dissenters, whether they be "recalcitrant Southerners," Mormons, or Indians.

Ever the student of Lincolnian rhetoric, Sherman beseeched new West Point graduates to act with "due regard to humanity and mercy" in the Indian wars, while at the same time supervising the appallingly inhumane policy of having his army murder defenseless Indian women and children.

"Most of the other generals who took a direct role in the Indian wars," writes Marszalek, "were, like Sherman, Civil War luminaries. . . . Their names were familiar from Civil War battles: John Pope, O. O. Howard, Nelson A. Miles, Alfred H. Terry, E. C. Ord, C. C. Augur, and Edward R. S. Canby. Among the colonels, George Armstrong Custer and Benjamin Grierson were the most famous."[48] And "other than Sherman, the most famous Indian fighter was Philip Sheridan, who fought the Indians the way he had fought Confederates in the Shenandoah Valley, all out."[49]

Marszalek is a little too kind to Sheridan here: Sheridan only went "all out" after the Confederate army had left the Shenandoah Valley and he was able to destroy the valley's economy in the presence of defenseless women and children.

In the American public's mind, Sherman and Sheridan were the two most famous Indian fighters, and their names were attached to a joint statement they issued that "the only good Indian is a dead Indian."[50] This, of course, seems to have been Sherman's opinion of Southern secessionists as well during the war, especially in light of his statement that to secessionists, "death is mercy."

Sherman and Sheridan purposely planned their raids during the winter months when they knew that entire families would be together. They killed all the animals as well as the people, ensuring that any survivors would not survive for very long. Drawing a further analogy to the War between the States, Marszalek comments that "During the Civil War, Sherman and Sheridan had practiced a total war of destruction of property; they had, however, spared the populace. Now the army, in its Indian warfare, often wiped out entire villages."[51] (This is not an entirely correct statement: Many Southerners, including quite a few women and children, were killed in the bombardment of Atlanta and other cities.)

One thing Lincoln and Sherman had in common was their personal friendship with Grenville Dodge, the chief engineer of the government-subsidized transcontinental railroads. Lincoln had been an attorney for the Illinois Central Railroad; and Sherman, as a bank president before the war, had invested some of his bank's money in a railroad. Sherman urged his brother, U.S. Senator John Sherman, to support government subsidies for the railroad. This was the reason the Plains Indians had to be killed en masse: to make way for the government-subsidized transcontinental railroad, which seems more and more like the sole reason the Republican Party was created in the first place.

One peculiar aspect of the war against the Plains Indians is the fact that hundreds of ex-slaves joined the U.S. Army (the "Buffalo Soldiers"). Here were men who, just a few years earlier, had suffered the inhumanity of slavery and were now inflicting upon another colored race the ultimate inhumanity: violent death or a concentration camp existence on "reservations."

The fact that the war against the Plains Indians began just three months after Lee's surrender calls into question yet again the notion that racial injustices in the South were the primary motivation for Northerners' willingness to wage such a long and destructive war. No political party purporting to be sensitive to racial injustice could possibly have even contemplated doing to the Indians what the United States government did to them.

Both the Southern Confederates and the Indians stood in the way of the Whig/Republican dream of a North American economic empire, complete with a subsidized transcontinental railroad, a nationalized banking system, and protectionist tariffs. Consequently, both groups were conquered and subjugated by the most violent means.

The character of the American state had changed almost overnight, from the one established by the founding fathers whose primary responsibility was protecting the lives, liberty, and property of its citizens, to an expansionist, imperialistic power that was more willing than ever to trample on individual rights and abandon the Constitution to achieve these ends. This was especially easy to accomplish once the check on centralized power that states' rights created was destroyed.

The kind of corruption that accompanied railroad "construction" in the South was multiplied many times over through the massive subsidies for transcontinental railroads funded by the federal government. As an apparent reward for mass-murdering the Plains Indians and confiscating their land for the benefit of the railroads, General Sherman was sold a vast expanse of land near Omaha, Nebraska, at less than one-third the market price.[52] Crédit Mobilier company stock was given to congressmen as a form of bribery; and during the Grant administrations (1869–1877), it was revealed that Schuyler Colfax, the former speaker of the House and Grant's vice president, had been given Crédit Mobilier stock, as had more than a dozen prominent Republican congressmen. Grant's Secretary of War, W. W. Belknap, was forced to resign for having accepted bribes; his private secretary, Orville Babcock, was involved with a ring of stock swindlers; Treasury Secretary W. W. Richardson was implicated in a tax swindle; and even Grant's ambassador to England, Robert Schenck, had to plead diplomatic immunity to avoid being arrested for selling Londoners worthless stock in American "mining companies."[53]

Republicans were not necessarily more corrupt than Democrats (or anyone else, for that matter), but the expanded size and scope of government, and its centralization in Washington, guaranteed corruption. Government power corrupts, and the more detached the citizens are from their government, when it becomes more centralized, the more corruption there will be. This expansion of government was exactly what the Southern secessionists feared. It was a major reason why they seceded and why the Confederate Constitution of 1861 outlawed protectionist tariffs and corporate welfare disguised as "internal improvement subsidies." Indeed, it is exactly this kind of corruption that the Jeffersonians first became alarmed over while Alexander Hamilton reveled in the political possibilities for himself and for the Federalist Party that such a British-style mercantilist system would create. The Whig Party always lusted after the political power that such a massive patronage system could give it, and the Republican Party of the 1860s and 1870s finally realized it.

The Whigs and Republicans never had solid public support; patronage was always their only hope to hang on to power, for each patronage job meant several votes (that is, the adult family members of the patronage job holder) as well as campaign contributions.

The expansion of government in general created "profit" opportunities for Republican Party operatives. High tariffs led many businessmen to bribe tariff inspectors, who were always patronage appointees, to look the other way when their goods were being imported. The massive excise taxation that was enacted during the war was only partly repealed after the war, leaving in place a large internal revenue bureaucracy that became another source of patronage jobs for the Republican Party faithful. The New York State Supervisor of Internal Revenue pocketed as much as $500,000 a year in bribes in the late 1860s.[54]

Between 1860 and 1864, population in the thirteen largest Northern cities rose by 70 percent, but taxes in those cities rose by 363 percent. Some of these taxes probably went for increased public services, but a rate of tax increase five times that of population growth was surely excessive. Most of the increased tax revenue likely went to paying for patronage jobs, which did not necessarily translate into increased services for the public.[55]

Federal employees became a powerful source of votes for the Republican Party. As Mark Summers writes, "Congressional nominating conventions became rallies for federal employees from navy yards and internal revenue offices, as they pushed for their candidate and promised offices on his behalf."[56] Ulysses S. Grant was notorious for using the expanded powers of government to employ almost all of his relatives, even including former Confederate General James Longstreet, whom he appointed federal railroad commissioner. (Grant and Longstreet were best friends as students at West Point. It was Longstreet who introduced Grant to his future wife, Longstreet's cousin. General Longstreet had no particular qualifications that were specific to the railroad business other than that he enjoyed riding on trains and was one of President Grant's oldest friends.)

The very term "lobbyist" was coined by Ulysses S. Grant, who used it to refer to the men who spent their days in the lobby of the Capitol building in Washington waiting their turn to bribe senators and congressmen. Such bribery was always a part of politics, of course, but with an expanded federal government came expanded lobbying and bribery. Since government was allocating significantly more funds than it ever had, it became more profitable to lobby to procure some of those funds for oneself. Railroad and banking lobbyists and protectionist manufacturers were especially influential, having been among the core supporters of the Republican Party from the very beginning of its existence.

This state of affairs proved inevitable once the Republican Party realized Lincoln's career-long dream of implementing the vaunted American System. Lobbying, patronage, and political corruption *were* the "American System."

Lincolnian election strategies continued to be practiced: Federal employment was expanded just prior to election day with the newly appointed jobholders instructed to vote Republican; and in 1871 the elections in the District of Columbia were affected by a government order that all federal employees were to register to vote in the District and vote Republican if they wanted to keep their jobs.[57] Many government jobholders were also required to contribute money to the Republican Party as a condition of their employment. (Interestingly, all of these corrupt election strategies were greatly expanded during the Franklin D. Roosevelt administration, as historian John D. Flynn demonstrated.)[58]

Lincoln's own Reconstruction ideas made a mockery of democracy. He believed that at least 10 percent of the Southern population probably had Unionist sympathies, and he wanted representatives of that group to be put into place by the Republican Party as the governors, mayors, and local public officials of the Southern states after the war. But what kind of democracy is it in which a 10 percent minority rules an effectively disenfranchised 90 percent majority? This was a very strange definition of "democracy" indeed.

In 1861 the federal government barely existed. As Richard Bensel wrote in *Yankee Leviathan,* "the American state emerged from the wreckage of the Civil War. The state that early American nationalists had previously attempted to establish at the Constitutional Convention in 1787 had become a mere shell by 1860—a government with only a token administrative presence in most of the nation and whose sovereignty was interpreted by the central administration as contingent on the consent of the individual states. . . . an account of the American state formation can begin with the Civil War."[59]

From 1861 until the 1880s, when Southern Democrats began to reassert their influence in Congress, the Republican Party *was* the state. It was a monopoly government that exercised its greatly expanded powers largely on behalf of the Northern industrial and financial interests that funded its political operations. It was a mercantilist state. Among the closest parallels to this situation, writes Richard Bensel, are the "PRI in Mexico, the Congress Party in India, and the Bolsheviks in the early years of the Soviet Union."[60]

Reconstruction ended in 1877, after which the Democratic Party in general, and Southern Democrats in particular, slowly gained influence in Washington. The result was a temporary slowdown of the relentless march toward the centralization of state power that was initiated by the Party of Lincoln. Many Americans once again became tax protesters, which helped slow down—at least temporarily—the growth and centralization of government.

Grover Cleveland was perhaps the last president of the United States (1885–1889) who waged principled battles against unconstitutional usurpations of power by the centralized state. He vetoed hundreds of bills that would have given pensions to thousands of "veterans" who had never seen combat, thereby creating a welfare-dependent class.

He vetoed income tax legislation and sought to cut tariffs, which he called "a vicious, inequitable, and illogical source of unnecessary taxation."[61]

But a mere decade later, William McKinley would declare war on Spain, with the result being the imperialistic acquisition of Puerto Rico, Guam, and the Philippines and the setting of the stage for further military intervention in World War I.

WHAT DID THE REVISIONISTS REVISE?

THE RECONSTRUCTION REVISIONISTS, the most prominent of whom is the Marxist historian Eric Foner, claim to have "overturned" the Dunning School's interpretation of Reconstruction while admittedly agreeing with most of the facts that Dunning and his disciples presented. They admit that government became greatly centralized (which they applaud); that there was massive corruption; that Southern property owners were effectively looted for twelve more years (which they also applaud); and that the railroad subsidies were a scandal. What, then, have they revised?

In his book, *Reconstruction*, Eric Foner summarizes what he believes are the reasons for the "demise" of the Dunning School. First, the revisionists claim to have uncovered the "real" Andrew Johnson as "a stubborn, racist politician" incapable of responding to the situation that confronted him. But Johnson did respond by explaining his veto of the Civil Rights bill as being based on his opposition to the federalization of law enforcement, something never before done in so bold a manner. It's not that Johnson didn't respond at all to the situation that confronted him; he just didn't respond in the way Foner would like.

Foner spends much of his 690-page book celebrating the political activism of the ex-slaves during Reconstruction, noting that black voter turnout exceeded 90 percent in many communities. But then he claims that revisionists like himself have "proven" that "Negro rule" was a myth concocted by the Dunning School. By Foner's own admission, however, black voters were indeed influential in the South during Reconstruction, just as the Dunning School said. The notion that they "ruled" the white population is a red herring. They may not have dominated politics, but they were certainly helpful to the Republican Party.

Foner next claims that because there were "efforts to revitalize the devastated Southern economy," the Dunning School is wrong in its critique of economic interventionism as well. Yes, "efforts" were made, but to the extent that the Southern economy recovered, it was despite, not because of, the high taxes and extraordinarily high levels of debt imposed on it by its conquerors. Reconstruction policies hampered the Southern recovery rather than helping it, just as similar policies had plunged the entire economy into a deep recession in the late 1830s when the Whigs had attempted a similar mercantilist scheme. Many Southern states took decades to pay off the debt burden that was placed on them by Reconstruction-era puppet governments run by the Republican Party.

Foner's claim that the revisionists have also "proven" that the Republican Party was not merely the political vehicle of Northern industrialists and financiers simply should not be taken seriously. Among the research Foner alludes to in this regard is an article by Stanley Cohen in an anthology of revisionist work edited by Kenneth Stampp and Leon Litwack.[62] In that article, Cohen argues that since there were disagreements among Northern business interests—that is, some wanted lower tariffs and others wanted higher tariffs—the Republican Party was not united in an effort to use its political power during Reconstruction to serve "Northern business interests," as the Dunning School had argued.

This argument hardly makes any sense, for the fact is that Northern business interests favoring higher tariffs and railroad subsidies did in fact have their way, despite some opposition among other Northern businesses. Of course, Northern business interests were not uniform in their preferences, but so what? The protectionists and central banking advocates dominated despite the lack of uniformity of interests (which never exists anywhere, for that matter).

Finally, Foner and the other revisionists admit that there was indeed massive corruption during Reconstruction, as documented in great detail by Dunning and his students. But the revisionists' "rebuttal" of this evidence is to argue that corruption was even worse in the North. "Corruption in the Reconstruction South paled before that of the Tweed Ring, Crédit Mobilier scandal, and Whiskey Rings in the post–Civil War North."[63]

Corruption was undoubtedly worse in the North, for there was more government there than in the South. The practice of granting government subsidies to private businesses was more common in the North (as was the attendant corruption), and it was this corrupt system that was introduced to the South on a massive scale during Reconstruction. The fact that corruption was even worse in the

North proves the Dunning School's point; since massive corporate welfare was relatively new to the South, it hadn't quite equaled the North in terms of political corruption. The expansion of government, which Reconstruction facilitated, caused such corruption.

As Richard Bensel says, virtually every program enacted under Reconstruction caused a permanent expansion of the power of the central government. Once one recognizes that the Republican Party politicians were the political heirs to the Whigs, who were themselves heirs to the Hamiltonians, it becomes clear that this result was not just a by-product of the quest for "social equality," as the revisionist historians argue, but the intended effect all along. William Archibald Dunning and his students got it right.

CHAPTER 9

THE GREAT CENTRALIZER: LINCOLN'S ECONOMIC LEGACY

By the 1850s the authority of all government in America was at a low point; government to the American was, at most, merely an institution with a negative role, a guardian of fair play.
—DAVID DONALD, *LINCOLN RECONSIDERED*

The war . . . has tended, more than any other event in the history of the country to militate against the Jeffersonian idea, that "the best government is that which governs least."
—ILLINOIS GOVERNOR RICHARD YATES, JANUARY 2, 1865

LINCOLN VETOED only two pieces of legislation during his four years as president, a fact some historians have interpreted as meaning that he effectively delegated domestic policy to Congress while focusing his efforts on the war. This interpretation, however, fails to take into account the historical context and Lincoln's deep, career-long involvement in

economic policy, particularly the Whig dream of implementing the American System. As we've seen in earlier chapters,
the Whig/Republican American System was blocked time
and again for decades by presidential vetoes, including the
vetoes of Whig President John Tyler. Jefferson, Madison,
Monroe, Jackson, Tyler, and others consistently made constitutional arguments in opposition to the mercantilist policies of the American System.

Lincoln seethed in frustration over this for two decades
as the Constitution stood squarely in the way of his (and
his party's) aspirations for political domination. Not only
did the federal Constitution stand in his way, but so did
most state constitutions. By 1860, in response to the gross
corruption of early experiments with such subsidies, most
states had amended their constitutions to prohibit taxpayer
subsidies for internal improvements (see chapter 4). The
real "American System" of constitutional liberty, as codified in federal and state constitutions, was in sharp conflict
with Lincoln's career dream of being the "DeWitt Clinton
of Illinois," if not of the entire United States.

So it is not surprising at all that Lincoln would have dis-
carded constitutional liberties the way he did (see chapter
6). It is almost as if he had a vendetta against the Constitution with his casual abolition of the writ of habeas corpus,
his pervasive censorship, and his scrapping of much of the
Bill of Rights. Once the Southerners had left the U.S. Congress and the Republican Party was firmly in control of the
federal government, Alexander Hamilton's old mercantilist
coalition was finally in charge. Now that the coalition
dominated Congress as well, its members were not about

to be stopped in their seventy-year quest to bring British-style mercantilism to America.

The Whigs had assumed they were in such a position in 1841 when the Whig William Henry Harrison was inaugurated as president and Henry Clay dominated Congress. Their plans for protectionist tariffs, a nationalized banking system, and internal improvement subsidies was foiled at that time by the states' rights Southerner, John Tyler, who became president after Harrison's untimely death just one month after his inauguration. But in 1860, the old Whig coalition was not about to let political victory slip away. They finally had their man—Lincoln—in the White House, and it was clear to all that he was not about to let the Constitution stand in the way of the centralization of governmental power and the adoption of mercantilism. There would be no vetoes of national banking, tariff, or internal improvement bills coming from Lincoln. He was a political fox guarding the constitutional henhouse.

From this perspective one takes a different view of Lincoln's role in seeming to delegate so much domestic policy authority to Congress. Congress was dominated by his party, and he did exactly what his party members expected him to do: acquiesce in all the legislation that had been deemed unconstitutional by all previous administrations. As Senator John Sherman of Ohio explained at the time,

> Those who elected Mr. Lincoln expect him . . . to secure to free labor its just right to the Territories of the United States; to protect . . . by wise revenue laws, the labor of our people; to secure the public lands to actual settlers . . . ; to develop

the internal resources of the country by opening new means of communication between the Atlantic and Pacific.[1]

David Donald translated this statement "from the politician's idiom" into plain English as meaning that Lincoln and the Republicans "intended to enact a high protective tariff that mothered monopoly, to pass a homestead law that invited speculators to loot the public domain, and to subsidize a transcontinental railroad that afforded infinite opportunities for jobbery" (that is, political patronage jobs).[2] In fact, that is exactly what they did. Lincoln awarded himself special "war powers" (that are mentioned nowhere in the Constitution) in order to adopt every mercantilist plank of the American System during the first two years of his administration.

PROTECTIONIST TARIFFS

IN HIS FIRST INAUGURAL ADDRESS Lincoln stated over and over again that he had no intention of disturbing Southern slavery, and even if he did, it would be unconstitutional to do so. He referred to all of his past speeches to make his point. On slavery, he was always willing to compromise.

But when it came to protectionist tariffs, Lincoln was totally uncompromising. In that same First Inaugural Address, he literally promised a military invasion of any state that failed to collect its share of tariff revenues: "The power confided in me will be used to hold, occupy, and possess the property, and places belonging to the government, and to collect the duties and imposts; *but beyond what may be necessary for these objects, there will be no invasion—no using force against, or among the people anywhere"* (emphasis added).[3]

To Lincoln, slavery was just another political issue subject to compromise. But protectionist tariffs—the keystone of the Republican Party platform—were nonnegotiable. He promised to wage war on any state that refused to collect enough tariff revenue, a truly bizarre stance. What other American president, in his first address to the American people, would have threatened a bloody war *on his own citizens* over the issue of tax collection? He was essentially threatening American citizens with death and annihilation unless they continued to pay a tribute (and at a considerably higher rate) to the central government. How else could one interpret his threat of a military invasion? Those Southerners who took Lincoln seriously and expected an invasion did not expect it to be a pleasant experience. They fully expected bloodshed to result from the spectacle of thousands of armed Federal troops marching into their communities to force them to collect federal tariff revenues, or else. The Republican Party had just tripled the rate of federal taxation (the average tariff rate), and Lincoln was saying to Southerners that if they refused to pay this increased rate of tribute, they would face an invasion by a federal army. Seen in this light, one can understand why there was such strong support for secession.

As soon as it was apparent that Lincoln had a good chance of winning the election of 1860, the Republicans in

Congress, led by Pennsylvania iron manufacturer Thaddeus Stevens and Senator Justin S. Morrill of Vermont, began working on the Morrill tariff. The House of Representatives passed the tariff bill in May 1860—before the election—and by the time Lincoln was inaugurated, it had passed the Senate as well.

Lincoln may have had very little to do with the tariff in an official capacity, but as the leader of the Republican Party one has to assume that Lincoln the master politician was involved in the political maneuvering over the tariff.

The Morrill tariff was a radical departure from existing tariff policy. As economist Frank Taussig wrote in *The Tariff History of the United States* (1931), by 1857 the maximum duty on imports had been reduced to 24 percent; many raw materials were tariff-free; and the "level of duties on the whole line of manufactured articles was brought down to the lowest point which [had] been reached in this country since 1815. It is not likely that we shall see, for a great many years to come, a nearer approach to the free-trade ideal."[4] This was the trend in Europe as well; England had repealed the so-called Corn Laws in 1850, and France was in the process of reducing its tariffs.

Taussig also explained how the Republican-controlled Congress went on a protectionist frenzy for the next several years (indeed, the next several decades). "In the next regular session, in December 1861, a still further increase of duties was made. From that time until 1865 no session, indeed, hardly a month of any session, passed in which some increase of duties on imports was not made."[5]

By 1862 the average tariff rate had crept up to 47.06 percent, which "established protective duties more extreme than had been ventured on in any previous tariff act in our country's history."[6] Great sacrifices (including the ultimate sacrifice) were being made by Northerners who were being taxed to finance the war and conscripted into the army; but most of the Northern manufacturers, who were the financial lifeblood of the Republican Party, were not only exempted from sacrifices but also thrived. As Taussig wrote, "Great fortunes were made by changes in legislation urged and brought about by those who were benefited by them." Congress enacted tariff legislation, "whose chief effect was to bring money into the pockets of private individuals" by protecting them from foreign competition.[7] Long after the war was over "almost any increase in duties demanded by domestic producers was readily made."[8] This came about because the Republican Party made very effective use of the war and Reconstruction to solidify its monopolistic grip on national politics. The first plank of the American System was finally nailed into place.

To put this all into historical context, it is important to recall that Southerners had been adamantly protesting protectionist tariffs since 1824. Southerners ended up paying the lion's share of all federal taxes (more than 90 percent of federal tax revenue came from tariffs at that time), since they relied so heavily on foreign trade, while most federal spending was occurring in the North. As mentioned earlier, most of the nonagricultural goods that Southerners purchased came from either Europe or the North. A tariff, which is a tax on imports, raised the price of virtually everything Southerners purchased. An average tariff rate of almost 50 percent was an extraordinarily burdensome level of taxation. Southerners had been protesting for some thirty-five years that they were being plundered by the government's tariff policy, primarily for the benefit of certain politically well connected Northern manufacturers, such as Thaddeus Stevens and his ilk. Even before the Morrill tariff of 1860, because of their reliance on foreign manufactured goods, Southerners were paying about 87 percent of all federal taxes, even though they had less than half the population of the North.

Southerners were such ardent free traders that protectionist tariffs were outlawed by the Confederate Constitution of 1861. Article I, Section 8, clause 1 stipulates that

> Congress shall have power to lay and collect taxes, imposts, and excises for revenue necessary to pay the debts, provide for the common defense, and carry on the Government of the Confederate States; but no bounties shall be granted from the Treasury; nor shall any duties or taxes on importations from foreign nations be laid to promote or foster any branch of industry; and all duties, imposts, and excises shall be uniform throughout the Confederate States.[9]

Free trade in the South would have brought about a substitution of shipping from New York, Boston, and Baltimore to Charleston, New Orleans, and Savannah. That is, European shipping merchants would not have imported their goods into, say, New York Harbor and paid a 47.06 percent tax on all goods that came off their ships for sale in the United States when they could have shipped their goods to the United States through, say, Charleston Harbor, where there was no tariff at all. Their goods would have therefore been sold much more cheaply in American markets, which is exactly why Northern manufacturers wanted to destroy free trade in the Southern ports. This is why New York City Mayor Fernando Wood proposed making his city a "free city" that was not a part of either the United States or the state of New York—so that it could be a Northern free-trade zone. The Republican Party could not tolerate this, and so it waged war to stop it. It was either that or political death, for as historian Richard Bensel observed, "the tariff was the centerpiece of the Republican program."[10]

This was the interpretation given by Representative Clement L. Vallandigham of Ohio on the floor of the U.S. House of Representatives on July 10, 1861, which would eventually incite Lincoln to have him arrested without a civil warrant, imprisoned without being charged, and deported. Vallandigham was the leader of the opposition in the House of Representatives and an advocate of free trade. In his speech he spoke of an "impelling cause, without which this horrid calamity of civil war might have been . . . averted."[11] One of the "last and worst acts of a Congress . . . which it ought not to have done . . . was the passage of an obscure, ill-considered, ill-digested, and unstatesmanlike high protective tariff act, commonly known as the Morrill Tariff," Vallandigham said.[12] Moreover,

> Just about the same time, too, the Confederate Congress . . . adopted our old tariff of 1857 . . . fixing their rate of duties at five, fifteen, and twenty percent lower than ours. The result was . . . trade and commerce . . . began to look to the South. . . . The city of New York, the great commercial emporium of the

Union, and the North-west, the chief granary of the Union, began to clamor now, loudly, for a repeal of the pernicious and
ruinous tariff. Threatened thus with the loss of both political
power and wealth, or the repeal of the tariff, and, at last, of
both, New England—and Pennsylvania . . . demanded, now,
coercion and civil war, with all its horrors, as the price of preserving either from destruction. . . . The subjugation of the
South, and the closing up of her ports—first, by force, in war,
and afterward, by tariff laws, in peace, was deliberately resolved upon by the East.[13]

In the mid-nineteenth century, newspapers were openly
associated with one political party or another, and numerous Republican newspapers in the North had been calling
for the bombardment of the Southern ports in order to destroy the South's free-trade policy long before Fort Sumter
(which was, by the way, a customs house).

On December 10, 1860, the *Daily Chicago Times* can-
didly admitted that the tariff was indeed a tool used by
Northerners for the purpose of plundering the South. The
editor of the newspaper warned that the benefits of this
political plunder would be threatened by the existence of
free trade in the South:

The South has furnished near three-fourths of the entire exports of the country. Last year she furnished seventy-two percent of the whole . . . we have a tariff that protects our
manufacturers from thirty to fifty percent, and enables us to
consume large quantities of Southern cotton, and to compete
in our whole home market with the skilled labor of Europe.
This operates to compel the South to pay an indirect bounty
to our skilled labor, of millions annually.[14]

"Let the South adopt the free-trade system," the Chicago paper ominously warned, and the North's "commerce must be reduced to less than half what it now is." In addition, "Our labor could not compete . . . with the labor of Europe" and "a large portion of our shipping interest would pass into the hands of the South," leading to "very general bankruptcy and ruin."[15] Unless, of course, the North competed by reducing its tariff rates, just as France was in the process of doing in order to compete with England's free-trade policy.

On March 12, 1861, another Republican Party mouthpiece, the *New York Evening Post*, advocated that the U.S. Navy "abolish all ports of entry" into the Southern states simply because sending hordes of customs inspectors there to enforce the Morrill tariff would be too expensive. Protectionist tariffs require "a collector, with his army of appraisers, clerks, examiners, inspectors, weighers, gaugers, measurers, and so forth."[16]

The *Newark Daily Advertiser* was clearly aware that the free-trade doctrines of Adam Smith had taken a strong hold in England, France, and the Southern states. On April 2, 1861, the paper warned that Southerners had apparently "taken to their bosoms the liberal and popular doctrine of free trade" and that they "might be willing to go . . . toward free trade with the European powers," which "must operate to the serious disadvantage of the North," as "commerce will be largely diverted to the Southern cities."[17] "We apprehend," the New Jersey editorialists wrote, that "the chief instigator of the present troubles—South Carolina—have all along for years been preparing the way for the adoption of free trade," and must be stopped by "the closing of the ports" by military force.[18]

It is likely that such editorializing by Republican Party newspapers was serving the purpose of getting the (Northern) public used to the idea that the government was about to unconstitutionally blockade Southern ports. It was either that or the Republican Party might possibly go the way of the Whig Party, an outcome that Lincoln was doggedly determined to avoid.

There were some voices of moderation among Northern editorialists. The *New Haven Daily Register,* for example, recognized that "while Congress is raising the duties for Northern ports, the Southern [Constitutional] Convention is doing away with all import duties for the Southern ports, leaving more than three-fifths of the seafront of the Atlantic States . . . beyond the reach of our . . . tariff."[19] The South would then "invite the free trade of the world," which would be economically devastating to the North.[20] But rather than advocating the tyrannical policy of threatening Southerners with annihilation by the U.S. military unless they paid an even larger tribute to the federal government, the *New Haven Daily Register* advocated political competition: lower the Northern tariff rate and allow free trade to flourish in both the North and the South.

This was an intolerable position to Lincoln, for it would have meant that he and his party failed to generate special privileges for its major base of political support—protectionist manufacturers in the Northern states. And if they couldn't have done that, their new political party, which was barely five years old, might well have become defunct. Vallandigham and other opponents of protectionist tariffs were branded as "traitors" by Thaddeus Stevens and Lincoln. (The reason that was given for deporting Vallandig-

ham was his allegedly "treasonous" speech.) In light of
what happened to Vallandigham, this was bound to have
intimidated others as well.

As we saw in chapter 4, Lincoln was a devoted protectionist over his entire political career. He and other Whigs
took this position because it created a stream of economic
benefits for a wealthy and powerful constituency group, and
it also provided the revenue to help finance the second plank
of the American System, internal improvements. That, in
turn, provided even more opportunities for "jobbery." Having the government dispense special privileges to the
wealthy and influential was always the core of the Whig political program to which Lincoln devoted his political career.

INTERNAL IMPROVEMENTS (AGAIN)

WHEN LINCOLN was elected in 1860, nearly every state
constitution prohibited the use of tax dollars for internal
improvement subsidies, and federal subsidies had never
materialized for constitutional reasons as well. By that
time, "internal improvement subsidies" meant subsidies for
railroad corporations, primarily, and the shipping industry
secondarily. But as of 1860 "no bill granting federal aid for
the construction of a railroad to the Pacific had ever managed to clear both houses of Congress" despite the persistent support for such subsidies by the Whigs and, later, the
Republicans.[21]

"Constitutional scruples," writes historian Leonard
Curry, "ranked high among the considerations that had
prevented Congress from passing a Pacific Railway Act

before 1861."²² But as we have seen, Lincoln had few constitutional scruples. He made many speeches throughout his political career denouncing the way in which the Constitution stood in the way of the American System. The same can apparently be said of his Republican compatriots in Congress. "Constitutional scruples rapidly disintegrated" once the Republicans controlled both the Senate and the White House, writes Curry.²³

Thus, even though by mid-1862 the military situation facing Lincoln was desperate—so desperate that he resorted to the trick of an emancipation proclamation that freed no one and decided to dramatically change his war strategy to target Southern civilians—the Lincoln administration and Congress diverted millions of dollars to the construction of a railroad in California. The major opposition to federal railroad subsidies had always come from Southerners—both on constitutional grounds and on the more practical political grounds that the proposed routes did not go through Southern states. Now that these Southern congressmen were no longer present, there was nothing stopping the Republicans from adopting the second plank of the American System, massive subsidies for railroad corporations. The Constitution was simply ignored once again by Lincoln and his party. And once again the plucky Congressman Vallandigham was the leader of the opposition, making futile constitutional arguments, in the spirit of Jefferson and Jackson, in opposition to this particular form of corporate welfare.

Such opposition was to no avail; by June 1862 both houses of Congress had passed the Pacific Railway Act authorizing the expenditure of millions of dollars to build a subsidized and government-regulated transcontinental railroad in the form of the Union Pacific and Central Pacific Railroad Corporations.

Myriad reasons, some of them quite specious, were offered for why such huge sums had to be diverted from the war effort to begin building a railroad in California. It was supposedly necessary for military purposes, just in case California seceded. California was said to be developing "a different culture," and multiculturalism was to be avoided at all costs. California had recently said "no thank you" to the government's issuance of paper money ("greenbacks"), preferring instead to remain on the gold standard. This opposition, too, needed to be crushed according to Lincoln and the Republicans in Congress.[24]

Most historians argue that the transcontinental railroads would never have been built if the only source of financing came from private capital markets, but that view is wrong. All of England's railroad lines were privately financed, and American railroad entrepreneur James J. Hill did in fact build a transcontinental railroad, the Great Northern, without government subsidies.[25] Hill's line was built fifteen years later than the government-subsidized ones, but it would likely have been built even sooner had his competitors not received millions of dollars in subsidies. The Great Northern was a famously efficient and profitable operation; by contrast, the Union Pacific and Central Pacific were so inefficient that they were bankrupt as soon as they were completed in 1869.

"Our own line in the north," Hill boasted, "was built without any government aid, even the right of way, through hundreds of miles of public lands, being paid for in cash."[26] Hill (naturally) resented the fact that his rivals were receiving millions of dollars in government subsidies. In an 1893 letter to a friend he complained, "The government should not furnish capital to these companies, in addition to their enormous land subsidies, to enable them to conduct their business in competition with enterprises that have received no aid from the public treasury."[27]

Whenever government subsidizes any industry, the inevitable result is inefficiency and corruption. The most extreme example of this phenomenon would be the former communist countries where *every* industry was entirely subsidized by government, and the result was economic disaster and a thorough corruption of society.

When private investors have their own funds at stake, they can be expected to do everything possible to assure that the funds are used economically. James J. Hill, for example, supervised in great detail the building of his railroads to minimize waste and inefficiency. This doesn't guarantee efficiency, but the proper incentives are in place with privately funded roads and railroads. Efficient railroad building rewards investors with profits; inefficiency penalizes them with losses or bankruptcy. No such incentives exist with government financing. In fact, government has a tendency to throw good money after bad.

With government financing, politics inevitably takes the place of economics as the main decision-making criterion. Legislators will always insist, as a condition of voting for the subsidies, that the railroad be built near where they live or at least near their constituents and contributors, even if it is uneconomical to do so. During the congressional debates over funding for the Union Pacific and Central Pacific

Railroads in 1862, a delegate to Congress from New Mexico (which was not yet a state) complained that "the wrangle of local interests" was such that many members of Congress refused to support the subsidy bill unless the railroad "starts in the corner of every man's farm and runs through all his neighbors' plantations" in every congressional district.[28]

On the free market, by contrast, railroads are built in a way that will serve consumers most effectively. If not, profits will decline. Consumer sovereignty prevails over the whims of politicians.

Historian Heather Cox Richardson has argued that all the corruption that accompanied the federally subsidized railroads was probably necessary as an extra financial incentive for investors.[29] This is a creative excuse for fraud and corruption, but it is very poor economics. The transcontinental railroads would have been built and financed by private capital markets, as James J. Hill proved. They most certainly would have been built more efficiently, and corruption would not have even been an issue since no taxpayers' funds would have been involved. As long as the federal government was subsidizing railroads, it was a certainty that they would be corrupt and inefficient, and they were. It was just such corruption that generations of Southern statesmen had warned about, but those arguments were being ignored by Lincoln and the leading congressional Republicans.

The Union Pacific and Central Pacific were given sections of land for each mile of track completed; $16,000 in low-interest loans for each mile of track on flat land; $32,000 for hilly terrain; and $48,000 per mile in the mountains. The chief engineer of the Union Pacific was Grenville

Dodge, a close friend of Lincoln's (and Sherman's) who had been appointed as a general in the Union army despite having no military experience. Dodge and Charles Durant, the president of the Union Pacific, built wastefully circuitous routes so as to collect more per-mile subsidies. They used the cheapest construction materials and stressed speed, not workmanship. Indians as well as farmers were evicted from their lands at gunpoint to make way for the railroad. James J. Hill, by contrast, paid cash to Indians, farmers, and anyone else for rights of way through their property.

Dodge laid track on the ice and snow during the winters, and when the line had to be rebuilt after the spring thaws, the corporation pocketed even more subsidy money by rebuilding. The officers of the two companies set up their own supply companies and used their government funds to purchase supplies from themselves at inflated prices. This practice was the source of the Crédit Mobilier scandal during the Grant administration.

Republican legislators routinely accepted bribes in return for appointing railroad commissioners, some of whom had no previous railroad experience. By the time the line was completed in May 1869, both the Union Pacific and the Central Pacific were bankrupt. A precedent of corruption was established that would be a drag on the U.S. economy for decades to come. As Leonard Curry explained,

> Throughout the remainder of the nineteenth century (and beyond), corporate interests—apparently insatiable—returned again and again to demand direct and indirect federal subsidies. To insure preferential treatment and noninterfer-

ence, national legislative and executive offices were corrupted
and representative government made a mockery . . . the corruption of the Grant era was sparked by . . . the activities of
those two companies and individuals connected to Pacific
railway scheme.[30]

The one individual most closely connected to the Pacific
railway "scheme" was, of course, Lincoln himself, who had
been battling for his vaunted internal improvement subsidies
ever since the day he entered politics in 1832. It was only after federal subsidies dried up in the latter part of the century
that the transcontinental railroad industry began to take on
some semblance of economically efficient operation.

The massive subsidies for internal improvements pin-
point yet another stark difference in the essential role of
government in society as viewed by Lincoln, on the one
hand, and the leaders of the Confederate government, on
the other. The Confederate Constitution was incompatible
with Lincoln's (and the Republicans') economic policy
objectives. Not only were protectionist tariffs ruled unconstitutional in the Confederacy, but so were internal improvement subsidies.

A NATIONALIZED BANKING SYSTEM
AT LAST

AS OF 1861 the central government was completely di-
vorced from the country's banking system despite decades
of agitation for a nationalized banking system by the
Hamiltonians, the Whigs, and the Republicans. There was

no central bank, and the only legally recognized money was gold or silver coins. The nation's currency consisted solely of state-chartered bank notes redeemable in gold or silver on demand.

Historians have long argued that this system created an unacceptable degree of financial instability, but this argument is a myth. It was in fact the best—the most stable—monetary system the United States ever had.[31] No monetary system is perfect, and there were bankruptcies, but most of these losses were the result of government regulation in the form of prohibitions on branch banking, mandates for minimum specie (gold and silver) reserves, restrictions on the issue of small-denomination bank notes, and requirements that banks purchase state bonds—requirements that were especially unwise when the bonds were issued to finance internal improvement boondoggles.[32]

On February 25, 1862, Lincoln signed into law the Legal Tender Act that empowered the Secretary of the Treasury (Salmon P. Chase) to issue paper money printed in green ink known as "greenbacks." The greenbacks were not immediately redeemable in gold or silver but were backed by a governmental promise to do so in the future. (After the war Chase became the chief justice of the U.S. Supreme Court and ruled greenbacks to be unconstitutional!)

The National Currency Acts of 1863 and 1864 created a system of nationally chartered banks that could issue bank notes supplied to them by the newly created comptroller of the currency. In addition, a prohibitive 10 percent tax on state bank notes was imposed to help create a federal monetary monopoly. Lincoln recruited financier Jay Cooke to take out (and pay for) newspaper ads throughout the country denouncing the private, state-chartered banking system while praising the Republican plan for nationalizing the nation's money supply.

The government's paper money flooded private banks so that the amount of money in circulation doubled in just the first year. The consequent inflation was so severe that by July 1864 greenback dollars were worth only thirty-five cents in gold.[33] So much for monetary "stability" through centralized banking.

Ohio Senator John Sherman was a top spokesman for the nationalized banking system. He was forthright and honest in the reasons he gave for the system: It would centralize power in Washington, which is to say, in his hands and in the hands of his Republican Party colleagues. He urged his congressional colleagues to "nationalize as much as possible," even the currency, so as to "make men love their country before their states." "All private interests, all local interests, all banking interests, the interests of individuals, everything, should be subordinate now to the interest of the Government."[34]

This is quite a remarkable statement, for it is a clear repudiation of the philosophy of government established by the founding fathers—namely, that government should be the servant, not the master, of the people. It is a precursor to twentieth-century collectivism, whereby individual rights were held to be subservient to the "national will" and where citizens were said to have "duties" to the state, rather than the other way around. Republican Party newspapers echoed Sherman's (and Lincoln's) collectivist philosophy throughout the land.

New York Congressman Elbridge G. Spaulding, an influential member of the House Ways and Means Committee (and a New York banker), was just as honest as Senator Sherman was. On February 19, 1863, speaking on the floor of the U.S. House of Representatives, he argued that the nationalized banking system would help to achieve the Hamiltonian system of a strong central government that could subsidize economic development by handing out subsidies to private corporations. Henry Clay himself could not have said it better.[35] The Republicans in Congress, with Lincoln's support, were clearly using the war as an excuse to enact the Hamiltonian mercantilist system.

Kentucky Democrat Lazarus Powell took Sherman, Spaulding, and Lincoln at their words. "The result of this course of [banking] legislation," Powell said, "is utterly to destroy all the rights of the States. It is asserting a power which if carried out to its logical result would enable the national Congress to destroy every institution of the States and cause all power to be consolidated and concentrated here."[36] That, of course, is exactly what Lincoln and the Republicans wanted. The third plank of the American System was finally and firmly set in place. On March 9, 1863, the *New York Times* triumphantly editorialized that "The legal tender act and the national currency bill crystallized . . . a centralization of power, such as Hamilton might have eulogized as magnificent."[37]

THE BIRTH OF THE INTERNAL REVENUE BUREAUCRACY

THE FIRST INCOME TAX in American history was signed into law by Lincoln, with a top rate of 10 percent on incomes over $10,000. It would be eliminated in 1872, but establishing such a precedent undoubtedly aided the cause of income taxation, and it eventually prevailed.

On July 1, 1862, Lincoln signed a tax bill that filled more than seventeen triple-column pages of very fine print. The bill contained 119 different sections, imposing hundreds of excise taxes, stamp taxes, inheritance taxes, gross receipts taxes, and license taxes on virtually every occupation, service, and commodity in the entire economy.[38] Congressman Vallandigham once again protested, and once again Thaddeus Stevens, Lincoln's point man in the Congress, branded all dissenters as traitors with the implicit threat of imprisonment (which was not so implicit in Vallandigham's case).

An internal revenue bureaucracy was created within the Treasury Department for the first time. Taxation on a scale never before seen in the United States was imposed on the population of the North. Most of these taxes remained in place after the war, as did the internal revenue bureaucracy, so that every American citizen would forever have direct contact with the federal government. As Leonard Curry concluded, "A great centralizing force had been set in motion."[39] Never again would the federal government's tax base be cut back to its 1861 level.

Historian Heather Cox Richardson quotes an "unhappy Democratic senator" who, despite his unhappiness, quite accurately described the implications of the Lincoln tax increases: "The Government is everything; it has become the end; and the people, and all their property, labor, efforts, and gains . . . are merely the means by which the Government is to continue . . . and its powers progressively augmented."[40]

The adoption of the vaunted American System, Lincoln's career-long dream, was complete by 1863. The predictions of all the opponents of Alexander Hamilton's mercantilist schemes were proven correct: The system of federalism that was created by the founding fathers was destroyed; and the protectionist tariff, pervasive federal taxation, and nationalized banking systems had a tremendous centralizing effect on American government.

The American public was also relentlessly propagandized by the government and its private sector accomplices, such as Jay Cooke, into believing that it could now look to the federal government for solutions to its problems. This made it easier for future generations of politicians to convince the American public to acquiesce in further expansions of government and further restrictions on personal liberty that would have caused the founding fathers to reach for their swords.

Lincoln will forever be known as The Great Emancipator, but he should also be thought of as The Great Centralizer.

CHAPTER 10

THE COSTS OF
LINCOLN'S WAR

Our government is not to be maintained or our Union preserved by invasions of the rights and powers of the several States . . . its true strength consists in leaving individuals and States as much as possible to themselves . . . ; not in binding the States more closely to the center.
—ANDREW JACKSON

LINCOLN DID NOT LAUNCH a military invasion of the South to free the slaves. No serious student of history could deny this fact. In 1861 Lincoln's position—and the position of the Republican Party—was that Southern slavery was secure: He had no intention of disturbing it; and even if he did, it would be unconstitutional to do so. This is what he said in his First Inaugural Address. The Republican Party, led by Lincoln, was *in favor of* Southern slavery because its leaders feared the spectacle of emancipated slaves residing in their own Northern states. Lincoln's own state of Illinois had recently amended its constitution to prohibit the emigration of black people into the state, as had several other Northern states. Most Northern states had adopted

Black Codes that discriminated in the most inhumane ways against freed blacks. Such discriminatory laws existed in the North decades before they were adopted in the South. There were very few blacks in the North in 1861, and most Northern voters wanted it to remain that way.

As of 1861 Lincoln and the Republicans were opposed only to the *extension* of slavery into the new territories. One reason they gave for this opposition was that they wanted to preserve the territories as the exclusive domain of the white race. A second reason articulated by Lincoln was the desire to avoid the further artificial inflation of Southern (i.e., Democratic Party) representation in Congress that was created by the three-fifths clause of the Constitution. The few abolitionists in the party undoubtedly believed that prohibiting slavery in the territories would quicken its overall demise, but few of them held any high elective offices.

The reason Lincoln gave for launching a military invasion of the South was to "save the Union." Translating from his obfuscating rhetoric, this means that he wanted to use military force to destroy once and for all the doctrines of federalism and states' rights that had, since the founding of the republic, frustrated ambitious politicians like himself who wanted a highly centralized and greatly enlarged state. As we've seen in earlier chapters, Lincoln spent his entire twenty-eight-year political career prior to becoming president working in the trenches of the Whig and Republican parties on behalf of a more centralized government that would dispense taxpayer subsidies to corporations and finance them with protectionist tariffs and a nationalized banking system (the "American System"). The major opposition to such plans, for some seventy years, had come mostly from Southern statesmen such as Jefferson, Madison, Monroe, Jackson, and Calhoun.

The war ended the constitutional logjam behind which the old Whig economic policy agenda had languished for decades. This is most likely the real reason why Lincoln decided that he *had* to wage war on the South and why he rebuffed any and all overtures from Southern statesmen to peaceably end the dispute. He wanted a war.

Lincoln believed that the war would last only a few months, after which he and the Republican Party could easily achieve their centralizing goals without even addressing the issue of slavery. It was the biggest political miscalculation in American history.

As Lincoln publicly stated on August 22, 1862, in his famous letter to *New York Tribune* editor Horace Greeley, his only concern with slavery was the extent to which the issue could be used to achieve his overriding goal of "saving the Union." He said in the letter that if he could do this without freeing a single slave, he would most certainly do so.

Lincoln adopted Daniel Webster's novel and ahistorical theory that the Union created the states, a theory that has no factual basis whatsoever. He then waged the bloodiest war in human history up to that point to "prove" that his theory was right. The war killed some 620,000 young men, including one-fourth of all the white males in the South between twenty and forty years of age. Standardizing for today's population of some 280 million (compared to 30 million in 1861), that would be the equivalent of about 5 million American deaths in four years—nearly a hundred times the number of Americans who died in Vietnam over a ten-year period.

Economic historian Jeffrey Rogers Hummel estimates that more than 50,000 Southern civilians perished during the war, and this number, even if it is off by a multiple of two, has to include thousands of slaves.[1] The indiscriminate bombing of Southern cities by federal armies did not distinguish between soldiers and civilians, let alone between black and white. Effective medicine was all but unheard of in the mid-nineteenth century, and yellow fever, malaria, and cholera plagued Southern cities during the summer months. The poor ex-slaves, who were undoubtedly affected more than the average white Southerner by the economically devastated postwar Southern economy, must have suffered disproportionately from disease. Food was scarce, and they must have also had a much harder time in fending off malnutrition and starvation.

Thousands of soldiers were maimed for life. The war essentially destroyed the Southern economy, including much of its livestock, farm machinery, and railroads. About two-thirds of Southern wealth was either destroyed or stolen by federal soldiers.[2] General Sherman boasted that his army alone, while passing through Georgia and South Carolina, destroyed $100 million in private property and stole another $20 million worth.

Industries that receive military contracts always prosper from war, giving parts of an economy a false sense of prosperity. But in reality the taxes that are used to pay for military procurement depress other areas of the economy. Moreover, during the War between the States the destruction of the Southern economy harmed the North as well as the South by depriving Northern businesses of Southern markets. This was such a large loss that, overall, the war erased at least five years of wealth accumulation nationwide.[3]

An even larger hidden cost, however, is all the foregone contributions to society that all those men (and their never-to-be-born offspring) would have made had they lived. Such things are incalculable.

Lincoln was victorious in the sense that he achieved what he always proclaimed to be his primary objective: Federalism and states' rights were destroyed. As we saw in earlier chapters, Thomas Jefferson was perhaps the most articulate defender of states' rights, followed by Andrew Jackson and John C. Calhoun. American political history since the founding had been divided into two great camps: the Hamiltonians, who favored a highly centralized state, and the Jeffersonians, who favored a highly decentralized and limited government constrained by state sovereignty. Beginning in the 1820s the debate over Hamiltonianism versus Jeffersonianism manifested itself in the economic debate over the American System. No one played a more outspoken role in that debate than Abraham Lincoln did for more than thirty years.

States' rights was an integral part of the federal system created by the founding fathers. The Hamiltonians, politically reincarnated as the Republican party of Abraham Lincoln, finally won this argument by force of arms during the War between the States. After decades of political failure, the Whig/Republican political coalition finally imposed its mercantilist American System on the country, literally at gunpoint.

Modern historians who are the intellectual descendants of the Hamiltonians continue to besmirch the Jeffersonian philosophy of states' rights. An especially specious example of this is a recent book edited by Gary W. Gallagher and Alan T. Nolan titled *The Myth of the Lost Cause and Civil War History*.[4] The book's premise is that the doctrine of states' rights had no real history but was fabricated after the war by disgruntled former Confederates to rationalize the secession of 1861.[5] In the first chapter Alan T. Nolan asserts that the issue of the right of secession as a cause of the war is a "legend" fabricated by former Confederates in order to "foster a heroic image" of themselves and the war.[6] The only "evidence" he offers of this, however, is a few quotations from Lincoln! (He doesn't even bother to mention Daniel Webster's—and Lincoln's—false notion that the federal government created the states, not vice versa.) Nolan does this so that he can offer what he calls the "real" history of the war, in which he claims that slavery was its sole cause. He ignores the fact that Lincoln never said that he was launching an invasion of the Southern states over the issue of slavery. Wars are always extraordinarily complicated events, and it is indeed odd for a historian to claim that this particular war, unlike virtually all others in history, had one and only one cause.

In the concluding chapter Lloyd A. Hunter claims that "mythmakers in gray" also fabricated another supposed falsehood—that the "Constitution of 1787 had been a compact among equally sovereign states."[7] Of course, the Constitution was in fact a compact among the thirteen sovereign states, as discussed in earlier chapters, several of which explicitly reserved their sovereign right to withdraw from the compact should the federal government become destructive of their liberties. Hunter dismisses this actual history as just another "myth" because of his desire to proclaim that there was never any such thing as a right of secession.

Gallagher and his eight co-authors all falsely maintain that the doctrine of states' rights was created out of thin air after the war by the likes of former Confederate General Jubal Early.[8] They accuse those who give credence to the states' rights view of "leaving truth behind" in a manner that "distorts our national memory."[9]

There may never have been a clearer example of the pot calling the kettle black. It is those who deny that states' rights and federalism had anything to do with the War between the States who are spreading untruths and distorting history. In 1999 the historian Forrest McDonald, who is one of the preeminent American historians of the Constitution, published a new book titled *States' Rights and the Union,* which catalogues the history of the states' rights doctrine from 1776 to 1876.[10] McDonald was named by the National Endowment for the Humanities as the sixteenth Jefferson Lecturer, the nation's highest honor in the humanities. If Gallagher and his co-authors have never heard of Forrest McDonald and are unfamiliar with his work, that would speak volumes about the shoddy scholarship that must have gone into their own book on "The Lost Cause." The notion that the doctrine of states' rights was invented out of thin air by disgruntled former Confederate soldiers should not be taken seriously.

Lincoln and the Republicans certainly had a cause: the cause of centralized government and the pursuit of empire. They said it over and over again; and then when they emerged victorious in the war, they continued to say it (and to implement the American System). They waged a war to see to it that *their* cause prevailed over the opposing cause of limited constitutional government—limited primarily by the sovereignty of the states. The cause of federalism and states' rights was lost, but it was in no way a myth. It was always an integral part of the federal system of government that was created by the founding fathers. The states' rights tradition has a long history and did not originate in the mind of a worn-out and elderly General Jubal Early.

THE DEATH OF FEDERALISM

PERHAPS THE biggest cost of Lincoln's war was the virtual destruction of states' rights, but the significance of this seems lost on most Americans. The loss of states' rights is important because it meant that the people, as citizens of their respective states, would no longer be sovereign; the federal government would be. The federal government became the master, rather than the servant, of the people—especially once it imposed military conscription and income taxation on the population.

Jefferson understood that the most important safeguard of the liberties of the people was "the support of the state governments in all their rights, as the most competent administrations for our domestic concerns and the surest bulwarks against anti-republican tendencies."[11] A generation later, John C. Calhoun clearly stated the value of states' rights to the preservation of liberty: "We contend, that the great conservative principle of our system is in the people of the States, as parties to the Constitutional compact, and our opponents that it is in the supreme court. . . . Without a full practical recognition of the rights and sovereignty of the States, our union and liberty must perish."[12]

States' rights is a universally acknowledged check on the arbitrary powers of the central state. It is not just a doctrine unique to the American South. Intellectual historian and constitutional scholar Forrest McDonald noted the universal appeal of states' rights and federalism when he wrote that

> Political scientists and historians are in agreement that federalism is the greatest contribution of the Founding Fathers to the science of government. It is also the only feature of the Constitution that has been successfully exported, that can be employed to protect liberty elsewhere in the world. Yet what we invented, and others imitate, no longer exists on its native shores.[13]

It no longer exists because it was destroyed by Lincoln's war. That such a distinguished scholar as Forrest McDonald would point out the importance of states' rights and federalism to the founding generation—and to much of the world—gives the lie to the work of such historians as Gary Gallagher who seem intent on promoting the preposterous myth that states' rights is something that was invented after the war by the defeated Confederates.

University of South Carolina historian Clyde Wilson has clearly explained just why it is that the founding fathers believed that states' rights were the "last best bulwark" of constitutional liberty. It is a question, says Wilson, of the sovereignty of the people.[14] Every political community must have a sovereign or a final authority. The sovereign may not rule over the people on a day-by-day basis, but it is the point of final authority on political matters.

In the United States, the people are said to be sovereign, but what people? How? As Professor Wilson explains,

> In American terms, the government of the people can only mean the people of the states as living, historical, corporate, indestructible, political communities. The whole of the Constitution rests upon its acceptance by the people acting through their states. The whole of the government reflects this by the representation of the states in every legitimate proceeding. There is no place in the Constitution as originally understood where a mere numerical majority in some branch of the government can do as it pleases. The sovereign power resides, ultimately, in the people of the states. Even today, three-fourths of the states can amend the Constitution. . . . In no other way can we say the sovereign people have spoken. . . . States' rights *is* the American government, however much in abeyance its practice may have become.[15]

The only real alternative, as John C. Calhoun pointed out, is to hand over sovereignty to the "black-robed deities of the Court" who disappear into their chambers and then tell us what orders we must obey, no matter how nonsensical or unpopular they may be. This, of course, is exactly the course that the American government has taken ever since 1865.

James Madison said that the meaning of the Constitution was to be sought "not in the opinions or intentions of the body which planned and proposed it, but in those of the state conventions where it received *all the authority which it possesses*" (emphasis added).[16] The father of the Constitution believed that the document gained *all* of its authority from the sovereign states and nothing else.

The federal government will never check its own power. That is the whole reason for federalism and the reason the founding fathers adopted a federal system of government. There is no check at all on the federal government unless state sovereignty exists, and state sovereignty is itself meaningless without the right of secession. Thus Lincoln's war, by destroying the right of secession, also destroyed the last check on the potentially tyrannical powers of the central state.

The great historian of liberty, Lord Acton, understood this. Lord Acton was a dominant intellectual force in Victorian England and viewed the South's defeat, conquest, and subsequent military occupation as a severe blow to the cause of liberty throughout the world, not just in the United States. Like most other British opinion makers, he did not believe the war was fought over slavery. On November 4, 1866, he wrote to General Robert E. Lee:

> I saw in States' rights the only availing check upon the absolutism of the sovereign will, and secession filled me with hope, not as the destruction but as the redemption of Democracy. The institutions of your Republic have not exercised on the old world the salutary and liberating influence which ought to have belonged to them, by reason of those defects and abuses of principle which the Confederate Constitution was expressly and wisely calculated to remedy. I believed that the example of that great Reform would have blessed all the races of mankind by establishing true freedom purged of the native dangers and disorders of Republics.

Therefore I deemed that you were fighting the battles of our liberty, our progress, and our civilization; and I mourn for the stake which was lost at Richmond more deeply than I rejoice over that which was saved at Waterloo.[17]

General Lee responded quite presciently to Lord Acton, writing on December 15, 1866:

While I have considered the preservation of the constitutional power of the General Government to be the foundation of our peace and safety at home and abroad, I yet believe that the maintenance of the rights and authority reserved to the states and to the people, not only are essential to the adjustment and balance of the general system, but the safeguard to the continuance of a free government. I consider it as the chief source of stability to our political system, whereas the consolidation of the states into one vast republic, sure to be aggressive abroad and despotic at home, will be the certain precursor of that ruin which has overwhelmed all those that have preceded it.[18]

The death of states' rights ultimately meant that Americans were forced to effectively give up the idea of government by consent. In its place was put the European idea that citizens owe obedience to the central state—the very idea that caused many of the original colonists to flee England in the first place.

It could not have been a mere accident or oversight that, in his Gettysburg Address, Lincoln quoted the dictum in the Declaration of Independence that all men are created equal but completely ignored the part about how governments derive their just powers from the consent of the governed and that whenever governments become destructive of liberty, it is the *duty* of the citizens to replace the existing government. The Federal victory in the war did irreparable damage to the concept that the powers of the American government are derived from the consent of the governed. As the founders understood it, consent of the governed had little meaning in the absence of state sovereignty and the right of secession.

Far from "saving the Union," Lincoln *destroyed* it in a philosophical sense, if by "Union" one means a *voluntary* confederation of states. Forcing a state (or states) to remain in the Union at gunpoint defeats the whole purpose of having a union in the first place. Horace Greeley once said that he wished to never live in a republic whereby one section is "pinned to the residue by bayonets." His wish did not come true.

The nineteenth century was the century of empire, and Lincoln transformed the American government from a constitutional republic to a consolidated empire, as General Lee observed. It became more and more despotic at home and adventurous abroad, just as Lee predicted in his letter to Lord Acton. As we saw in chapter 7, as soon as the war ended General Grant planned an invasion of Mexico and the government began agitating England—demanding reparations for its having traded with the South during the war.

President Grant proposed annexing Santo Domingo, and a campaign of ethnic genocide was waged against the Plains Indians by the U.S. army under the direction of Generals Sherman, Sheridan, and Custer. This "campaign" was waged for the benefit of the railroad industry. There was

much talk of extending "the American empire" all the way
to China.

The Lincolnian spirit of conquest, subjugation, and
imperialism was evident when the army, under the direction of William McKinley (a major in Lincoln's army during the War between the States) took over the Philippines
in the late nineteenth century, resulting in the slaughter of
some three thousand Filipinos. This occupation was a consequence of the Spanish-American War, instigated by the
United States government, after which Spain ceded to the
United States ownership of Puerto Rico, Guam, and the
Philippine Islands, thus allowing the government to consolidate its empire in the Western hemisphere and establish a stepping-stone to the Chinese markets (such as they
were) at last.

Theodore Roosevelt and Woodrow Wilson would invoke Lincoln's name as they unabashedly advocated wars
of empire and "righteousness." Thus, American foreign
policy was also overturned by the precedents Lincoln established—moving from one that sought to defend American
liberty to one that sought empire and constant meddling in
other countries' affairs. George Washington, who believed
that the American government should encourage commercial relationships with all nations but avoid any and all
"entangling alliances" would be shocked and appalled to
learn that that the U.S. government is now commonly referred to as "the world's policeman."

The death of federalism resulted in the federal judiciary
becoming the final arbiter of constitutional interpretation.
Judicial review already existed, of course, but until 1865
there was an ongoing debate over who would be the final

arbiters over what was and was not constitutional—the citizens of the sovereign states or the federal judiciary. Lincoln's war ended that debate. This was Jefferson's greatest fear, and for good reason. Lincoln's crackdown on constitutional liberties in the North during the War between the States established further precedents that would be taken advantage of by political demagogues who had little respect for constitutional liberty. Right up to the present day, the advocates of ever-greater governmental powers (and correspondingly smaller degrees of liberty) continue to invoke the name of Lincoln. As discussed in chapter 5, historian Garry Wills and Columbia University law professor George Fletcher have recently written books celebrating the fact that Lincoln's disregard for constitutional liberties opened the door to the whole array of unconstitutional government interventions that form the modern Leviathan state Americans labor under today.

So-called economic nationalists (largely a euphemism for "protectionists") such as Patrick J. Buchanan and Michael Lind praise Lincoln precisely because he successfully destroyed the founding fathers' federal Constitution and put America on the road to empire. Lind denounces the "cult of Thomas Jefferson" and its advocacy of a limited federal government, while praising Lincoln and FDR as "great American statesmen."[19]

In his book, *Takings*, University of Chicago law professor Richard Epstein bemoaned the fact that virtually all New Deal legislation, which we still live with, was strictly unconstitutional according to his interpretation of the Constitution.[20] Wills and Fletcher might agree with Epstein on the constitutionality issue, but *praise* the outcome and give the ultimate credit to Lincoln and the precedents that he established. They do so because they want the purpose of American government to be the pursuit of "egalitarianism" (i.e., socialism), not the defense of liberty.

WHAT IF THE SOUTH HAD BEEN ALLOWED TO LEAVE IN PEACE?

LINCOLN'S ADMONITION that secession would lead to "anarchy" and "destroy" democratic government was pure sophistry. Had the South been permitted to go in peace, as was the wish of the majority of Northern opinion makers before Fort Sumter according to historian Joseph Perkins, democracy would have continued to thrive in the two nations. Moreover, the act of secession would have had exactly the effect the founding fathers expected it to have; it would have tempered the imperialistic proclivities of the central state. The federal government would have been forced to moderate its high-tariff policies and to slow down or abandon its quest for empire. Commercial relationships with the South would have been continued and expanded. After a number of years, the same reasons that led the colonists to form a Union in the first place would likely have become more appealing to both sections, and the Union would probably have been reunited.

After that, knowing that secession was a real threat, the federal government would have stuck closer to its constitutional bearings. The mere *threat* of peaceful secession would have had that effect on it. Its imperialistic tendencies, and the large tax increases necessary to finance such adventures, would have been checked. We may never have had a Spanish-American War. We may also have never had a president like Woodrow Wilson, who was so eager to involve Americans in a foreign war. Economist Hans-Hermann Hoppe argues in a recent book that if America had not intervened in World War I, the European monarchies would have eventually worked out a peace agreement that was not so punishing on Germany, and that may have even precluded the rise of the Nazi Party, which itself was partly a reaction to the Versailles treaty of World War I.[21]

The Confederate Constitution explicitly outlawed protectionist tariffs and internal improvement subsidies and eliminated the general welfare clause of the U.S. Constitution. It had always been the contention of Jefferson, Madison, and others that the U.S. Constitution did not provide for any of these things, either. But the Whig Party and, later, the Republican Party, began slowly violating the Constitution, as these Southerners saw it, by getting legislation passed that imposed discriminatory tariffs, in violation of the clause in the Constitution that calls for uniform taxation, and spending on internal improvement and other programs that they believed were not provided for in the Constitution as it was then written. That's why the Confederate government was so explicit about these items in its own constitution. This would have made for a much smaller government with a traditionally minimal role in economic policy affairs, and that would have been more conducive to economic growth than the Northern mercantilist state. The elimination of the general welfare clause was momentous, for thousands of special-interest expenditure items have been inserted into the federal budget over the years under the most specious and bizarre reasoning with regard to how they supposedly serve the "general welfare." This would have been avoided with the Confederate Constitution.

The Confederate Constitution also required a two-thirds majority vote for all congressional appropriations; gave the president (who was limited to one six-year term) a line-item veto; and allowed for the impeachment of federal officials by state legislatures as well as the House of Representatives. These things would also have helped in keeping the federal government of the Southern states in check.

With a smaller and more efficient government just to its south, with its thriving free-trade ports and no cumbersome federal bureaucracy meddling in every industry's affairs, the U.S. government would have been forced to compete by sticking closer to the original intent of the U.S. Constitution as designed by the founding fathers. The Leviathan state would have been indefinitely delayed, if it came into creation at all, especially if involvement in World War I could have been avoided.

Lincoln theorized that allowing the Southern states to secede might cause a rash of copycat secessions. But this never happened, either in the United States or anywhere else. Even if it had, it would have been beneficial for the same reasons just described. Multiple secessions (by the California republic, for example) would have exerted even greater (and much needed) competitive pressures on the central state and forced it to comply more with the will of the people and the letter of the Constitution.

SLAVERY

THE ONE unequivocal good that came of Lincoln's war was the abolition of slavery. But the way in which Lincoln chose to end slavery could not possibly have been more divisive. During the nineteenth century dozens of countries throughout the world, including the British Empire, ended slavery peacefully through compensated emancipation. The United States was the only country that made slavery an issue of war (eighteen months into the war) between 1800 and 1863. In light of the almost unfathomable costs of the war, an important question becomes, Why didn't America do what every other nation on earth did with regard to slavery during the first sixty years of the nineteenth century and end it peacefully?

We may never know the answer to this question, but the monetary costs of the war alone would have been enough to purchase the freedom of every last Southern slave (and give each 40 acres and a mule). Lincoln failed to use his legendary political skills to achieve compensated emancipation. He did attempt, however, to colonize all of the freed blacks in Haiti, Africa, and elsewhere. His plans were spoiled because the man he appointed to spearhead his colonization program made off with much of the money Congress had appropriated for it.

The large majority of Northerners feared emancipation because it might have meant that the freed blacks would have come to live among them. This is an ugly fact but a fact nonetheless. Even after emancipation, the Republican Party during Reconstruction did all it could to keep the ex-slaves in the South (by making false promises of giving them land, giving them political patronage jobs, electing them to local political office, and so on). They were not welcomed in the North, which is likely the reason they were never given the land they were promised under the Homestead Act. That would have required many of the ex-slaves to immediately settle in the Northern states.

The *political* support for slavery was breaking down by 1860 thanks to the Enlightenment philosophy of freedom and the increasing recognition by more and more Americans that that philosophy, which they professed to believe in, was profoundly contradicted by the existence of slavery. Support for the Fugitive Slave Law was waning, as was support for myriad state and local laws, such as the prohibition of manumission, that artificially propped up slavery. Indeed, one of the chief complaints of the states of the deep South was about what they perceived as insufficiently strong enforcement of the Fugitive Slave Law in the North.

Slavery was already in sharp decline in the border states, which made it less costly for runaway slaves to escape (they didn't have as far to go). The underground railroad was thriving and would have gained more and more support. These things were all increasing the costs of owning slaves, which is another way of saying that slavery was becoming less profitable and was on its way out.

State legislatures would probably have ended slavery in the border states altogether before long, which would have made it even easier for slaves in the Southern states to escape. This in fact is how slavery ended in Brazil and many other countries—province by province. As slavery ended in the northern provinces it made it easier for slaves to escape as freedom moved south.

The advance of the industrial revolution in the South would have also made slavery more and more uneconomical compared to capital-intensive agriculture and manufacturing, as it had in the North several decades earlier. All of these things combined—the power of the Enlightenment philosophy in the American mind, the waning support for laws that artificially propped up slavery, the fact that slave labor is inherently less productive than free labor, and the increasing cost of maintaining and policing the slave system in general—would probably have led to the institution's demise long before the end of the century.

If this had happened, race relations in the South would not have been so irreparably poisoned as they were during Reconstruction. If the Republican Party had not used the ex-slaves as political pawns in the South and turned them against the whites, acts of violence against the ex-slaves and the institution of Jim Crow laws might never have happened. The ex-slaves would then have been able to economically integrate into Southern society more quickly; and once economic integration took place, social integration would have been that much easier. Peaceful separation in 1861 may well have resulted in black Americans receiving justice (in addition to freedom) much sooner while preserving more of the freedoms of *all* Americans.

Even some prominent Northern abolitionists were harshly critical of how Lincoln and the Republicans used the slavery issue to disguise their ulterior motives. One such critic was the Massachusetts abolitionist and legal scholar

Lysander Spooner. Spooner's entire family had been abolitionists for years when, in 1845, he wrote *The Unconstitu-
tionality of Slavery,* a book that won him the everlasting
esteem of the abolitionists. In 1849 the Liberty Party
passed a resolution honoring Spooner for publishing "a
perfectly conclusive legal argument against the constitutionality of slavery" and recommended that every lawyer in
Massachusetts be given a copy of it.[22]

Spooner was also an articulate opponent of the Fugitive
Slave Act and the author of *A Defence for Fugitive Slaves*
(1850), which was meant to assist in the legal defense of
runaway slaves. He was also an early advocate of jury nullification in the case of enforcement of the Fugitive Slave
Act. Should a jury find the act to be unjust, he advised, it
had a perfect right to nullify it and grant the runaway slave
his freedom.

Nevertheless, after witnessing the behavior of Lincoln
and the Republicans during the war and for the first five
years of Reconstruction, Spooner wrote that

> All these cries of having "abolished slavery," of having "saved
> the country," of having "preserved the union," of establishing
> a "government of consent," and of "maintaining the national
> honor" are all gross, shameless, transparent cheats—so trans-
> parent that they ought to deceive no one.[23]

Spooner's natural rights arguments were popular and
influential in New England prior to the war, but were soon
to be drowned out by supporters of the growing American
empire. Ironically, they were discredited for having been,
essentially, the same arguments for limited government that
were made by the Southern secessionists. The federalized

education system made sure that such arguments would all be eliminated from the American educational system for generations to come.

Despite an unspeakably bloody war, the demolition of constitutional liberties, and the conquest and subjugation of the South for twelve years after the war, Lincoln and his party still failed to completely destroy federalism and states' rights. Because the ideas were so ingrained in the American psyche, something of a revolt against centralized governmental authority occurred in the postwar years, personified by the presidency of Grover Cleveland, who vetoed the income tax and dozens of tariff bills. This temporarily slowed down the march toward the centralized, militaristic state that the founding fathers feared, but not for long. Lincoln's war had let the genie of centralization out of the bottle, never to be returned.

NOTES

CHAPTER 1

1. David Donald, *Lincoln Reconsidered* (New York: Vintage Books, 1961).

2. Richard Bensel, *Yankee Leviathan: The Origins of Central State Authority in America, 1859–1877* (Cambridge: Cambridge University Press, 1990).

3. Roy P. Basler, ed., *Abraham Lincoln: His Speeches and Writings* (New York: Da Capo Press, 1946).

CHAPTER 2

1. David Donald, *Lincoln* (New York: Simon and Schuster, 1996), p. 66.

2. Essay by William H. Herndon, in *The Lincoln Reader,* ed. Paul M. Angle (New York: Da Capo Press, 1947), p. 83.

3. Ibid., p. 65.

4. Murray Rothbard, "America's Two Just Wars: 1776 and 1861," in *The Costs of War: America's Pyrrhic Victories,* ed. John Denson (New Brunswick, N.J.: Transaction, 1997), p. 131.

5. Harry V. Jaffa, *A New Birth of Freedom* (New York: Roman and Littlefield, 2000).

6. Abraham Lincoln, "Lincoln's Reply to Douglas, Ottawa, Illinois, Aug. 21, 1858," in *Abraham Lincoln: His Speeches and Writings,* ed. Roy P. Basler (New York: Da Capo Press, 1990), p. 445.

7. Lincoln, "First Debate at Ottawa, Illinois, Aug. 21, 1858," in *The Collected Works of Abraham Lincoln,* ed. Roy Basler (New Brunswick, N.J.: Rutgers University Press, 1953), pp. 145–146.

8. Lincoln, "Lincoln's Reply to Douglas," p. 444.

9. Lerone Bennett, Jr., *Forced into Glory: Abraham Lincoln's White Dream* (Chicago: Johnson Publishing Co., 2000), p. 132.

10. Abraham Lincoln's Reply to Stephan Douglas, First Debate at Ottawa, Illinois, August 21, 1858, in *Abraham Lincoln: His Speeches and Writings*, ed. Roy P. Basler (New York: Da Capo Press, 1990), p. 444.

11. Ibid.

12. Ibid., p. 442.

13. Lincoln, "First Debate" p. 460.

14. Lincoln, "Eulogy on Henry Clay," delivered in the State House at Springfield, Illinois, July 6, 1852, in *Abraham Lincoln: His Speeches and Writings*, ed. Roy P. Basler (New York: Da Capo Press, 1990), p. 264.

15. Ibid., p. 265.

16. Robert W. Johannsen, *Lincoln, the South, and Slavery* (Baton Rouge: Louisiana State University Press, 1991), p. 21.

17. Lincoln, "Speech at Carlinville, Illinois, Aug. 31, 1858," in *The Collected Works of Abraham Lincoln,* vol. 3, ed. Roy Basler (New Brunswick, N.J.: Rutgers University Press, 1953), p. 79.

18. Johannsen, p. 22.

19. Lincoln, "Eulogy on Henry Clay," p. 274.

20. Ibid.

21. Ibid., pp. 274–275.

22. Webb Garrison, *The Lincoln No One Knows* (Nashville, Tenn.: Rutledge Hill Press, 1993), p. 48.

23. Ibid., p. 36.

24. Basler, *Collected Works,* p. 23.

25. Ibid., pp. 255–256.

26. Ibid., pp. 370–375.

27. Lincoln, "Eulogy on Henry Clay," p. 276.

28. Ibid., p. 277.

29. Ibid.

30. Ibid.

31. Lincoln, "Annual Message to Congress, Dec. 1, 1862," in *The Collected Works of Abraham Lincoln,* ed. Roy Basler (New Brunswick, N.J.: Rutgers University Press, 1953), p. 685.

32. Lincoln, "Eulogy on Henry Clay," p. 277.

33. Lincoln, "Address at Cooper Institute, New York, Feb. 27, 1860," in *The Collected Works of Abraham Lincoln,* ed. Roy Basler (New Brunswick, N.J.: Rutgers University Press, 1953), p. 541.

34. Eugene Berwanger, *The Frontier against Slavery* (Urbana: University of Illinois Press, 1967), p. 5.

35. P. J. Staudenraus, *The African Colonization Movement, 1816–1865* (New York: Octagon Books, 1980), p. 246.

36. Ibid.

37. Ibid., p. 247.

38. Ibid., p. 248.

39. Henry Mayer, *William Lloyd Garrison and the Abolition of Slavery* (New York: St. Martin's Press, 1998), p. 531.

40. Ibid., p. 538.

41. Gabor Boritt, "Did He Dream of a Lily-White America? The Voyage to Linconia," in *The Lincoln Enigma,* ed. Gabor Boritt (New York: Oxford University Press, 2000), p. 5.

42. Ibid., p. 7.

43. Ibid., pp. 7–16.

44. Lincoln, "First Inaugural Address," in *The Collected Works of Abraham Lincoln,* ed. Roy Basler (New Brunswick, N.J.: Rutgers University Press, 1953), p. 580.

45. Lincoln, "Speech at Peoria, Illinois, in Reply to Senator Douglas, Oct. 16, 1854," in *Abraham Lincoln: His Speeches and*

Writings, ed. Roy P. Basler (New York: Da Capo Press, 1990), p. 306.

46. James McPherson, *The Struggle for Equality: Abolitionists and the Negro in the Civil War and Reconstruction* (Princeton, N.J.: Princeton University Press, 1966), p. 24.

47. Horace Greeley, Editorial, *New York Tribune,* 17 December 1860.

48. Berwanger, p. 133.

49. Ibid., p. 134.

50. Ibid.

51. Ibid., p. 137.

52. Leon Litwack, *North of Slavery: The Negro in the Free States, 1790–1860* (Chicago: University of Chicago Press, 1961), p. 47.

53. Basler, *Abraham Lincoln,* p. 307.

54. William A. DeGregorio, *The Complete Book of U.S. Presidents* (New York: Wings Books, 1996), p. 238.

55. Berwanger, p. 97.

56. Alexis de Tocqueville, *Democracy in America* (New York: Macmillan, 1945), p. 359.

57. *Congressional Globe* 36, no. 1 (2 May 1860): 1903, cited in Richard Bensel, *Yankee Leviathan* (New York: Cambridge University Press, 1990), p. 22.

58. Litwack, p. 70.

59. Ibid.

60. C. Vann Woodward, *The Strange Career of Jim Crow* (New York: Oxford University Press, 1974), p. 20.

61. Litwack, p. 79.

62. Ibid., p. 71.

63. Leonard P. Curry, *Blueprint for Modern America: Nonmilitary Legislation of the First Civil War Congress* (Nashville, Tenn.: Vanderbilt University Press, 1968), p. 79.

64. Litwack, p. 277.

65. Ibid., p. 91.

66. Ibid., p. 161.

67. Howard Cecil Perkins, *Northern Editorials on Secession* (Gloucester, Mass.: Peter Smith, 1964), p. 425.

68. Ibid., p. 499.

69. Ibid., p. 431.

70. Ibid., p. 438.

71. Ibid., p. 441.

72. Ibid., p. 454.

73. Ibid., p. 455.

74. Ibid., p. 456.

75. Ibid., p. 469.

76. Ibid., p. 472.

CHAPTER 3

1. James G. Randall and David H. Donald, *The Civil War and Reconstruction* (Lexington, Mass.: D.C. Heath, 1969), p. 371.

2. Ibid., p. 372.

3. James McPherson, *For Cause and Comrades: Why Men Fought the Civil War* (New York: Oxford University Press, 1997), p. 119.

4. Allan Nevins, *Ordeal of the Union, vol. 3, The Improvised War* (New York: Macmillan, 1959), p. 340.

5. Abraham Lincoln, "Letter to Horace Greeley, August 22, 1862," in *Abraham Lincoln: His Speeches and Writings,* ed. Roy Basler (New York: Da Capo Press, 1946), p. 652.

6. James G. Randall and David H. Donald, *The Civil War and Reconstruction* (Lexington, Mass.: D.C. Heath, 1969), p. 371.

7. "The Emancipation Proclamation," in *The Harvard Classics, vol. 43, American Historical Documents,* ed. Charles Eliot (New York: P. F. Collier, 1910), p. 324.

8. Editorial, *New York World,* 7 January 1863.

9. Ibid.

10. Randall and Donald, p. 381.

11. Ibid.

12. Ibid.

13. Ibid.

14. Paul M. Angle, ed. *The American Reader* (New Brunswick, N.J.: Rutgers University Press, 1947), p. 407.

15. Ibid.

16. James I. Robertson, Jr., *Stonewall Jackson* (New York: Macmillan, 1997), p. 268.

17. Ibid., p. 269.

18. Ibid.

19. Shelby Foote, *The Civil War,* vol. 1, *Fort Sumter to Perryville* (New York: Vintage Books, 1986), p. 350.

20. Robertson, xiii.

21. Ibid., p. 516.

22. Randall and Donald, p. 225.

23. Sheldon Vanauken, *The Glittering Illusion: English Sympathy for the Southern Confederacy* (Washington, D.C.: Regnery/Gateway, 1989), p. 67.

24. Iver Bernstein, *The New York City Draft Riots* (New York: Oxford University Press, 1990).

25. Arthur J. L. Fremantle, *Three Months in the Southern States: April–June 1863* (Lincoln: University of Nebraska Press, 1991), p. 302.

26. Ibid., p. 300.

27. Bernstein, p. 13.

28. Ibid., p. 21.

29. Ibid.

30. Gary Gallagher, *The Confederate War* (Cambridge, Mass.: Harvard University Press, 1997), p. 67.

31. James McPherson, *What They Fought For: 1861–1865* (Baton Rouge: Louisiana State University Press, 1994), p. 63.

32. McPherson, *For Cause and Comrades,* p. 120.

33. Ibid., pp. 122–124.

34. Ludwig von Mises, *Human Action: A Treatise on Economics* (Auburn, Ala.: Mises Institute, 1998), p. 625.

35. Ibid., pp. 624–630.

36. Robert Fogel and Stanley Engerman, *Time on the Cross: The Economics of American Negro Slavery* (New York: Norton, 1974), p. 34.

37. Ibid., pp. 35–36.

38. Ibid., p. 36.

39. Ibid.

40. Claudia Goldin and Frank Lewis, "The Economic Cost of the American Civil War: Estimates and Implications," *Journal of Economic History,* June 1975, pp. 299–322.

41. Jeffrey Rogers Hummel, *Emancipating Slaves, Enslaving Free Men* (Chicago: Open Court, 1996), p. 353.

CHAPTER 4

1. Roy P. Basler, ed., *Abraham Lincoln: His Speeches and Writings* (New York: Da Capo Press, 1946), p. 23.

2. Michael F. Holt, *The Rise and Fall of the American Whig Party* (New York: Oxford University Press, 1999), p. 288.

3. David Donald, *Lincoln* (New York: Simon and Schuster, 1996), p. 94.

4. Ibid., p. 18.

5. Robert W. Johannsen, *Lincoln, the South, and Slavery: The Political Dimension* (Baton Rouge: Louisiana State University Press, 1991), p. 14.

6. Ibid., p. 45.

7. Ibid., p. 81.

8. Ibid., p. 92.

9. Murray N. Rothbard, *The Logic of Action II* (Cheltenham, England: Edward Elgar, 1997), p. 43.

10. Edgar Lee Masters, *Lincoln the Man* (Columbia, S.C.: Foundation for American Education, 1997), p. 27.

11. James McPherson, *Abraham Lincoln and the Second American Revolution* (New York: Oxford University Press, 1991), p. 40.

12. Adam Smith, *An Inquiry into the Nature and Causes of the Wealth of Nations* (Indianapolis: Liberty Classics, 1776/1981).

13. Gabor Boritt, "Lincoln and the Economics of the American Dream," in *The Historian's Lincoln,* ed. Gabor Boritt (Urbana: University of Illinois Press, 1996), pp. 87–106.

14. McPherson, p. 40.

15. Maurice Baxter, *Henry Clay and the American System* (Lexington: University Press of Kentucky, 1995), p. 209.

16. David Osterfeld, *Planning versus Prosperity* (New York: Oxford University Press, 1991).

17. John Taylor, *Tyranny Unmasked* (Indianapolis: Liberty Fund, 1992), p. xvi.

18. Robert V. Remini, *Henry Clay: Statesman for the Union* (New York: Norton, 1991), p. 226.

19. Ibid.

20. Ibid., p. 232.

21. Baxter, p. 75.

22. Robert V. Remini, *Andrew Jackson* (New York: Harper and Row, 1966), p. 141.

23. Ibid., p. 142.

24. Ibid., p. 144.

25. Ibid.

26. Ibid., p. 145.

27. Oliver Chitwood, *John Tyler: Champion of the Old South* (New York: Russell and Russell, 1964), p. 184.

28. Ibid., pp. 226–227.

29. Remini, *Henry Clay,* p. 314.

30. Roy P. Basler, ed., *Abraham Lincoln: His Speeches and Writings* (New York: Da Capo Press, 1990), p. 90.

31. Ibid., p. 233.

32. Ibid., p. 352.

33. Donald, *Lincoln,* p. 77.

34. Ibid.

35. Joseph Dorfman, *The Economic Mind in American Civilization, 1606–1865* (New York: Viking Press, 1946), p. 384.

36. Abraham Lincoln, "Fragments on the Tariff," in *Abraham Lincoln: Speeches and Writings, 1832–1858* (New York: Library of America, 1989), p. 149.

37. Ibid., p. 153.

38. Ibid., p. 156.

39. Richard Bensel, *Yankee Leviathan* (New York: Cambridge University Press, 1990), p. 73.

40. Lincoln, *Speeches and Writings,* p. 1.

41. Ibid., p. 188.

42. Paul M. Angle, ed., *The Lincoln Reader* (New York: Da Capo Press, 1947), p. 82.

43. Ibid., pp. 100–101.

44. Ibid., p. 83.

45. Ibid., p. 102.

46. William H. Herndon and Jesse W. Weik, *Life of Lincoln* (New York: Da Capo Press, 1983), p. 161.

47. John Bach McMaster, *A History of the People of the United States* (New York: D. Appleton, 1914), p. 628.

48. Angle, p. 65.

49. F. Thornton Miller, "Foreword," in John Taylor, *Tyranny Unmasked* (Indianapolis: Liberty Fund, 1992), p. xvi.

50. Taylor, p. 11.

51. Alexander Hamilton, "The Report on Manufactures," in *Hamilton's Republic,* ed. Michael Lind (New York: Free Press, 1997), p. 31.

52. Carter Goodrich, *Government Promotion of American Canals and Railroads, 1800–1890* (Westport, Conn.: Greenwood Press, 1960), p. 19.

53. John Quincy Adams, "Letter to Charles W. Upham, 2 February 1837," in *John Quincy Adams and American Continental Empire,* ed. Walter Lafeber (Chicago: Quadrangle Books, 1965), pp. 146–147.

54. Ibid.

55. Ibid.

56. Cited in Robert Rutland, *The Presidency of James Madison* (Lawrence: University Press of Kansas, 1990), p. 205.

57. Andrew Jackson, "Farewell Address of Andrew Jackson," in *Social Theories of Jacksonian Democracy,* ed. Joseph L. Blau (New York: Hafner, 1947), p. 305.

58. Daniel B. Klein, "The Voluntary Provision of Public Goods? The Turnpike Companies of Early America," *Economic Inquiry,* October 1990, pp. 788–812.

59. Goodrich, p. 138.

60. Ibid., p. 139.

61. Ibid., p. 231.

62. Ibid., p. 182.

63. Marshall DeRosa, *The Confederate Constitution of 1861: An Inquiry into American Constitutionalism* (Columbia: University of Missouri Press, 1991), p. 94.

CHAPTER 5

1. Thomas Jefferson, "First Inaugural Address," in *Thomas Jefferson: Writings,* ed. Merrill D. Peterson (New York: Library of America, 1984), p. 493.

2. Thomas Jefferson, "Letter to James Madison, January 30, 1787," in *Thomas Jefferson: Writings,* ed. Merrill D. Peterson (New York: Library of America, 1984), p. 882.

3. Thomas Jefferson, "Letter to W. Crawford, June 20, 1816," in *The Writings of Thomas Jefferson,* vol. 15, ed. Albert Bergh (Washington, D.C.: Thomas Jefferson Memorial Association of the United States, 1905), p. 27.

4. Thomas Jefferson, "Draft Declaration and Protest of the Commonwealth of Virginia, on the Principles of the Constitution of the United States of America, and on the Violations of Them," December 1825, in *Thomas Jefferson: Writings,* ed. Merrill D. Peterson (New York: Library of America, 1984), p. 484.

5. John Quincy Adams, *The Jubilee of the Constitution* (New York: Samuel Coleman, 1839), pp. 66–69.

6. Alexis de Tocqueville, *Democracy in America* (New Rochelle, N.Y.: Arlington House, 1945), p. 381.

7. *The Federalist Papers,* number 81.

8. James McClellan and Mel Bradford, eds., *Jonathan Elliot's Debates in the Several State Conventions on the Adoption of the Federal Constitution* (Richmond, Va.: J. River Press, 1989), p. 232.

9. Ibid., p. 389.

10. John Curtis, *Life of Webster* (New York: Macmillan, 1930), p. 518.

11. Kenneth Stampp, *The Imperiled Union* (New York: Oxford University Press, 1980), p. 15.

12. William Rawle, *A View of the Constitution* (Simsboro, La.: Old South Books, 1825/1993).

13. Ibid., pp. 234–235.

14. James Banner, *To the Hartford Convention: The Federalists and the Origins of Party Politics in Massachusetts* (New York: Knopf, 1970), p. 35.

15. "Letter from Timothy Pickering to Richard Peters," in *Documents Relating to New-England Federalism, 1800–1815,* ed. Henry Adams (Boston: Little, Brown, 1877), p. 338.

16. Ibid.

17. Cited in Claude G. Bowers, *Jefferson in Power: The Death Strug-gle of the Federalists* (Boston: Riverside Press, 1936), p. 235.

18. Ibid., p. 243.

19. Banner, p. 48.

20. Ibid., p. 117.

21. Douglas Southall Freeman, *Lee* (New York: Charles Scribner's Sons, 1991), p. 110.

22. "Letter from Roger Griswold to Oliver Wolcott," March 11, 1804, in *Documents Relating to New-England Federalism, 1800–1815,* ed. Henry Adams (Boston: Little, Brown, 1877), p. 376.

23. "Letter from William Smith Shaw to Abigail Adams," May 20, 1798, in James Banner, *To the Hartford Convention: The Feder-alists and the Origins of Party Politics in Massachusetts* (New York: Knopf, 1970), p. 90.

24. Daniel Waite Howe, *Political History of Secession* (New York: Negro University Press, 1914), p. 13.

25. "Letter from Timothy Pickering to George Cabot," January 29, 1804, in *Documents Relating to New-England Federalism, 1800–1815,* ed. Henry Adams (Boston: Little, Brown, 1877), p. 338.

26. Ibid.

27. "Letter from Timothy Pickering to Theodore Lyman," February 11, 1804, in *Documents Relating to New-England Federalism, 1800–1815,* ed. Henry Adams (Boston: Little, Brown, 1877), p. 338.

28. Bowers, p. 245.

29. Banner, p. 301.

30. Ibid., p. 102.

31. Ibid., p. 107.

32. Edward Powell, *Nullification and Secession in the United States* (New York: Putnam's Sons, 1897), p. 219.

33. William C. Wright, *The Secession Movement in the Middle Atlantic States* (Rutherford, N.J.: Fairleigh Dickinson University Press, 1973).

34. Ibid., p. 207.

35. Ibid., p. 41.

36. Ibid., p. 44.

37. Ibid., p. 59.

38. Ibid., p. 174.

39. Ibid., p. 198.

40. Ibid., p. 135.

41. Ibid., p. 137.

42. Ibid., p. 147.

43. Ibid., p. 107.

44. Howard Cecil Perkins, *Northern Editorials on Secession* (Gloucester, Mass.: Peter Smith, 1964).

45. Ibid., p. 10.

46. Ibid., p. 18.

47. Daniel Waite Howe, *Political History of Secession* (New York: Negro University Press, 1914).

48. Charles Eliot, ed., *The Harvard Classics, vol. 43, American Historical Documents* (New York: P. F. Collier, 1910), p. 158.

49. Donald W. Livingston, "The Secession Tradition in America," in *Secession, State and Liberty,* ed. David Gordon (New Brunswick, N.J.: Transaction, 1998), p. 9.

50. H. L. Mencken, "Gettysburg," *The Smart Set,* May 1920.

51. Max Farrand, ed., *The Records of the Federal Convention,* vol. 1 (New Haven, Conn.: Yale University Press, 1911), p. 47.

52. *The Federalist Papers,* number 36.

53. James Ostrowski, "Was Invasion of the Confederate States a Lawful Act?" in *Secession, State and Liberty,* ed. David Gordon (New Brunswick, N.J.: Transaction, 1998), p. 169.

54. Ibid., p. 179.

55. Ibid., p. 183.

56. Abraham Lincoln to Gustavus Fox, May 1, 1861, in *Gustavus Fox Papers,* The New York Historical Society.

57. Bruce Catton, *The Coming Fury* (Garden City, N.Y.: Doubleday, 1961), p. 297.

58. Shelby Foote, *The Civil War* (New York: Vintage Books, 1986), pp. 47–48.

59. Perkins, p. 716.

60. Ibid., p. 718.

61. Ibid., pp. 711–713.

62. Ibid., pp. 706–708.

63. Charles W. Ramsdell, "Lincoln and Fort Sumter," *The Journal of Southern History* 3, February–November 1937, p. 286.

64. Abraham Lincoln, "Message to Congress in Special Session," July 4, 1861, in *Abraham Lincoln: His Speeches and Writings,* ed. Roy P. Basler (New York: Da Capo Press, 1946), p. 609.

65. James G. Randall, *Constitutional Problems under Lincoln* (Urbana: University of Illinois Press, 1926/1964), pp. 63–64.

66. Carl Sandburg, *Abraham Lincoln: The War Years* (New York: Harcourt Brace, 1939), p. 206.

67. Jefferson Davis, *The Rise and Decline of the Confederate Government* (Richmond, Va.: Garrett and Massie, 1938), p. 80.

68. Alexander H. Stephens, *A Constitutional View of the Late War between the States* (Philadelphia: National Publishing Company, 1870), p. 9.

69. Robert Toombs, "Speech before the Legislature of Georgia, November 1860," in *The Causes of the Civil War,* ed. Kenneth Stampp (New York: Simon and Schuster, 1991), pp. 86–88.

70. Ibid., p. 87.

71. Ibid.

72. Ibid.

73. Ibid., p. 88.

74. "The Imperial North," *Vicksburg Daily Whig,* January 18, 1860, in *The Causes of the Civil War,* ed. Kenneth Stampp (New York: Simon and Schuster, 1991), p. 88.

75. Speech of Representative John H. Reagan, January 15, 1861, *Congressional Globe,* 36 Congress, Session I, p. 391.

76. "The Southern Bid for Commercial Power," *Boston Transcript,* March 18, 1861.

CHAPTER 6

1. Clinton Rossiter, *Constitutional Dictatorship* (New York: Harcourt Brace, 1948), p. 226.

2. James Ford Rhodes, *History of the United States from the Compromise of 1850 to the Final Restoration of Home Rule at the South in 1877* (New York: Macmillan, 1900), p. 441.

3. James G. Randall, *Constitutional Problems under Lincoln* (Urbana: University of Illinois Press, 1926/1964), p. 30.

4. Dean Sprague, *Freedom under Lincoln* (Boston: Houghton Mifflin, 1965).

5. Edward S. Corwin, *Total War and the Constitution* (Ann Arbor: University of Michigan Press, 1947), p. 16.

6. Randall, p. 133.

7. Ibid., p. 121.

8. Ibid., p. 136.

9. Rossiter, p. 227.

10. Randall, p. 150.

11. Ibid., p. 155.

12. Ibid.

13. Ibid., p. 91.

14. Sprague, p. 29.

15. Ibid., p. 159.

16. Ibid., p. 160.

17. Randall, p. 193.

18. Ibid., p. 203.

19. Sprague, p. 281.

20. Ibid., p. 282.

21. Ibid., pp. 178–179.

22. Ibid., p. 188.

23. Ibid., p. 203.

24. Ibid.

25. Ibid., p. 204.

26. Ibid., p. 206.

27. David Donald, *Lincoln Reconsidered* (New York: Vintage Books, 1961), p. 81.

28. Bart Rhett Talbert, *Maryland: The South's First Casualty* (Berryville, Va.: Rockbridge, 1995), pp. 55–56.

29. Ibid.

30. Sprague, p. 143.

31. Ibid., p. 145.

32. Randall, p. 493.

33. Ibid., p. 459.

34. Ibid., p. 226.

35. William L. Burton, *Melting Pot Soldiers: The Union's Ethnic Regiments* (New York: Fordham University Press, 1998).

36. Clement L. Vallandigham, "Executive Usurpation," Speech Delivered in the U.S. House of Representatives, July 10, 1861, in *The Record of Hon. C. L. Vallandigham: Abolition, the Union, and the Civil War* (Wiggins, Miss.: Crown Rights, 1998), pp. 94–109.

37. Ibid.

38. Ibid.

39. Ibid.

40. Ibid.

41. Ibid.

42. Ibid.

43. David A. Nichols, *Lincoln and the Indians* (Columbia: University of Missouri Press, 1978), p. 87.

44. Rossiter, p. 236.

45. Randall, p. 183.

46. Ibid., pp. 184–185.

47. Ibid., p. 503.

48. Sprague, p. 291.

49. Ibid., p. 299.

50. Ibid. p. 300.

51. Ibid., p. 301.

52. Ibid., p. 131.

53. Garry Wills, *Lincoln at Gettysburg: The Words That Remade America* (New York: Simon and Schuster, 1992).

54. George P. Fletcher, *Our Secret Constitution: How Lincoln Redefined American Democracy* (New York: Oxford University Press, 2001).

55. Ibid., p. 2.

56. Ibid., p. 5.

57. Ibid.

58. Ibid., p. 12.

59. Randall, p. 4.

60. Ibid., p. 5.

61. Ibid.

62. Ibid.

63. On the perversion of the commerce clause, see Edward S. Corwin, *The Commerce Power versus States Rights* (Gloucester, Mass.: Peter Smith, 1962).

64. Randall, p. xiv.

65. Ibid.

66. Ibid., p. xxiii.

67. For a discussion of this distinction see *Reassessing the Presidency,* ed. John Denson (Auburn, Ala.: Mises Institute, 2001).

68. W. B. Allen, ed., *George Washington: A Collection* (Indianapolis: Liberty Fund, 1980), p. 521.

69. Mark E. Neely, Jr., *Fate of Liberty: Abraham Lincoln and Civil Rights* (New York: Oxford University Press, 1991), p. 212.

70. Edmund Wilson, *Patriotic Gore: Studies in the Literature of the American Civil War* (New York: Oxford University Press, 1962).

71. Ibid. pp. xvi–xvii.

72. Ibid., pp. xviii–xix.

73. Neely, p. 231.

CHAPTER 7

1. James McPherson, "Tried by War," *Civil War Times,* December 1995, p. 66.

2. James McPherson, *Abraham Lincoln and the Second American Revolution* (New York: Oxford University Press, 1991), p. 66.

3. Ibid.

4. Stephen Oates, "The Man at the White House Window," *Civil War Times,* December 1995, p. 52.

5. Emmerich de Vattel, *The Law of Nations* (London: G. G. and J. Robinson, 1797).

6. Ibid., p. 364.

7. Henry W. Halleck, *International Law; or, Rules Regulating the Intercourse of States in Peace and War* (New York: Van Nostrand, 1861).

8. Mark Grimsley, *The Hard Hand of War: Union Military Policy toward Southern Civilians, 1861–1865* (Cambridge: Cambridge University Press, 1995), p. 16.

9. Francis Lieber, "Nationalism," in *Hamilton's Republic,* ed. Michael Lind (New York: Free Press, 1997), p. 119.

10. Grimsley, p. 45.

11. Ibid., p. 72.

12. Ibid.

13. "Letter from General McClellan to Lincoln," June 20, 1862, in Mark Grimsley, *The Hard Hand of War: Union Military Policy toward Southern Civilians, 1861–1865* (Cambridge: Cambridge University Press, 1995), p. 75.

14. Grimsley, p. 78.

15. Ibid., p. 80.

16. Ibid., p. 86.

17. Ibid., p. 88.

18. Ibid., p. 108.

19. James G. Randall, *Constitutional Problems under Lincoln* (Urbana: University of Illinois Press, 1926/1964), p. 148.

20. John F. Marszalek, *Sherman: A Soldier's Passion for Order* (New York: Vintage Books, 1993), p. 194.

21. John Bennett Walters, *Merchant of Terror: General Sherman and Total War* (New York: Bobbs-Merrill, 1973), p. 63.

22. Grimsley, p. 115.

23. Ibid., p. 116.

24. "Letter from Sherman to Mrs. Sherman," July 31, 1862, cited in Walters, p. 61.

25. Marszalek, p. 194.

26. Ibid.

27. Walters, p. 78.

28. Ibid., p. 96.

29. Ibid., p. 101.

30. Ibid., p. 110.

31. Ibid., p. 116.

32. Grimsley, p. 164.

33. Michael Fellman, *Citizen Sherman: A Life of William Tecumseh Sherman* (Lawrence: University Press of Kansas, 1995), p. 184.

34. Walker, p. 152.

35. Ibid., pp. 137–138.

36. Lee Kennett, *Marching through Georgia: The Story of Soldiers and Civilians during Sherman's Campaign* (New York: Harper-Collins, 1995), p. 279.

37. Grimsley, p. 196.

38. Kennett, p. 303.

39. Kennett, p. 276.

40. Ibid., p. 277.

41. Ibid.

42. Grimsley, p. 202.

43. Ibid.

44. Shelby Foote, *The Civil War* (New York: Vintage Books, 1986), p. 795.

45. Ibid.

46. Michael Fellman, ed., *Memoirs of General W. T. Sherman* (New York: Penguin Books, 2000), p. 644.

47. Ibid., p. 280.

48. Ibid., p. 291.

49. Ibid., pp. 310–311.

50. Earl Schenk Miers, ed., *When the World Ended: The Diary of Emma LeConte* (Lincoln: University of Nebraska Press, 1987).

51. Ibid., p. 39.

52. Ibid., p. 43.

53. Ibid., p. 45.

54. Ibid.

55. Ibid., pp. 45–46.

56. Ibid., p. 46.

57. Ibid., p. 58.

58. Charles Royster, ed., *Memoirs of General William T. Sherman* (New York: Macmillan, 1990), p. 810, cited in Marszalek, p. 336.

59. Foote, p. 562.

60. Roy Morris, Jr., *Sheridan* (New York: Vintage Books, 1992), p. 183.

61. Ibid., p. 563.

62. Ibid., p. 564.

63. Grimsley, p. 178.

64. Ibid., p. 183.

65. Ibid.

66. Ibid., p. 184.

67. Kennett, p. 286.

68. Stig Forster and Jorg Nagler, eds., *On the Road to Total War: The American Civil War and the German Wars of Unification, 1861–1871* (Cambridge: Cambridge University Press, 1997), p. 51.

CHAPTER 8

1. Thomas Nelson Page, *Robert E. Lee* (New York: Macmillan, 1908), p. 656.

2. Claude Bowers, *The Tragic Era: The Revolution after Lincoln* (New York: Houghton Mifflin, 1929); William Archibald Dunning, *Reconstruction: Political and Economic* (New York: Harper Brothers, 1907); and William Archibald Dunning, *Essays on the Civil War and Reconstruction* (New York: Harper Brothers, 1965).

3. James Ford Rhodes, *History of the United States from the Compromise of 1850 to the Final Restoration of Home Rule at the South in 1877* (New York: Macmillan, 1900); James G. Randall, *The Civil War and Reconstruction* (Lexington, Mass.: D.C. Heath, 1951).

4. Kenneth M. Stampp, *The Era of Reconstruction: 1865–1877* (New York: Knopf, 1966), p. 9.

5. Eric Foner, *Reconstruction: America's Unfinished Revolution* (New York: Harper and Row, 1988).

6. Stampp, p. 9.

7. Dunning (Reconstruction, p. 175) wrote, for example, that "It was plausibly argued [by Southerners] that the right of intelligent white women to vote was as worthy an object of a constitutional guarantee as the right of ignorant and degraded black men." Words like "ignorant" and "degraded" were surely quite accurate descriptions of the illiterate and propertyless ex-slaves in 1866, but they have generated outrage in the Marxist revisionists.

8. Stampp, p. 20.

9. Walter L. Fleming, ed., *Documentary History of Reconstruction* (New York: McGraw-Hill, 1966), p. 9.

10. Ibid., p. 10.

11. Ibid., p. 21.

12. Dunning, *Reconstruction,* p. 35.

13. Charles Adams, *When in the Course of Human Events: Arguing the Case for Southern Secession* (New York: Roman and Littlefield, 2000), pp. 177–192.

14. Dunning, *Reconstruction,* p. 64.

15. Dunning, *Essays on the Civil War,* p. 93.

16. Dunning, *Reconstruction,* p. 84.

17. Dunning, *Essays on the Civil War,* p. 181.

18. Ibid., p. 120.

19. Ibid., p. 152.

20. Ibid., p. 206.

21. Ross M. Lence, *Union and Liberty: The Political Philosophy of John C. Calhoun* (Indianapolis: Liberty Fund, 1992).

22. Dunning, *Reconstruction,* p. 206.

23. Marshall DeRosa, *The Confederate Constitution of 1861* (Columbia: University of Missouri Press, 1991).

24. Dunning, *Reconstruction*, p. 208.

25. Merton L. Coulter, *The South during Reconstruction* (Baton Rouge: Louisiana State University Press, 1947), p. 150.

26. Dunning, *Reconstruction*, p. 208.

27. Ibid., p. 209.

28. Mark Wahlgren Summers, *The Era of Good Stealings* (New York: Oxford University Press, 1993), p. 154.

29. Ibid.

30. Coulter, p. 151.

31. Foner, p. 380.

32. Coulter, pp. 148–149.

33. Ibid., p. 155.

34. Ibid., p. 156; Foner, p. 376.

35. Coulter, p. 156.

36. Fleming, p. 28.

37. Ibid., p. 31.

38. Bowers, p. 363.

39. *New York Times*, 26 May 1874, cited in Summers, p. 162.

40. *Washington, D.C. Sunday Capital*, 21 March 1874, cited in Summers, p. 163.

41. Robert V. Remini, *Henry Clay: Statesman for the Union* (New York: Norton, 1991).

42. Dunning, *Reconstruction*, p. 153.

43. Ibid., p. 160.

44. Ibid.

45. Michael Fellman, *Citizen Sherman: A Life of William Tecumseh Sherman* (Lawrence: University Press of Kansas, 1995), p. 264.

46. John F. Marszalek, *Sherman: A Soldier's Passion for Order* (New York: Vintage Books, 1993), p. 379.

47. Ibid., p. 380.

48. Ibid., pp. 380–381.

49. Ibid., p. 381.

50. Ibid.

51. Ibid., p. 382.

52. Burton Folsom, *Entrepreneurs vs. the State* (Herndon, Va.: Young America's Foundation, 1988), p. 21.

53. Paul Johnson, *A History of the American People* (New York: HarperCollins, 1998), p. 544.

54. Summers, p. 92.

55. Ibid., p. 127.

56. Ibid., p. 93.

57. Ibid.

58. John D. Flynn, *The Roosevelt Myth* (San Francisco: Fox and Wilkes, 1950).

59. Richard Bensel, *Yankee Leviathan* (Cambridge: Cambridge University Press, 1990), p. ix.

60. Ibid., p. x.

61. William A. DeGregorio, *The Complete Book of U.S. Presidents* (New York: Wings Books, 1996), p. 328.

62. Kenneth Stampp and Leon Litwack, eds., *Reconstruction: An Anthology of Revisionist Writings* (Baton Rouge: Louisiana State University Press, 1969).

63. Foner, p. xxii.

CHAPTER 9

1. Quoted in David Donald, *Lincoln Reconsidered* (New York: Vintage Books, 1961), pp. 105–106.

2. Ibid., p. 106.

3. Roy P. Basler, ed., *Abraham Lincoln: His Speeches and Writings* (New York: Da Capo Press, 1946), p. 583.

4. Frank Taussig, *The Tariff History of the United States*, 8th ed. (New York: Putnam, 1931), p. 157.

5. Ibid., p. 258.

6. Ibid., p. 167.

7. Ibid.

8. Ibid., p. 166.

9. Marshall DeRosa, *The Confederate Constitution of 1861* (Columbia: University of Missouri Press, 1991), p. 94.

10. Richard Bensel, *Yankee Leviathan* (Cambridge: Cambridge University Press, 1990), p. 73.

11. "Executive Usurpation," speech by Clement L. Vallandigham, Congressman from Ohio, July 10, 1861, in *Reassessing the Presidency*, ed. John Denson (Auburn, Ala.: Mises Institute, 2001), pp. 711–731.

12. Ibid., p. 719.

13. Ibid., p. 720.

14. Howard Cecil Perkins, *Northern Editorials on Secession* (Gloucester, Mass.: Peter Smith, 1964), p. 573.

15. Ibid., p. 574.

16. Ibid., p. 600.

17. Ibid., p. 601.

18. Ibid., p. 602.

19. Ibid., pp. 589–590.

20. Ibid.

21. Leonard P. Curry, *Blueprint for Modern America: Nonmilitary Legislation of the First Civil War Congress* (Nashville, Tenn.: Vanderbilt University Press, 1968), p. 116.

22. Ibid.

23. Ibid.

24. Heather Cox Richardson, *The Greatest Nation on the Earth: Republican Economic Policies during the Civil War* (Cambridge, Mass.: Harvard University Press, 1997), p. 195.

25. Albro Martin, *James J. Hill and the Opening of the Northwest* (New York: Oxford University Press, 1976); and Burton Folsom, *The Myth of the Robber Barons* (Herndon, Va.: Young America's Foundation, 1991).

26. Martin, pp. 410–411.

27. Ibid.

28. *Congressional Globe,* 37th Congress, 2nd Session, pp. 2808, 1707.

29. Richardson, p. 196.

30. Curry, p. 247.

31. Hugh Rockoff, "The Free Banking Era: A Reexamination," *Journal of Money, Credit and Banking,* 6 (May 1974), pp. 149–151.

32. Jeffrey Rogers Hummel, *Emancipating Slaves, Enslaving Free Men: A History of the American Civil War* (Chicago: Open Court, 1996), p. 224.

33. Ibid., p. 226.

34. Richardson, p. 87.

35. Ibid., p. 90.

36. Ibid., p. 101.

37. *New York Times,* 9 March 1863, cited in Richardson, p. 94.

38. Curry, p. 179.

39. Ibid.

40. Richardson, p. 138.

CHAPTER 10

1. Jeffrey Rogers Hummel, *Emancipating Slaves, Enslaving Free Men* (Chicago: Open Court, 1996), p. 279.

2. James McPherson, *Ordeal by Fire* (New York: Knopf, 1982), p. 476.

3. Hummel, p. 235.

4. Gary Gallagher and Alan T. Nolan, *The Myth of the Lost Cause and Civil War History* (Bloomington: Indiana University Press, 2000).

5. Ibid., flap copy.

6. Ibid., p. 14.

7. Lloyd A. Hunter, "The Immortal Confederacy," in Gallagher and Nolan, p. 207.

8. Ibid.

9. Ibid.

10. Forrest McDonald, *States' Rights and the Union: Imperium in Imperio, 1776–1876* (Lawrence: University Press of Kansas, 1999).

11. Adrienne Koch and William Peden, eds., *Selected Writings of Thomas Jefferson* (New York: Modern Library, 1944), p. 323.

12. Clyde Wilson, ed., *The Essential Calhoun* (New Brunswick, N.J.: Transaction, 1992), p. 299.

13. Forrest McDonald, "Federalism in America," in *Requiem: Variations on Eighteenth Century Themes,* by Forrest McDonald (Lawrence: University Press of Kansas, 1989).

14. Clyde Wilson, "Secession: The Last, Best Bulwark of Our Liberties," in *Secession, State and Liberty,* ed. David Gordon (New Brunswick, N.J.: Transaction, 1998), pp. 89–98.

15. Ibid., p. 93.

16. Gaillard Hunt, ed., *Writings of James Madison* (New York: Putnam's Sons, 1900), p. 372.

17. J. Rufus Fears, ed., *Selected Writings of Lord Acton,* vol. I, *Essays in the History of Liberty* (Indianapolis: Liberty Fund, 1985), p. 363.

18. Ibid., p. 365.

19. Michael Lind, ed., *Hamilton's Republic* (New York: Free Press, 1997), pp. 1–2.

20. Richard Epstein, *Takings* (Cambridge, Mass.: Harvard University Press, 1980).

21. Hans-Hermann Hoppe, *Democracy: The God That Failed* (New Brunswick, N.J.: Transaction, 2001).

22. George H. Smith, ed., *The Lysander Spooner Reader* (San Francisco: Fox and Wilkes, 1992), p. xi.

23. Lysander Spooner, "No Treason: The Constitution of No Authority," in *The Lysander Spooner Reader,* ed. George W. Smith (San Francisco: Fox and Wilkes, 1992), p. 121.

SELECTED
BIBLIOGRAPHY

Adams, Charles. 2000. *When in the Course of Human Events: Arguing the Case for Southern Secession*. New York: Roman and Littlefield.

Adams, Henry, ed. 1877. *Documents Relating to New-England Federalism, 1800– 1815*. Boston: Little, Brown.

Angle, Paul M. ed. 1947. *The Lincoln Reader*. New York: Da Capo.

Banner, James. 1970. *To the Hartford Convention: The Federalists and the Origins of Party Politics in Massachusetts*. New York: Knopf.

Basler, Roy P. ed.1946. *Abraham Lincoln: His Speeches and Writings*. New York: Da Capo Press.

―――. 1953. *The Collected Works of Abraham Lincoln*. New Brunswick, N.J.: Rutgers University Press.

Baxter, Maurice. 1995. *Henry Clay and the American System*. Lexington: University Press of Kentucky.

Bensel, Richard. 1990. *Yankee Leviathan: The Origins of Central State Authority in America*. Cambridge: Cambridge University Press.

Berger, Raoul. *Government by Judiciary: The Transformation of the Fourteenth Amendment*. Cambridge, Mass.: Harvard University Press.

Bernstein, Iver. 1990. *The New York City Draft Riots*. New York: Oxford University Press.

Berwanger, Eugene. 1967. *The Frontier Against Slavery*. Urbana: University of Illinois Press.

Blau, Joseph L., ed. 1947. *Social Theories of Jacksonian Democracy.* New York: Hafner.

Bowers, Claude. 1929. *The Tragic Era: The Revolution after Lincoln.* New York: Houghton Mifflin.

Chitwood, Oliver. 1964. *John Tyler: Champion of the Old South.* New York: Russell and Russell.

Corwin, Edward S. 1947. *Total War and the Constitution.* Ann Arbor: University of Michigan Press.

————. 1962. *The Commerce Power versus States Rights.* Gloucester, Mass.: Peter Smith.

Coulter, Merton L. 1947. *The South during Reconstruction.* Baton Rouge: Louisiana State University Press.

Curry, Leonard P. 1968. *Blueprint for Modern America: Nonmilitary Legislation of the First Civil War Congress.* Nashville: Vanderbilt University Press.

Curtis, John. 1930. *Life of Webster.* New York: Macmillan.

Davis, Jefferson. 1938. *The Rise and Decline of the Confederate Government.* Richmond, Va.: Garrett and Massie.

Denson, John, ed. 1997. *The Costs of War.* New Brunswick, N.J.: Transaction.

DeRosa, Marshall. 1991. *The Confederate Constitution of 1861: An Inquiry into American Constitutionalism.* Columbia: University of Missouri Press.

————, ed. 1998. *The Politics of Dissolution: The Quest for a National Identity and the American Civil War.* New Brunswick, N.J.: Transaction.

Donald, David. 1961. *Lincoln Reconsidered.* New York: Vintage Books.

————. *Lincoln.* 1996. New York: Simon and Schuster.

Dunning, William Archibald. 1907. *Essays on the Civil War and Reconstruction.* New York: Harper and Brothers.

Fears, J. Rufus. 1985. *Selected Writings of Lord Acton.* Indianapolis: Liberty Fund.

Fellman, Michael. 1995. *Citizen Sherman: A Life of William Tecumseh Sherman*. Lawrence: University of Kansas Press.

———. 2000. *Memoirs of General W.T. Sherman*. New York: Penguin Books.

Fletcher, George P. 2001. *Our Secret Constitution: How Lincoln Remade America*. New York: Oxford University Press.

Fogel, Robert, and Stanley Engermann. 1974. *Time on the Cross: The Economics of American Negro Slavery*. New York: Norton.

Foner, Eric. 1988. *Reconstruction: America's Unfinished Revolution*. New York: Harper and Row.

Fleming, Walter L. 1966. *Documentary History of Reconstruction*. New York: McGraw-Hill.

Foote, Shelby. 1986. *The Civil War*. New York: Vintage Books.

Forster, Stig and Jorg Nagler, eds. 1997. *On the Road to Total War: The American Civil War and the German Wars of Unification, 1861–1871*. Cambridge: Cambridge University Press.

Freeman, Douglas Southall. 1961/1991. *Lee*. New York: Charles Scribner's Sons.

Fremantle, Arthur J.L. 1864/1991. *Three Months in the Southern States: April– June 1863*. Lincoln: University of Nebraska Press.

Gallagher, Gary. 1997. *The Confederate War*. Cambridge, Mass.: Harvard University Press.

Garrison, Webb. 1993. *The Lincoln No One Knows*. Nashville, Tenn.: Rutledge Hill Press.

Goodrich, Carter. 1960. *Government Promotion of American Canals and Railroads, 1800–1890*. Westport, Conn.: Greenwood Press.

Gordon, David, ed. 1998. *Secession, State and Liberty*. New Brunswick, N.J.: Transaction.

Grimsley, Mark. 1995. *The Hard Hand of War: Union Military Policy toward Southern Civilians, 1861–1865*. Cambridge: Cambridge University Press.

Herndon, William H. and Jesse W. Weik. 1983. *Life of Lincoln*. New York: Da Capo Press.

Holt, Michael F. 1999. *The Rise and Fall of the American Whig Party.* New York: Oxford University Press.

Howe, Daniel Waite. 1914. *Political History of Secession.* New York: Negro University Press.

Hummel, Jeffrey. 1996. *Emancipating Slaves, Enslaving Free Men.* Chicago: Open Court.

Jaffa, Harry V. 2000. *A New Birth of Freedom.* New York: Roman and Littlefield.

Johannsen, Robert W. 1990. *Lincoln, the South, and Slavery.* Baton Rouge: Louisiana State University Press.

Kennett, Lee. 1995. *Marching through Georgia: The Story of Soldiers and Civilians during Sherman's Campaign.* New York: Harper-Collins.

Lafeber, Walter, ed. 1965. *John Quincy Adams and the American Continental Empire.* Chicago: Quadrangle Books.

Lence, Ross M. 1992. *Union and Liberty: The Political Philosophy of John C. Calhoun.* Indianapolis: Liberty Fund.

Lind, Michael. 1997. *Hamilton's Republic.* New York: Free Press.

Litwack, Leon. 1961. *North of Slavery: The Negro in the Free States, 1790-1860.* Chicago: University of Chicago Press.

Marshall, John A. 1881/1996. *American Bastille.* Wiggins, Miss.: Crown Rights Book Company.

Marszalek, John F. 1994. *Sherman: A Soldier's Passion for Order.* New York: Vintage Books.

Masters, Edgar Lee. 1997. *Lincoln the Man.* Columbia, S.C.: Foundation for American Education.

Mayer, Henry. 1998. *William Lloyd Garrison and the Abolition of Slavery.* New York: St. Martin's Press.

McClellan, James, and Mel Bradford, eds. 1989. *Jonathan Elliot's Debates in the Several State Conventions on the Adoption of the Federal Constitution.* Richmond, Va.: J. River Press.

McDonald, Forrest. 1999. *States' Rights and the Union: Imperium in Imperio, 1776–1876.* Lawrence: University Press of Kansas.

McPherson, James. 1966. *The Struggle for Equality: Abolitionists and the Negro in the Civil War and Reconstruction*. Princeton, N.J.: Princeton University Press.

———. 1997. *For Cause and Comrades: Why Men Fought the Civil War*. New York: Oxford University Press.

———. 1994. *What they Fought For: 1861-1865*. Baton Rouge: Louisiana State University Press.

———. 1991. *Abraham Lincoln and the Second American Revolution*. New York: Oxford University Press.

———. 1982. *Ordeal by Fire*. New York: Alfred A. Knopf.

Miers, Earl S. ed. 1987. *When the World Ended: The Diary of Emma LeConte*. Lincoln: University of Nebraska Press.

Morris, Roy, Jr. 1992. *Sheridan*. New York: Vintage Books.

Neely, Mark E., Jr. 1991. *Fate of Liberty: Abraham Lincoln and Civil Rights*. New York: Oxford University Press.

———. 1993. *The Last Best Hope of Earth: Abraham Lincoln and the Promise of America*. Cambridge, Mass.: Harvard University Press.

Nichols, David A. 1978. *Lincoln and the Indians*. Columbia: University of Missouri Press.

Perkins, Howard. 1964. *Northern Editorials on Secession*. Gloucester, Mass.: Peter Smith.

Peterson, Merrill D. 1984. *Thomas Jefferson: Writings*. New York: Library of America.

Powell, Edward. 1897. *Nullification and Secession in the United States*. New York: Putnam's Sons.

Randall, James G. and David Donald. 1969. *The Civil War and Reconstruction*. Lexington, Mass.: D.C. Heath.

———. 1964. *Constitutional Problems Under Lincoln*. Urbana: University of Illinois Press.

Rawle, William. 1825/1993. *A View of the Constitution*. Simsboro, La.: Old South Books.

Remini, Robert. 1991. *Henry Clay: Statesman for the Union*. New York: Norton.

————. 1966. *Andrew Jackson.* New York: Harper and Row.

Richardson, Heather Cox. 1997. *The Greatest Nation on the Earth: Republican Economic Policies during the Civil War.* Cambridge, Mass.: Harvard University Press.

Robertson, James I. 1997. *Stonewall Jackson.* New York: Macmillan.

Rossiter, Clinton. 1948. *Constitutional Dictatorship.* New York: Harcourt Brace.

Rutland, Robert. 1990. *The Presidency of James Madison.* Lawrence: University of Kansas Press.

Sandburg, Carl. 1939. *Abraham Lincoln: The War Years.* New York: Harcourt Brace.

Smith, George H. 1992. *The Lysander Spooner Reader.* San Francisco: Fox and Wilkes.

Sprague, Dean. 1965. *Freedom Under Lincoln.* Boston: Houghton Mifflin.

Stampp, Kenneth. 1980. *The Imperiled Union.* New York: Oxford University Press.

————, ed. 1991.*The Causes of the Civil War.* New York: Simon and Schuster.

————. 1966. *The Era of Reconstruction: 1865–1877.* New York: Alfred A. Knopf.

———— and Leon Litwack, eds. 1969. *Reconstruction: An Anthology of Revisionist Writings.* Baton Rouge: Louisiana State University Press.

Staudenraus, P.J. 1980. *The African Colonization Movement, 1816–1865.* New York: Octagon Books.

Stephens, Alexander H. 1870. *A Constitutional View of the Late War between the States.* Philadelphia: National Publishing Company.

Summers, Mark W. 1993. *The Era of Good Stealings.* New York: Oxford University Press.

Taussig, Frank. 1931. *The Tariff History of the United States.* New York: Putnam.

Vallandigham, Clement L. 1998. *The Record of Hon. C.L. Val-landigham: Abolition, the Union, and the Civil War*. Wiggins, Miss.: Crown Rights Book Company.

Vanauken, Sheldon. 1989. *The Glittering Illusion: English Sympathy for the Southern Confederacy*. Washington, D.C.: Regnery/Gateway.

Van der Linden, Frank. 1998. *Lincoln: The Road to War*. Golden, Co.: Fulcrum Publishing.

Vidal, Gore. 1984. *Lincoln: A Novel*. New York: Random House.

Walters, John Bennett. 1973. *Merchant of Terror: General Sherman and Total War*. New York: Bobbs-Merrill.

Wills, Garry. 1992. *Lincoln at Gettysburg: The Words that Remade America*. New York: Simon and Schuster.

Wilson, Clyde, ed. 1992. *The Essential Calhoun*. New Brunswick, N.J.: Transaction.

Wilson, Edmund. 1962. *Patriotic Gore: Studies in the Literature of the Civil War*. New York: Oxford University Press.

Woldman, Albert A. 1936. *Lawyer Lincoln*. New York: Carrol and Graff.

Woodward, C. Vann. 1974. *The Strange Career of Jim Crow*. New York: Oxford University Press.

Wright, William C. 1973. *The Secession Movement in the Middle Atlantic States*. Rutherford, N.J.: Farleigh Dickinson University Press.

INDEX

Index